Small-scale Research in Prim Schools

Small-scale Research in Primary Schools provides guidance and inspiration for students and professionals undertaking practical investigations and workplace enquiry in the primary school. The 30 chapters are carefully selected to illustrate a variety of approaches to educational enquiry, and are particularly relevant to the range of practitioners who may carry out school-based research as part of a course of study: teachers, trainee and newly-qualified teachers, teaching assistants, learning mentors and staff who support children with individual needs.

Research topics addressed in chapters include children's learning in the core curriculum subjects as well as themes central to teaching and learning. Important concepts and terminology are highlighted throughout. More specifically, areas of research explored include:

- play
- special educational needs
- working with parents and families
- English as an additional language
- creativity
- language development
- learning environments.

Small-scale Research in Primary Schools provides a straightforward, highly accessible introduction to enquiry approaches and research methodologies, embedded in the questions and challenges adults in schools encounter about children's learning. It shows how small-scale research in primary education can impact on professional thinking and learning. It aims to provide constructive support for students and practitioners in extending their knowledge and understanding through workplace enquiry.

Kimberly Safford is Head of Awards, Primary Teaching and Learning in the Faculty of Education and Language Studies at The Open University, UK.

Mary Stacey is a writer and educational consultant working with teaching assistants and early years practitioners.

Roger Hancock is a Senior Lecturer and Researcher in the Faculty of Education and Language Studies at The Open University, UK.

This Reader forms part of the Open University course *Learning through enquiry in primary schools* (E101). This is a 60 point course and is part of the Foundation Degree in Primary Teaching and Learning.

Details of this and other Open University courses can be obtained from the Student Registration and Enquiry Service, The Open University, PO Box 197, Milton Keynes MK7 6BJ, United Kingdom: tel. +44 (0)845 300 6090, e-mail general-enquiries@open.ac.uk

Alternatively, you may visit the Open University website at http://www.open.ac.uk where you can learn more about the wide range of courses and packs offered at all levels by The Open University.

Small-scale Research in Primary Schools

A Reader for learning and professional development

Edited by
Kimberly Safford, Mary Stacey
and Roger Hancock

LONDON AND NEW YORK

First published 2011
by Routledge
2 Park Square, Milton Park, Abingdon, Oxon OX14 4RN
in association with The Open University, Walton Hall, Milton Keynes MK7 6AA, United Kingdom

Simultaneously published in the USA and Canada
by Routledge
270 Madison Avenue, New York, NY 10016

Routledge is an imprint of the Taylor & Francis Group, an informa business

Typeset in Sabon by Glyph International Ltd.
Printed and bound in Great Britain by TJ International Ltd, Padstow, Cornwall

British Library Cataloguing in Publication Data
A catalogue record for this book is available from the British Library

Library of Congress Cataloging-in-Publication Data
Small-scale research in primary schools: a reader for learning and professional development/edited by Kimberly Safford, Mary Stacey and Roger Hancock.
p. cm.
1. Education, Primary–Research. 2. Child development–Research.
I. Safford, Kimberly. II. Stacey, Mary, 1943– III. Hancock, Roger.

LB1507.S63 2010
372.24'1072–dc22 2010004124

ISBN 10: 0-415-58559-7 (hbk)
ISBN 10: 0-415-58560-0 (pbk)

ISBN 13: 978-0-415-58559-0 (hbk)
ISBN 13: 978-0-415-58560-6 (pbk)

Contents

Figures

Tables

Acknowledgements

The publishers would like to thank the following for permission to reprint their material:

SAGE Publications for permission to reprint extracts from 'Remodelling schools – experiences from within change teams', Linda Hammersley-Fletcher and Michelle Lowe, 2006, *Management in Education* Vol. 20, Issue 2. Copyright © 2006 Linda Hammersley-Fletcher and Michelle Lowe. Reprinted by permission of SAGE. Also reprinted with permission of Education Publishing (EPC).

Taylor & Francis Journals for permission to reprint extracts from 'Children's views of teaching assistants in primary schools', Clare Fraser and Sara Meadows, *Education 3–13*, 2008, Vol. 36, No. 4, 351–363. Copyright © Association for the Study of Primary Education, reprinted by permission of Taylor & Francis Ltd. (http://www.tandf.co.uk/journals) on behalf of the Association for the Study of Primary Education.

Michael Tedder and Gert Biesta for permission to reprint 'Learning without teaching? Opportunities and limitations in biographical learning for adults', Tedder and Biesta, 2008, a paper for The European Conference on Educational Research From Teaching to Learning? in Gothenburg, Sweden, 10–12 September 2008.

Taylor & Francis Ltd. for permission to reprint extracts from 'Boxes, bags and videotape: enhancing home–school communication through knowledge exchange activities', Martin Hughes and Pamela Greenhough, *Educational Review*, 2006, Vol. 58, No. 4, 471–487, reprinted by permission of Taylor & Francis Ltd., http://www.tandf.co.uk/journals

Taylor & Francis Ltd. for permission to reprint extracts from '"It's different…because you are getting older and growing up": how children make sense of the transition to Year 1', Gabrielle White and Caroline Sharp, 2007, in *European Early Childhood Education Research Journal* Vol. 15, No. 1. Copyright © European Early Childhood Education Research Association, reprinted by permission of Taylor & Francis Ltd (http://www.tandf.co.uk/journals) on behalf of the European Early Childhood Education Research Association.

John Wiley & Sons, Inc. for kind permission to reprint extracts from 'Listen to me! Children's experiences of domestic violence', Helen Buckley, Stephanie Holt and Sadhbh Whelan, 2007 in *Child Abuse Review* Vol. 16, 296–310.

Emerald Group Publishing for permission to reprint extracts from 'Active travel to school: views of 10–13 year old schoolchildren in Scotland', Joanna Kirby and Joanna Inchley, 2009, in *Health Education* Vol. 109, No. 2, 169–183.

Taylor & Francis for permission to reprint extracts from 'Gender roles in televisions commercials and primary school children in the UK', Jenny Lewin-Jones and Barbara Mitra, 2009, in *Journal of Children and Media* Vol. 3, No. 1, 35–50. Reprinted by permission of the publisher (Taylor & Francis Ltd., http://www.tandf.co.uk/journals).

SAGE Publications for permission to reprint extracts from '"If Michael Owen drinks it, why can't I?": 9 and 10 year olds' perceptions of physical activity and healthy eating', Rachael Gosling, Debbi Stanistreet and Viren Swami in 2008, in *Health Education Journal* Vol. 67, No. 3, 167–181. Copyright © Rachael Gosling, Debbi Stanistreet and Viren Swami, 2008. Reprinted by permission of SAGE.

Taylor & Francis for permission to reprint extracts from '"Playtime in the borderlands": children's representations of school, gender and bullying through photographs and interviews', Michelle Newman, Andree Woodcock and Philip Dunham, 2006 in *Children's Geographies* Vol. 4, No. 3, 289–302. Reprinted by permission of the publisher (Taylor & Francis Ltd., http://www.tandf.co.uk/journals).

Scottish Educational Review and the author for kind permission to reprint 'Supporting our most challenging pupils with our lowest status staff: can additional staff in Scottish schools offer a distinctive kind of help?' Stead *et al.* 2007 in *Educational Review* Vol. 39, No. 2.

The School Food Trust for kind permission to reprint 'The impact of breakfast clubs in a deprived neighbourhood' (2008) and 'School lunches and behaviour' (2008): These are web-publications www.schoolfoodtrust.org.uk

Centre for Literacy in Primary Education for permission to reprint extracts from 'What language do you speak at home? Linguistic journeys in school', Raymonde Sneddon, 1997 in *Language Matters* CLPE: 1996–1997 with a 2009 update from the author.

Multiverse for kind permission to reprint extracts from 'Achieving successful home–school links with refugees', Jill Rutter (2006). This is a web-publication www.multiverse.ac.uk

Taylor & Francis for permission to reprint extracts from 'Assistance to pupils with physical disabilities in regular schools: promoting inclusion or creating dependency?', Snaefridur Thora Egilson and Rannveig Traustadottir, 2009 in *European Journal of Special Needs Education* Vol. 24, No. 1, 21–36. Reprinted by permission of the publisher (Taylor & Francis Ltd., http://www.tandf.co.uk/journals).

Taylor & Francis for permission to reprint extracts from ‘Going outside together: good practice with respect to the inclusion of disabled children in primary school playgrounds’, Helen Woolley, Marc Armitage, Julia Bishop, Mavis Curtis and Jane Ginsborg, 2006 in *Children’s Geographies* Vol. 4, No. 3, 303–318. Reprinted by permission of the publisher (Taylor & Francis Ltd., http://www.tandf.co.uk/journals).

Wiley Blackwell for kind permission to reprint extracts from ‘Including students with ADHD in mainstream schools’, *British Journal of Special Education*, Vol. 36, No. 1. Copyright © 2009 Neil Humphrey, Journal compilation © NASEN.

British Institute of Learning Disabilities for permission to reprint extracts from ‘Improving our use of objects of reference and touch cues’, Anna Kilberg and Ros How. Reproduced from *The SLD Experience*, Spring 2007, Issue 47, 11–14, with permission of the British Institute of Learning Disabilities.

British Institute of Learning Disabilities for permission to reprint extracts from ‘To what extent can an Individual Management Plan overcome barriers to learning in an inclusive classroom?’, Simon Knight. Reproduced from *The SLD Experience*, Autumn 2008, Issue 52, 17–21, with permission of the British Institute of Learning Disabilities.

Sue Cottam for permission to reprint extracts from ‘Birds and flights; a research project’, Sue Cottam, *Dance Matters*, Summer 2008, No. 52, 4–5.

Peacock Press and Gitika Partington for kind permission to reprint ‘Primary singing days’, Gitika Partington, *Primary Music Today*, 2008, Issue 39.

Peacock Press and Ruth Wright for kind permission to reprint ‘Practice pals make perfect’, Ruth Wright, *Primary Music Today*, 2008, Issue 41.

Reproduced by permission of SAGE Publications, London, Los Angeles, New Delhi and Singapore, extracts from ‘Analysing the data’, Min Wilkie, in *Doing Action Research: A Guide for School Support Staff*, Claire Taylor, Min Wilkie and Judith Baser. Copyright © Claire Taylor, Min Wilkie and Judith Baser 2006.

Sense Publishers for permission to reprint an extract from *Understanding Teacher Expertise in Primary Science*, Anna Traianou, 2007.

Primary Science Today for kind permission to reprint ‘Progression in children’s ideas about evaporation and condensation’, Georgina Harcourt-Brown, 2004 in *Primary Science Today*, Issue 24.

Literacy: A Journal of the United Kingdom Literacy Association for permission to reprint extracts from ‘Does teaching complex sentences have to be complicated? Lessons from children’s online writing’, Alison Kelly and Kimberly Safford, *Literacy*, November 2009, 43, 3, 118–122. Reprinted by permission of the Journals of the United Kingdom Literacy Association.

Centre for Literacy in Primary Education for permission to reprint extracts from 'Creativity and verbal development in the early years', Ann Bailey and Brita Little, 2005 in *Animating Literacy: Inspiring Children's Learning through Teacher and Artist Partnerships*, Sue Ellis and Kimberly Safford (eds) London: CLPE.

Centre for Literacy in Primary Education for permission to reprint extracts from 'Who should ask the questions? How arts partnerships help develop children's critical thinking', Adam Hickman, 2005 in *Animating Literacy: Inspiring Children's Learning through Teacher and Artist Partnerships*, Sue Ellis and Kimberly Safford (eds) London: CLPE.

Disclaimer

Introduction

Kimberly Safford

The focus of this Reader is small-scale enquiry and research in primary schools and its aim is to inspire the thinking, practice and professional development of adults who teach and support children's learning. The 30 chapters collected here present a variety of investigative approaches to better understand teaching practice and children's learning.

Every adult in primary schools can be seen as part of a network of professionals in the children's workforce who share responsibility for children's health, safety, learning and development, and this Reader is relevant to this considerable range of roles. You may be a qualified teacher, training to teach or returning to teaching. You may be a teaching assistant or classroom assistant in a paid or voluntary post where you work with children in particular areas of the curriculum. You may provide one-to-one support for a child with a physical impairment or complex learning needs. You may mentor pupils identified as 'challenging' or at risk of underachieving or exclusion. You may help children who are learning to use English as an additional language, or enable recently-arrived pupils and families adjust to a new school, a new community or a new culture. You may teach or support children in a Saturday school, a pupil referral unit, a hospital school or be involved in home education. You may work across age phases and activities at different times of the school day: in class, during play or lunch times, in breakfast clubs, in after-school or half-term activities. The multi-authored accounts in this Reader will enable you to develop your knowledge of how appropriately focused small-scale enquiry can promote your own learning and your understanding of how children learn.

This Reader begins with a discussion of the nature and purpose of small-scale practitioner enquiry, and approaches which are appropriate to the active social and educational community of the primary school. The three readings which follow in Part 1 – on changes in the schools workforce, children's views of teaching assistants and how adults understand their 'learning lives' – highlight some of the personal and professional contexts in which small-scale research can take place.

Part 2 presents enquiries into children's learning environments, and the ways in which the world outside the classroom influences their dispositions for learning; this section focuses on enquiries which explore the transitions – and gaps – which children may experience between home, community and school. Part 3 contains enquiries which examine diversity, inclusion and barriers to learning and the ways in which adults discover more about children's individual needs. Part 4 enquiries investigate children's learning in the primary curriculum's 'core' subjects and includes accounts of activities in dance, music and singing where adults, of course, may learn alongside children.

Most chapters are edited versions of original academic papers, and in editing we have tried to make these readings more accessible to students and school-based staff who are beginning to undertake small-scale enquiries and research, often in the context of their studies and career development. Editor introductions to each chapter provide an overview of the focus, key ideas, terminology and approaches (methodologies) of the enquiry.

A focus on additional staff

One of the most significant changes in primary education has been the expansion of roles and responsibilities undertaken by additional staff, largely brought about by initiatives to promote the inclusion of children with a range of individual needs in mainstream schools and, more recently, to reduce the workload of class teachers. Whilst many of the enquiries in this Reader are undertaken by class teachers, they also reflect the overlapping work of classroom and teaching assistants: where teachers are referred to, additional staff who support children's learning and who also support teachers will almost always be present and involved.

Research has identified the positive impact of support staff on children's learning in an array of contexts, from one-to-one curriculum support to nurturing children's social skills (Burgess and Mayes, 2009; Groom, 2006). The largest study undertaken to date in the UK (Blatchford *et al.*, 2009) reports that 50% of the schools workforce is support staff, and that one in four of this workforce is a teaching assistant. The same study has identified the distinct pedagogic role of additional staff in supporting and interacting with pupils: over 50% of teaching assistant time is spent on direct support for children's learning, providing both 'additional' and 'alternative' teaching. Many of the enquiries in this Reader relate to one of the key findings of Blatchford *et al.* (2009): the greater a child's individual need, the more likely the child is to work with a teaching assistant.

Small-scale enquiry in the workplace offers opportunities for teaching assistants and other kinds of support staff to explore their unique roles and relationships with children, and the 'insider' knowledge they often have of the children they come into contact with. In this Reader, for example, children express their views about working with teaching assistants and provide thoughtful representations of the nature and range of their support. Teaching and classroom assistants and other additional staff often have particular perspectives on the learning process through their close work with children (Sasia, 2007). There are often distinctive characteristics of supporting learning such as the use of first names, opportunities for one-to-one conversations with children and opportunities to mediate or advocate which can play a critical role in keeping some children in education. The very 'marginality' of school support staff can, sometimes unexpectedly, also create positive informal relationships with parents (Stead *et al.*, 2007).

The professional development of school support staff increasingly reflects models of teacher education and training, where adult learners acquire theoretical perspectives in relation to pedagogic skills, apply this knowledge and understanding in practice and progress towards enhanced roles, higher status and qualifications. Research into the training of teaching assistants (Burgess and Mayes, 2009; Burgess, 2006) found that support staff value the acquisition, through work-based learning, of reflective and theoretical perspectives to underpin their existing practical skills. As standards and expectations of classroom support staff increasingly mirror those of teachers, it is important that adults in support roles are able to promote their own professional growth. Small-scale, practice-based enquiry is an effective pathway for this kind of adult learning and development.

Whatever your role in primary school – teacher, student- or newly-qualified teacher, teaching assistant, classroom assistant, special needs assistant, behaviour support, cover supervisor, learning mentor, higher level teaching assistant, parent-helper, lunchtime supervisor or play worker – we hope that this Reader encourages you to become an active enquirer as you explore the learning lives of children and your own learning journey in these accounts of small-scale research.

References

Blatchford, P., Bassett, P., Brown, P., Martin, C., Russell, A. and Webster, R. (2009). *Deployment and Impact of Support Staff in Schools (2003–2008)* London: DCSF and Institute of Education, University of London.

Burgess, H. and Shelton Mayes, A. (2009). 'An exploration of the higher level teaching assistants' perceptions of their training and development in the context of school workforce reform'. *British Journal of Learning Support* 24(1): 19–25.

Burgess, H. (2006). 'The Butterfly Effect: teaching assistants and workforce reform in primary schools', Chapter 12 in *Changing Teaching and Learning in the Primary School* (edited by Webb, R.). Oxford: Oxford University Press.

Groom, B. (2006). 'Building relationships for learning: the developing role of the teaching assistant'. *Support for Learning* 21(4): 199–203.

Sasia, A. (2007). 'Communication between primary school teachers and teaching assistants: an exploratory study investigating communication about teaching assistants' pedagogical interaction with students'. Unpublished dissertation, Institute of Education, University of London.

Stead, J., Lloyd, G., Munn, P., Kane, J. and MacLeod, G. (2007). 'Supporting our most challenging pupils with our lowest status staff: can additional staff in Scottish schools offer a distinctive kind of help?' *Scottish Educational Review*, November.

Part 1

Contexts for small-scale research

Learning lives and professional roles

Chapter 1

Approaches to small-scale enquiry and research in primary schools

Kimberly Safford and Roger Hancock

Personal enquiry in professional contexts

The term 'action research' was coined by Kurt Lewin in 1944. It is a form of enquiry which can involve research with – rather than 'on' – others. It is now recognised as a significant means of academic and professional development for school staff, and a way of better understanding school routines and practices which may sometimes be taken for granted (see, for example, Shakir-Costa and Haddad, 2009; Taylor *et al.*, 2006). The accounts in this Reader cover a large territory in educational enquiry, but chapters have a clear unifying aspect: they all arise from questions, concerns, puzzles or problems encountered by practitioners who then carried out enquiries 'at the chalk face' in and around school settings to better understand what they practice and experience.

The enquiries gathered here are evidence of the many opportunities practitioners have for investigations into children's learning and school life. These opportunities are sometimes because a concern or problem emerges from a specific child or a group of children (Chapter 18 on including children with ADHD in mainstream schools); other enquiries involve collaboration between school staff and outside researchers (Chapter 5 on home–school knowledge exchange activities). In other cases, school staff create participatory enquiries, where children and adults work together on shared projects (Chapter 14, What language do you speak at home?). Enquiries can explore the links between children's experiences in school and outside school (Chapter 9 on children and television gender roles; Chapter 28 on children's online writing). They can examine school practices and effective pedagogies (Chapter 15, Achieving successful home–school links with refugees). They may reflect collective aims for professional development (Chapter 17 on including disabled children in school playgrounds) and small steps in understanding one child who frustrates or fascinates (Chapter 20 on individual management plans). All of these focuses for learning – in and around school, in personal and professional contexts, with groups and individuals – are opportunities where, through enquiry, adults who work with children can develop what Nancy Martin has called 'conscious competence – a heightened awareness of what you do'.

> If I set out to find an answer to some classroom matter, I am a learner; but in engaging in this enquiry, I am initiating a small piece of research: I am both learner and researcher – two sides of the same coin.
>
> (Nancy Martin 1987: 204)

The small-scale enquiries that we bring together here can be seen as forms of personalised learning which place 'the self in research' (Conteh *et al.*, 2005). In the same way that we acknowledge different starting points for children's development and understanding, enquiry-based learning takes account of adults' different starting points, histories, careers, roles and learning pathways. Throughout this Reader we suggest the notions of enquiry, investigation or 'research' therefore have a dual meaning: enquiry into children's learning, and enquiry into further adult understanding and learning.

Approaches and methodologies

Stenhouse (1981) defined research as 'systematic enquiry, made public'. This perspective of what 'counts' as research enables school staff to consider small, even idiosyncratic features of children's learning and behaviour. According to Walter Humes of the University of Strathclyde (2001), in small-scale research based on personal and professional experience 'methodological purity is an illusion'. Enquiries need to take place in active, unpredictable places (classrooms and schools) and rely chiefly on observational and behavioural data, particularly language data. They may be seen to lack the rigour of a scientific investigation, of course, but they are not usually set up in ways which endeavour to follow scientific methods. Such investigations usually have a short time frame and must take place within day-to-day routines. Results may not be generalizable or replicable, because small-scale inquiries tend to be studies of single instances or cases; conclusions may be subjective, because data is gathered and evaluated by those who are intimately involved in a particular process or context.

Such research however can contribute significantly to the practice and knowledge of the enquirers and of others within the focus of the study. The 'learner-researcher' role (as Nancy Martin earlier characterised practice-based enquiry) highlights deeply personal as well as professional dimensions of development. Interpretations of data will reflect specific local circumstances and individuals, and are unlikely to make grand claims. In small-scale workplace enquiry, issues of size and subjectivity, validity and reliability are approached and defined differently to what John Furlong of the British Educational Research Association (BERA) characterised as the 'Big Science' model of research, as Table 1.1 below indicates.

Table 1.1 Differences between personal workplace enquiry and 'Big Science' research*

Topic	*'Big Science' research*	*Personal workplace enquiry*
Goals of the research	Knowledge which advances current thinking, can be generalised and have wide impact	Understanding which helps make sense of a specific situation, can influence a local context and personal practice
Training which the researcher requires	Background of training in a variety of research methods	Experience gained through the process of supported study and workplace enquiry
Method of identifying the question to be studied	Extensive review of previous research (literature review) and a wish to add to this body of knowledge	Curiosity about something observed or experienced in practice; a puzzle or problem in practice

Table 1.1 Cont'd

Topic	*'Big Science' research*	*Personal workplace enquiry*
Approach to research 'informants' (those to be 'studied')	Random or representative sample; no direct relationship to researcher	Collaborative, possibly drawing upon those you know and work with
Approach to research design and validity	Control of variables, control groups, lengthy time frame, consistency of method for collecting data	Diverse perspectives, short time frame, mixed methods which take account of individual and local circumstances
Analysis of data	Use of quantitative and/or qualitative theoretical frameworks to identify significant statistical trends	Looking for themes or patterns which highlight practical rather than statistical relevance
Application of results	Significance for theory building, impact on policy	Significance for personal understanding (What did I learn?) and potential developments in practice (What might I change?)

* Adapted from Indiana University, 'Classroom Action Research Overview' http://mypage.iusb.edu/~gmetteta/Classroom_Action_Research.html

In his 2003 inaugural presidential address to BERA, Furlong argued for greater recognition of practitioner enquiry in educational contexts and less privileging of the 'Big Science' model of research. A key aspect of personal enquiry in relation to this Reader is that adults who teach and support children are not detached and looking from a distance but are potentially privileged 'insider' enquirers; this is arguably a sound researcher position or 'stance' which makes such workplace enquiries more, not less, valid for those involved.

Questions arising from experience

As we have said, enquiry-based learning begins with a query arising from practice, and all adults who teach and support children's learning frequently encounter such queries and puzzles:

- Why does a child find learning maths quite easy but writing and spelling quite hard?
- Why does a child behave well when working with me alone but not well when working with me in a group?
- What does a child with a physical disability think about my support in PE lessons?

Questions such as these create an instant interplay between children's learning and adults' learning, where gaining an understanding of the child's experience is linked to the practitioner's personal and professional insights and capacities, for example:

- I want to find out why a child finds writing difficult because this will help me support her more effectively, and our school development plan is for improvements in writing;

- I want to learn how children decide where to play as this will enable me to plan creatively and inclusively for playground activities and resources;
- I want to better understand children's singing development so I can confidently lead music sessions.

Small-scale enquiries like the ones above aim of course to shed light on issues which regularly arise in day-to-day practice. As a result, they have great potential to enhance the knowledge, skills and understanding of practitioners.

It is often the nature of small-scale enquiry to be more concerned with words rather than numbers, so information from such enquiries tends to be qualitative and interpretive rather than quantitative and 'countable'. Classroom research, when reported to others, is often presented as a narrative or story, drawing upon children's and adults' words and actions (see, for example, Chapter 29 by Ann Bailey and Britta Little on creativity and verbal development, and Chapter 25 by Anna Traianou on the classroom discussions and language that support children's learning of a scientific concept like 'friction'). This type of account, focusing on language and behaviour, is usually created through gathering observations, interviews and collection of relevant documents such as children's writing or drawings, school records or classroom planning. Qualitative, interpretive research can also be carried out with photographs (see Chapter 11 by Michelle Newman and colleagues). Quantitative research, lends itself to graphic presentations (see Chapter 24 by Min Wilkie) and such countable information can also strengthen narrative, interpretive information. Small-scale enquiry can, of course, combine numerical and narrative approaches, and drawing upon a range of information enables adults to create more holistic responses to puzzles and questions which arise in classrooms.

As an example: a teacher and a teaching assistant notice that some Year 3 children always seem to prefer to stay in the classroom during playtime. They are curious about why this is so, because the school has recently refurbished and improved the playground to make it more attractive to all children. They plan a small enquiry which they can undertake in their day-to-day work. As a first step, the teaching assistant counts, over a week, how many boys and girls go outside and how many children stay inside during the morning playtime; this initial activity informs her that there is a gendered pattern to the children's behaviour. In the second week, the teaching assistant and the teacher make two playtime observations of what children do in the playground and in the classroom during playtime; they make notes during the observations and later discuss and write down further thoughts about what they observed. The teaching assistant then organises an informal, voluntary 'focus group' discussion during a lunch time, inviting four children (two girls and two boys) to talk with her about their choices for playtime and she takes notes on their views. Later that afternoon, the teacher invites the whole class to complete a simple, anonymous questionnaire about their playtime likes and dislikes.

Within a short period of time the teacher and the teaching assistant have created four interesting 'sets' of information, or data: counting, observation, discussion and questionnaire. To place their information in a wider context and to compare their local experiences to other perspectives, they look on the internet for what government policy and other researchers have to say about school playgrounds and playtimes; in this process they may also read about the history of playground provision.

The teacher and teaching assistant review all of their information and look for themes and patterns emerging from it. They will look for key messages, and implications, for their personal understanding and their professional practice which they might share with other teachers, teaching assistants, play- and lunchtime supervisors and other school staff. Their findings might inform provision or policy-making in their school.

The varied enquiries in this Reader present a wide range of practical approaches to finding out about the ways in which children learn and experience the world of school. In addition to gathering numerical data, making observations and carrying out interviews and questionnaires, there are examples of enquiries which involve collecting examples of children's work and inviting children to comment on these, scrutinizing records such as test scores and attendance, and reviewing policies and practices (such as school dinners and playground provision) which impact on school life. In some enquiries, school staff seek the views of parents as an important source of information about children's learning.

The accounts presented here serve to foreground the diverse methods of small-scale enquiry, and collectively provide substantial indication of the value of this form of research. Within this Reader, personal enquiry in the workplace is conceptualised as an active, flexible and self-evaluative undertaking which enables adults to think purposefully about queries and dilemmas they encounter as they work with and support children. The 30 enquiries to be found in the following chapters, we believe, do much to promote the professional and personal reflection of adults in primary schools who are endeavoring to better understand and improve the very important role they play in children's learning.

References

Conteh, J., Gregory, E., Kearney, C. and Mor-Sommerfeld, A. (2005). *On Writing Educational Ethnographies: The Art of Collusion*. Stoke-on-Trent: Trentham Books.

Furlong, J. (2004). 'Bera at 30. Have we come of age?' *British Educational Research Journal*, 30(3): 343–358.

Humes, W. (June 2001). Unpublished seminar report to the Scottish Educational Research Association, University of Strathclyde.

Martin, N. (1987). 'On the move: teacher-researchers', in *Reclaiming the Classroom: Teacher Research as an Agency for Change* (edited by Goswami, D. and Stillman, P.). Portsmouth NH: Heinemann.

Shakir-Costa, K. and Haddad, L. (2009). 'Practitioner research: an inside look at using classroom research to inform and improve teaching'. *Science and Children*, 44(5): 25–27.

Stenhouse, L. (1981). 'What counts as research?' *British Journal of Educational Studies*, 29(2).

Taylor, C., Wilkie, M. and Baser, J. (2006). *Doing Action Research: A Guide for School Support Staff*. London: Paul Chapman.

Chapter 2

Workforce remodelling

The view from the school

Linda Hammersley-Fletcher and Michelle Lowe

The employment of adults other than teachers in schools has proceeded steadily since the mid 1990s. Teachers and head teachers have welcomed the classroom and administrative support that an additional workforce provides, but this significant workforce development has, it can be argued, happened in a somewhat piece-meal way. This is not, however, meant as a criticism of schools as they have had to manage and implement many reforms at the same time as employing and integrating additional staff to help progress these reforms. Workforce remodelling, in theory, is an opportunity for schools to bring about a more effective organisation of all staff. This chapter explores the gap that can occur between policy and practice. Linda Hammersley-Fletcher and Michelle Lowe consider findings from a small-scale study of eight Staffordshire schools. They find that the legislative requirements of remodelling are being addressed in a range of ways, with a tendency to prioritise cover for teachers' 'planning, preparation and assessment' (PPA) time rather than the wider purposes of remodelling embracing the work–life balance of all employees. They describe varied approaches to the establishment of school 'change teams' and question the extent to which all staff across the eight schools are truly represented and consulted.

Workforce remodelling is at the heart of the government's change agenda in maintained schools (Collarbone, 2004). It is presented as a process that will enable schools to think both creatively and flexibly about ways to introduce sustainable and beneficial changes in employment patterns and to improve teaching and learning practices. For the processes of change to take place all staff need to engage with the idea of 'remodelling'. The research reported here considers the reality of remodelling processes as they are practiced in schools and the extent to which all staff are involved.

This chapter considers evidence about the process of introducing workforce remodelling in four high schools and four primary schools in Staffordshire Local Authority through 48 interviews with headteachers, senior managers, teaching and support staff.

Background

The National Agreement between Government, employers and school workforce unions was intended to introduce significant changes to teachers' conditions of service. This was in some ways a response to the identification of workload as a major reason cited by teachers for leaving the profession; an attempt to address specific teacher shortages in a number of key subjects; the recognition that over 30 percent of a teacher's working week prior to the National Agreement was spent on non-teaching activities; and that teachers generally had a poor work–life balance (DfES, 2003). Furthermore, schools are employing increasing numbers of support staff for whom there is a need for professional development (DfES, 2001). The National Remodelling Team (NRT) was established by the DfES to provide a change management programme in a form appropriate to schools' needs. They describe remodelling as a self-directed approach that places the school in control of its own change agenda. Enshrined in the remodelling agreement was a promise of joint action to help every school across the country raise standards and tackle workload issues. This action was to take account of the different circumstances of each school.

The remodelling of the school workforce was designed to take place through three phases. Phase 1 included the changes made to teachers' contracts which were to promote a reduction in overall hours, introduce new work–life balance clauses, ensure the delegation of administrative and clerical tasks and provide leadership and management time. In phase 2 new limits on covering for absent teachers were introduced and in 2005 (phase 3) there was the introduction of guaranteed professional time for 'planning, preparation and assessment' (PPA time) which equates to 10 per cent of a teacher's time. For the change programme to be successful and sustainable there must be "a compelling reason to change, a clear vision for the future and a coherent plan for getting there" (see: www.remodelling.org/how.php). To enter into such a programme the NRT recommend establishing school 'change teams' which should contain representatives from all staff within the school and should be willing to consider the political, emotional and practical factors associated with each prospective change.

There are a number of questions raised about the process of remodelling. Stewart (2003) sees remodelling as a means of reducing education costs whilst solving teacher recruitment problems by employing unqualified staff to teach, thus enabling a smaller qualified teacher workforce to become focused on 'expert' teaching, planning and pupil assessment. Gunter (2004) has noted that the main issue is not the employment of such staff but the allocation of resources that will enable schools to appoint, train and develop these staff appropriately although she highlights the potential benefits that can be derived from the clarification of roles and workload audits which will enable schools to work more efficiently and effectively. What is important is that teachers are given time to reflect on the nature of their work to make any change effective (Lawn and Grace, 1987). It is therefore necessary for any research to establish whether the reforms envisaged by the government are actually taking place, the extent to which schools' are taking ownership of their own reform agenda and the extent to which the reform agenda is shared by all staff. This chapter explores these issues from research conducted within eight schools.

Are the reforms taking place?

All the schools visited were working on the legislative elements of workforce remodelling. There was considerable agreement with the notion of adjusting the work–life balance to something more sympathetic to having a 'life beyond school' but there was alongside this a mis-trust of the current model of remodelling meeting this need. It was acknowledged, however, that this at least was some kind of public acknowledgement of the workload faced by teaching staff. Phase one of the reform had been implemented and all the schools were working on phase two and particularly the element of PPA time. All staff seemed to have some understanding of how this would be managed. The primary schools' responses however, demonstrated some concerns with the expense involved in covering PPA time. In addition, teaching assistants who were expecting to cover teachers during PPA time expressed a deep concern with and commitment to doing the job well:

> ... the teacher obviously is being given time out ... so the input has got to be as strong as when the teacher is there ... if not better, because you are there to stimulate the child. ...
>
> (Support staff – primary)

The high schools were finding the organisation of PPA time easier. Teachers had the advantage of a situation where they have always had non-contact time although this was often eaten into by doing cover for other classes. Primary schools on the other hand had to make creative use of current staff resources and were more insecure about how they would meet the demands of PPA time in the future. There were also indications from a number of the schools visited from both phases that remodelling was something that was done and then completed, rather than seeing it as an ongoing process.

Do schools own their own reform process?

If, as recommended by the government, schools are to own the reform process and adopt change to meet their particular needs then the model of remodelling adopted in each school should look and feel individual. The models of remodelling adopted by schools researched did seem to vary particularly in terms of size and the phase of education involved. This can be illustrated (Table 2.1) by looking at a selection of four of the eight schools visited, two primary schools and two secondary schools. As Table 2.1 demonstrates the solutions for working on remodelling differ according to the circumstances of the school and, in particular, the preferred approach of the headteacher.

Is the reform agenda shared?

In the schools studied all those interviewed had heard about workforce remodelling but the depth of their knowledge about it was variable, particularly when it came to practice in their school. Those in the schools' senior management were much more likely to have a fuller knowledge of remodelling than other members of staff with support staff and teachers having only a very basic knowledge about it. There was, in addition, a feeling that explanations about remodelling needed reinforcing, particularly

Table 2.1 Models of remodelling

	Medium-sized urban primary school	*Medium-sized rural primary school*	*Medium-sized rural high school*	*Medium-sized urban high school*
Change Team	All staff excluding headteacher	Senior Managers plus all staff invited plus	None – Senior managers + selected representatives	None – Staff information meetings by Headteacher
Chair	Elected by team	Deputy head	Senior Manager	Administrator and Head
Responsibilities of Team	Available for discussion and to report on developments	Ensures agreed changes come into force	Ensures agreed changes come into force	Convey messages and ensure changes come into force
Approach of Team	Encouragement of open and frank debate (at times involved differences of opinion). Seen as part of their on-going development	Vehicle through which issues could be raised and solutions formulated. Staff audited about changes wanted and completed	Looking for ways of extending roles. Communication problems recognised	Keeping costs down. Communication problems recognised

amongst support staff. The high schools appeared to rely more heavily on smaller teams making decisions and then imparting these decisions to the rest of the staff rather than ensuring whole staff involvement. The lack of change teams also meant that teachers and support staff were less aware of what remodelling looked like in their school. There was, in some instances, a feeling from the support staff that the decisions around remodelling were not necessarily fully inclusive of them:

> ... basically it felt like 'this is how we're going to do it, and you've got to have a go at doing this sort of thing' ...
>
> (Support staff – primary)

This was in direct contrast to the teachers' view of staff involvement in remodelling:

> because it's a small school ... the whole staff was used as a change team. We all went through it together ...
>
> (Teacher – primary)

This may be indicative of the levels of empowerment felt by support staff in contrast to teaching staff and could also indicate the degree to which staff further down in what is perceived to be the hierarchy feel excluded from decision making.

Conclusion

The schools visited were all working to ensure that all the legislative requirements of the workforce remodelling agenda were being implemented. Issues around workload had been discussed but chiefly in terms of how to manage the introduction of PPA time rather than more general discussion about work–life balance. As Lawn and Grace (1987) point out, staff need time to reflect and reach understandings about what they are being asked to do in order to be clear about their commitment or otherwise, to change processes. Some of the schools visited seemed simply to be working to meet a government legislative agenda which raises questions about their understandings of the full implications of remodelling and as a consequence, their long-term commitment to it and the sustainability of the reform.

The communication of knowledge and understandings of remodelling was very variable as was the communication about how the workforce remodelling agenda was being met. Because channels of communication were not always open some members of staff did not feel involved in contributing to the decision making process. The varied approaches taken by schools may be appropriate in terms of the different cultures of each institution and the preferences of the headteacher (which was undoubtedly a strong influence on the approach adopted). However issues of communication in situations of change would seem to be extremely important. Clear understandings are necessary for all those involved in change as is a need to see where the school is going. It seems important for all schools to think very carefully about how such communication channels might be improved and perhaps reach an understanding that what they think of as good communication may in reality only be touching the edges of genuinely open interactions.

References

Collarbone, P. (2004) *Governors News April 2004*, National Association of School Governors, web-based journal, Birmingham available at: www.nagm.org.uk/govern-apr04.html

DfES (2001) *Teacher Workload Study*. London: PriceWaterhouseCoopers.

DfES (2003) *Time for Standards – Raising standards and tackling workload: a national agreement*. London: DfES.

Gunter, H. (2004) 'Remodelling the school workforce'. Paper presented at the School Leadership and Social Justice Seminar Society for Educational Studies, 4 November.

Lawn, M. and Grace, G. (eds) (1987) *Teachers: The Culture and Politics of Work*. London: Falmer Press.

National Remodelling Team: www.remodelling.org

Stewart, W. (2003) 'Storm out of blue skies'. *Times Educational Supplement*. 5 December 2003.

Chapter 3

Children's views of teaching assistants

Clare Fraser and Sara Meadows

After a long period of some neglect, researchers are now seeking the views of children about a range of educational issues. Government too feels it important to consult young people and this is reflected in the Every Child Matters agenda which originated from children's needs. Children in classrooms have, over a relatively short period, needed to adjust to the fact that adults other than qualified teachers can teach them. This is particularly so for those children who find school learning difficult or who cannot comply with the behavioural expectations of school life. Building on the small existing literature, Clare Fraser and Sara Meadows focus on three English primary schools to investigate the perceptions that children have of the role of teaching assistants. A questionnaire was completed by 419 junior children and 86 infant and junior pupils were interviewed. The study is of particular interest because it finds that even very young primary children can offer responses that are revealing of the similarities and differences between teaching assistants and teachers. The finding that when children do not understand something or are confused a 'teaching assistant explains things more clearly' seems worthy of further research.

The aim of this study was to elicit children's views of teaching assistants and to give children a 'voice' about a world which they are compelled to inhabit for a large percentage of their day. The responses that the children gave in interviews and questionnaires revealed a clear, coherent and sensible view of teaching assistants, at all ages.

1. Perceptions of the role of the teaching assistant

Interviews began by establishing that all children understood the term 'teaching assistant' and that assistants would be referred to as 'she'/'her' (because these children had only worked with female assistants). In answer to the question, 'Can you tell me all the jobs that she does?', the children listed a wide and varied range of duties covered by the role.

Taylor & Francis Journals for permission to reprint extracts from 'Children's views of teaching assistants in primary schools', Clare Fraser and Sara Meadows, *Education 3–13*, 2008, Vol. 36, No. 4, 351–363.

Children's answers offer a thoughtful representation of the wide range of activities that assistants can now reasonably expect to do in the classroom and, in particular, of the ways the assistant 'helps'.

The answers to the open-ended questionnaire question, 'Can you think of one important job a teaching assistant does to help a pupil?' are displayed in Table 3.1 below. This shows that the majority of children think that directly supporting their class work is an important job for an assistant. Nevertheless, as in the infant school study by Moyles and Suschitzky (1997), a significant number of children cited the role of the teaching assistant as being much more than just a helper. The assistant occupies a very powerful role in the eyes of some pupils and for a number of children, indeed, they seem to provide a pivotal role as a 'significant other'. A few pupils during the interview implied that they had already 'tested' their assistants' trustworthiness and reliability:

> If you don't feel comfortable talking to your teacher for any reason you can talk to her (assistant) and she keeps secrets as well!
>
> [Janet, age 10]

> She feels like a friend as well. We don't feel embarrassed to go up to her; I think everyone in our class, it would be safe to say, thinks Miss Hart isn't there to teach us, she's there as a friend.
>
> [Carol, age 10]

The majority of children thought that teaching assistants are employed to help everyone – both pupils and teachers. Some children even widened the field to include parents:

> I think parents as well because they can come in and they can speak to the parents.
>
> [John, age 8]

Table 3.1 Children's views on an important job the TA does to help a pupil

Code		*Frequency*	*Percent*
0	Missing = no entry	26	6.2
1	Helping with work; spellings if stuck, reads words and questions, helps to learn, solves problems, explains questions, gives ideas/clues, helps people concentrate, reads stories	307	73.3
2	Helps one pupil, group, special pupils, disabled	28	6.7
3	Listens when upset, helps when sad/hurt/in trouble, takes care of us, keeps secrets, makes sure we are all out if there's a fire	14	3.6
4	Helps teacher, same as teacher	15	3.5
5	Teaches, gives more work	13	3.1
6	Marks work, writes on whiteboard, changes reading books, sorts things out (child-centred duties)	8	1.9
7	Photocopying, classroom activities, cuts up paper, makes costumes for plays	4	1.0
8	Encourages pupils, makes you confident, gives incentives	4	1.0
	Total	419	100.0

> They are very important because they help everybody in the whole school not just like the teacher does, say 30 children, they help everybody.
>
> [George, age 11]

Almost all children said teaching assistants were important members of their school community, doing a useful or very useful job, and preferred to have at least one assistant in their classroom.

When asked, 'What do you think makes a good teaching assistant?', the children gave a wide range of thoughtful answers. The assistant should be a caring, happy and friendly woman, of comparable intelligence to a teacher, helpful, kind, with a good personality and, importantly, who is good at listening. Two themes that emerged from the interviews were that many children thought it was important for the assistant to like children and it was also important for the assistant to pay attention to the children. Some children gave more detail:

> If they ignore you they wouldn't be very good, because they've got to pay attention to what you are saying.
>
> [Bruce, age 8]

> Well, they have to get down to the child's level almost and not make them feel nervous and cope with child problems like 'they keep kicking my ball'.
>
> [Daniel, age 11]

It was generally agreed that teaching assistants need to be helpful and to be clever/brainy and know lots of things. The range of activities pupils thought assistants needed to be able to cover was probably indicative of the range of jobs they carry out on a daily basis: they have to be good at typing, writing, spelling, computers, cooking, art and teaching.

Personal characteristics were important qualities sought by some children: assistants need to know how to tell people off without upsetting them too much and to be calm, lovely, patient, understanding, funny, bright and happy, caring, not too strict and not get too 'eggy'. Additionally:

> If people fight she can make them become friends again.
>
> [Kyle, age 9]

Some older children recognised that boundaries were needed and suggested some discipline tempered with a fun-loving side:

> She should have some strict rules and also a sense of humour.
>
> [Neil, age 11]

2. What distinction do children make between their teacher and a teaching assistant?

Children of all ages in our study were able to distinguish between the roles of teacher and teaching assistant. They expressed a clear distinction in the power balance between these two adult roles. As in Hancock and Eyres (2004), there was a general sense that the teacher has an overall responsibility for the class and that assistants were 'on the periphery'. Concurring with the findings of Eyres *et al.* (2004), the children in this study perceived their class teachers not simply as 'more important' per se but, also, to have a management role, setting them above the assistant. During interviews children often depicted the teacher as 'leading the lesson', with the assistant carrying out the clarification on any given exercise. Class teachers were the people most commonly said to 'tell the teaching assistant what to do'. The idea of the teacher's ownership and responsibility for the class is mooted by some pupils as a crucial difference:

> The teacher teaches you all the time and they have the responsibility of properly looking after you and the other one would look after you when the teacher is busy.
>
> [Francesca, age 10]

Unsurprisingly, the word 'teaches' features quite heavily in the children's vocabulary when discussing the differences between the teacher and assistant; it is often applied solely for the teacher with the assistant as 'just' helping. Although the following quotes do not highlight what the assistant does to help, there is a clear distinction in the minds of the children in their perceptions of the two roles:

> The teacher teaches you things and the teaching assistant helps you a bit.
>
> [Mark, age 5]

> She doesn't actually teach, she doesn't actually write up what the teachers say, she doesn't go in the classroom and stand up and go at the front and talk the work out.
>
> [Jason, age 8]

A number of the teaching assistants were on part-time contracts and this was cited by pupils as a distinction between the two adult roles:

> She's not a teacher because she doesn't stay in the classroom all the time.
>
> [Alex, age 6]

It was found that some children thought that teaching assistants were 'teachers in training':

> She's learning to be a real teacher and to look after children.
>
> [Tim, age 6]

> I don't know, but I'm thinking that the teaching assistant is just learning how to be a teacher and hasn't really got qualifications or anything yet.
>
> [Isobel, age 11]

Other incisive differences that were suggested were:

> They don't get paid as much and I don't think they dedicate as much time as teachers normally do, whereas a teacher goes home and marks books every night

> and plans what she's going to do for the rest of the week, the teaching assistants well, they just come in and help on that day.
>
> [Robbie, age 11]

We found examples of symbolism used to distinguish between the two adult roles. In one group of Reception children, the notion of the 'teacher's chair' was developed as a distinction between the role of the teacher and the assistant:

> The teacher actually sits on the chair and the helper doesn't, so that's why the helper isn't the teacher.
>
> [Paul, age 5]

This notion of territory or priority was mainly, but not exclusively, expressed by younger children:

> She is not the teacher because Miss Morris was there before her.
>
> [Sam, age 5]

> Is it because we've got a teacher and she can't just move in on our teacher?
>
> [Liam, age 8]

3. Who do children work harder for?

Given that children are able to distinguish between their teacher's more managerial status and the teaching assistant's more peripheral role, it was surprising to find that 83% of children reported that they would work equally hard for either adult and make no such distinction. There was a significant gender difference here, with 20% of boys but only 8% of girls saying they would work harder for the teacher.

4. What kinds of things does a teaching assistant do to help children when they are stuck?

We asked in the interview, 'What kinds of things does a teaching assistant do to help you when you are stuck?' The children were able to articulate different ways in which assistants work in the classroom, mainly by supporting pupils when they are 'stuck' and explaining things more clearly.

5. How do children feel being withdrawn from the classroom?

The majority of the children in this study did not feel embarrassed to be taken out of class for extra help and a number of children even reported in the interview that they would prefer to be taught 'outside' the classroom for a number of reasons:

> I would prefer to be taken out because if you are trying to concentrate there is quite a lot of noise with all the children in one room, so if you want to concentrate you could come out with an assistant – I would prefer it.
>
> [James, age 11]

Contrary to popular teaching opinion that there may be a 'stigma' attached if you are taken from the class for extra help, this pupil found a sense of security in this action:

> I would like to be taken out because people in our class, well if you do something wrong they just laugh at you, so I would like to be taken out.
>
> [Peter, age 11]

The children in one of the schools were asked an additional question about how they felt when they got help with their work. Two year groups expressed positive feelings but older children were more likely to express feelings of embarrassment.

6. Children's perceptions of how they feel in the classroom

The children were asked to describe how they perceive themselves when they need help in the classroom and who they would ask for help. Most children expressed a healthy, confident image – willing to ask teachers or assistants for help when needed. The youngest children did not discriminate between the teacher or the assistant when asking for help when stuck with their work. Worryingly, around 25% of this sample reported that they would be worried about asking for help or feel too shy and nervous to do so. These were mostly junior children and they reported that they would prefer to ask a friend or neighbour first, before seeking adult help. Some of the pupils highlighted how their seeking assistance depended on the task and the quality of support that was available:

> It depends what the subject is, it depends whether the teaching assistant knows what you are doing and has been in the room.
>
> [Michael, age 10]

7. Teaching assistants and gender roles

The children in our study had only worked with female assistants and there were some signs of gender-stereotyping in their views. When asked whether they would like to be a teaching assistant 'when you grow up', very few said definitely 'yes'. Seventy eight per cent of boys and 51% of girls said definitely 'no' but 43% of girls and 17% of boys were prepared to say 'maybe'. In one interview group, children were asked 'why do you think there were not many men teaching assistants':

> Ladies like children more and maybe men like electricity more than girls.
>
> [Jane, age 7]

> Because men do the best jobs – like rally racing, flying and stuff.
>
> [Alistair, age 7]

> Maybe, because ladies know more than men?
>
> [Emma, age 7]

Conclusion and recommendations

It was found that children's views are fluently expressed and they can offer intelligible and realistic ideas about teaching assistants and their work, even at five years of age. Although a wide age range is included in this sample, the only age differences were in the amount of detail children offered, the coherence of their sentences and where they thought to expand upon ideas. Given free rein to express themselves they gave sensible and considered answers.

The main perceptions which the children agree on about the role of the teaching assistant, are that they view the role of the assistant as useful and helpful and feel that assistants are important members of the school community. Children are able to distinguish between the role of the teacher and the assistant and offer reasoned views to substantiate their distinctions.

The wide range of jobs which the children listed that a teaching assistant may carry out, concurs with the current expectation that the role the assistant plays has shifted from an ancillary role to one of directly supporting the pupil. Many children commented on the extra responsibility the teacher carries in comparison to the assistant. The children's main citation of an important job performed by the assistant is when they help them with their work and, more specifically, when they do not understand or are confused and the assistant explains things more clearly. Most children viewed working individually with a teaching assistant as a positive rather than a stigmatizing experience but further consideration needs to be given to the problem of those children who were anxious about asking for help. Those children who did not themselves work with a teaching assistant nevertheless felt that the work of the assistant freed up the work of the teacher and was, in turn, helpful to them.

Finally, the children's clear and insightful views of the roles of their teaching assistants were impressive. Researching children's perspectives is both a rewarding and an interesting thing for adults to do. It is an area that is still quite undeveloped but one vital in ensuring children's voices are heard, especially with respect to their schooling. So often adults decide what is best for children and make decisions on their behalf. It is right and proper in that parents, teachers and carers have responsibilities towards children but it should also be remembered that children have unique rights, opinions and perspectives and therefore need to be heard.

References

Department for Education and Skills. 2003. *Time for standards: Guidance accompanying the section 133 regulations issued under the Education Act 2002*. Nottingham: DfES publications.

Eyres, I., Cable, C., Hancock, R. and Turner, J. 2004. 'Whoops, I forgot David': Children's perceptions of the adults who work in their classrooms. *Early Years* 24, no. 2: 149–62.

Hancock, R. and Eyres, I. 2004. Implementing a required curriculum reform: Teachers at the core, teaching assistants on the periphery? *Westminster Studies in Education* 27, no. 2: 223–35.

Moyles, J. and Suschitzky, W. 1997. *Jills of all trades? Classroom assistants in KS1 classes.* London: ATL.

Chapter 4

Adult learning lives and biographies

Michael Tedder and Gert Biesta

We all have lives that have potential interest for a listener. The central argument of this chapter and the research study from which it arises is that, by talking to another about our lives we can take part in important biographical learning and develop understanding of what our lives have involved and mean. Our life-stories can have a 'plot' which serves, amongst other things, to organise our lives sequentially and thematically. The plots we construct can indicate, to ourselves and to others, what we have learned from our lives and what we consider significant. The Learning Lives Project explored these themes through in-depth interviews with about 125 adults who were interviewed up to eight times. It is suggested that when we construct our biographies – which is to some extent carrying out research on ourselves – we are, in fact, engaging in a valuable learning process.

Introduction

Lifelong learning is sometimes defined as an 'economic transaction' in which education is seen as a commodity 'a thing' for consumption. An important task for adult education researchers is to highlight the significance of the broad range of learning processes and practices that occur in the lives of adults so as to show that there is more to learning than this. The Learning Lives project, therefore, gave the participants opportunities to tell stories about their earlier lives and enabled the researchers to hear and discuss stories about changes in the participants' lives.

We became particularly interested in the role of life-stories and life "storying" in learning processes and in the relationship between the narrative quality of such stories and their learning potential. Unsurprisingly, we found that some people were more adept at telling stories about their lives than others, suggesting that the potential for their learning from their life-stories also varies. Our analysis revealed that a significant number of participants had come to some kind of understanding about their lives and

Michael Tedder and Gert Biesta for permission to reprint 'Learning without teaching? Opportunities and limitations in biographical learning for adults', Tedder and Biesta, 2008, a paper for The European Conference on Educational Research From Teaching to Learning? in Gothenburg, Sweden, 10–12 September 2008.

themselves and that this learning had had an impact on the ways in which they led their lives.

Biographical learning and narrative theory

The idea that life itself can be or can become an 'object' of learning is not new. Alheit and Dausien (2002) call it biographical learning and highlight three aspects: the implicit dimension, the social dimension and the 'self-willed' dimension. They note that the implicit dimension "forms a person's *biographical stock of knowledge*" (ibid., p. 15) and that we can reflect on and retrieve such learning "when we find ourselves stumbling or at crossroads" (ibid.). They emphasise that such reflexive learning processes do not exclusively take place 'inside' the individual "but depend on communication and interaction with others" (ibid., p. 16). And they argue that while learning within and through one's life history is interactive and socially structured, it also follows its own 'individual logic' generated by the specific, biographically layered structure of experience.

Although the stories people tell about their lives can be taken simply as accounts or descriptions of these lives, they may already reflect aspects of what people have learned from their lives, either in a more self-aware or implicit manner. It seems reasonable to assume that the construction and telling becomes an important part of such learning processes. To think of the life-story as a 'site' for biographical learning and to think of life-story*ing* as central to this activity, is captured in the notion of 'narrative learning' (Biesta *et al.*, 2008; Goodson *et al.*, 2010). Narratives, to put it briefly, are those stories that are characterised by a *plot* (Polkinghorne, 1988). Plots can organise stories either in a sequential or in a thematic, non-seqential manner but they provide structure to a story and enable the narrator to select relevant events in the story – thus making the story into an understandable narrative.

This raises the possibility that the presence of a particular plot – or particular plots – may be an expression of what narrators have learned from their lives. Sometimes the narrator seems to be aware of the plot and actively uses it to construct a particular 'version' of his or her life; at other times the plot can be reconstructed by the researcher – but does not seem to be part of the narrator's narrative 'strategy'. Bruner has suggested that we construct narrative – both at an individual and societal level – in order to justify the *departure* from established norms and patterns of belief (see Bruner, 1990, p. 47). Autobiographical accounts are therefore not simply descriptions of one's life but should be understood as accounts "of what one thinks one did in what settings in what ways for what felt reasons" (ibid., p. 119). Narratives thus reveal why it was necessary (morally, socially, psychologically) why the life had gone in a particular way" (ibid., p. 121).

This means that narration is not only about the construction of a particular 'version' of one's life and at the same time a construction of a particular 'version' of oneself. Although stories about one's life are about the past, Bruner argues that "an enormous amount of work is going on here and now as the story is being put together" (ibid., p. 122). This is not so much because the narrator needs to work hard to bring events back from memory, but more importantly because in telling about the past the narrator must decide "what to make of the past narratively at the moment of telling" (ibid.). Thus the narration is not simply to be seen as the outcome of a learning process, but can be seen as (narrative) learning-in-action.

A narrative perspective on biographical learning

In our reading and analysis of participants' life-stories we made use of the foregoing ideas in order to characterise and explore processes and outcomes of narrative learning. One reason for this was our interest in the question whether a focus on the narrative quality of life-stories could reveal something about the 'learning potential' of different narrative forms. Another reason was that we were interested in the 'action potential' of life-stories, i.e., the way in which and the extent to which particular narrative forms or characteristics relate to the ability to exert agency over and give direction to one's life.

Perhaps our most significant finding is that the differences between the stories people tell about their lives do indeed connect with ways in which people learn from their lives and that such learning affects how they conduct their lives. This not only suggests that life-stories and life-storying are important 'vehicles' or 'sites' for learning from life. It also suggests that the differences between stories matter for such learning.

One relevant dimension in this regard is the *narrative intensity* of life-stories. Narrative intensity refers to the length of the life-story and to the amount of detail and 'depth' of the account offered. The extent to which life-stories are more or less elaborate not only has to do with length and detail but also with the question whether the life-story is predominantly *descriptive* or whether it is more *analytical or evaluative*. We found stories that were at the more descriptive end of the spectrum and stories that presented themselves more explicitly as attempts to 'make sense' of the life.

To make sense of one's life – or, to be more precise: to construct a story which presents the life as 'making sense' – is related to the ideas of '*plot*' and '*emplotment*'. If we see the plot of a (life) story as an organising principle, then we can see that the presence of a plot is a strong indication that the narrator has learned something from his or her life. In most stories we were able to identify a plot and this coincided with the narrative being more evaluative and analytical than descriptive. Some participants appeared to be aware of the plot in their life narrative from the outset; for others the plot only emerged throughout the interviews. In some cases a plot was only discernible from the point of view of the researcher but there was little evidence that the narrator was aware of this plot. Not all stories carried a single plot and in cases with multiple plots we could also see that they functioned differently in the narrator's self-understanding. The absence of a plot does not automatically mean the absence of learning. We found examples of life-stories that lacked any emplotment but there was still evidence that the person had learned from life. This suggests that narration is only one of the possible ways of learning from one's life. It also highlights the fact that the life-story is a particular genre that is unfamiliar to some people.

The question of the awareness of a plot can be connected to the question of the *efficacy* of the life-story; that is, what is the 'learning potential' of life-narratives, i.e., the extent to which particular narratives make learning from one's life possible, and the extent to which such learning 'translates' into action? It seems as if in some cases people are 'caught' in their story so that their story and storying does not help them to 'move on'. Being 'stuck' in their life-story, and having a 'strong' version of one's life, can sometimes prevent further learning.

Important from the perspective of the learning potential of life-stories is the question of *flexibility*. We call a life-story scripted when there is little flexibility in the storying, when the life is lived and understood in relation to one particular 'version'. There is, as such, nothing wrong with this and the research provides evidence that for some people it is very important to have a 'strong' story about themselves and their lives as this gives them direction, orientation and a sense of self. This may become a problem in those situations where the 'fit' between the story and the conditions under which the life (and perhaps we could also say, the story) is lived begins to shift. We are not saying that narrative learning is the only way in which people can respond to change and transition but it can be an important resource, provided that there is a degree of flexibility in the story or, that there is a 'capacity' for narrative learning from life. Some participants clearly developed their ability to use narration as a way to reflect upon their lives. A certain familiarity with the 'genre' and perhaps even practising storying may be an element that can help develop the ability to learn narratively from one's life.

The question of the 'action potential' of life-stories is not necessarily connected to an ability to change one's story in relation to changing circumstances. We found evidence where holding on to a particular story or version of the life – often based on strong ideas about what a good life should look like – was effective for individuals to achieve a degree of agency control in particular situations.

Case study

Anne Wakelin – a participant in the project – told a story that illustrates some of the foregoing themes. Anne was a willing and fluent story teller and undergoing a significant transition in her life.

She was interviewed six times between November 2004 and May 2007. With her husband and three children, Anne had uprooted in 2002 from one part of the country to another. The Learning Lives project gave Anne the opportunity to tell stories about this life-changing transition.

Anne, aged 38 and married for 16 years, was the mother of a teenage daughter and two infant sons. The family came originally from the urban Midlands of England where Anne had lived all her life until she and her husband decided to move to a village in the rural South West. She came from a close-knit family where she was accustomed to visiting parents, grandparents and sisters regularly and, despite close family ties and an established pattern of life, Anne and her husband took the risks involved in making a major change. They had no previous connection with the village they moved to and yet were willing to leave behind their familiar lives for the sake of living somewhere new that was close to the sea.

When she left school, Anne had trained and worked for several years as a hairdresser. She described herself as being a 'people person' who found enjoyment in that profession. In the village and through her son's primary school, Anne came into contact with the government initiative Sure Start, becoming a volunteer mentor for the scheme. Subsequently she was invited to become 'parent rep' for the village at Sure Start organisational meetings and became active in a number of community groups. In time Sure Start employed her as a community development officer with responsibility for leading several projects for parents and children. Alongside her workplace learning were elements of formal education, including an NVQ 3 in Early Years Education. When the Sure Start initiative came to an end, Anne continued to be employed by her local authority as a community development officer.

Narrative quality

Anne is an enthusiast for life and the interview transcripts frequently quote her saying that things are 'fab', 'fantastic', 'lovely', 'brilliant'. Anne's narratives were primarily *descriptive* of events and the most distinctive characteristic of her stories was an intense *dialogic quality:* as an enthusiastic narrator of events in her life, she would frequently reconstruct conversations between key players in these. There was usually little analysis or reflection in Anne's stories, although the final interview achieved an unprecedented depth in terms of its *analytical* and *evaluative* quality when Anne was asked to comment on her experiences of taking part in the Learning Lives project.

Plot

The plot that emerges from Anne's narrative is of a wife and mother resuming her career after moving to a different part of the country. She presented as a vigorous, active, enthusiastic and sociable person engaged in an exuberant quest to engage in life's opportunities. Even the interviews were scarcely episodes of quiet reflection: she emerged as the epitome of the uninhibited multitasking mother, attending to her toddler, taking care of a pet, dealing with phone calls from work and phone calls about house improvements. She was excited by life and its possibilities and this exuberance characterises her stories about her own life, even when talking about family problems and conflicts. Most striking during the research period was Anne's resumption of her identity as a woman with a career. This resulted in stories about changes to routines, knowledge and skills and in her physical change.

The clue to Anne's perspective on the existence of a plot in her narrative is contained in the frequently used comment that she sees herself as a 'people person'. In her new location, becoming a community development worker enables Anne to pursue her interest in people in new ways – going into housing estates and caravans to locate small children and ensuring their carers are aware of their rights and responsibilities. Anne relishes 'being on a mission' and meeting the challenge of co-ordinating people and resources in projects. She loves doing this in a work environment where she can co-operate with others she finds congenial. However, she has a daily challenge of reconciling her aspirations and preferences with her concerns about her domestic life.

Learning potential

In early interviews we heard many stories *about* Anne's learning as a result of moving to a new home. Some adjustments were material such as how to cope with everyday matters like transport and shopping in a rural area. Others involved the way she related to her husband and children as she started to develop a new sense of identity in her new home and community. We heard of the skills and knowledge she gained from her voluntary and then her employed work for Sure Start. Anne's stories were of the experiences in which and from which she learned.

During the final interview Anne was asked to reflect on the experience of taking part in the project and this shifted the quality of her responses, away from a descriptive account to a more reflective stance. She commented on what a rare opportunity it had been:

> I've really enjoyed doing it. I've enjoyed doing it because it's, it's not very often that somebody sits there and lets you tell them about what you are and what you do and how you do your [pause] how your life has been, has been really.
>
> (Interview 6, June 2007)

It was suggested that perhaps the experience was like talking with friends or with relatives. While she agreed that friends may well get together and reminisce, it was never to the extent that someone talks about themselves at length. She added that family members have so many interests and commitments that they would not listen to each other for long.

Action potential

There was an embodied manifestation of the changes that Anne had experienced by our fifth interview. Anne had started attending a slimming club and lost three stone in weight. She resembled far more the glamorous young hairdresser featured in photographs in the family home. She spoke of having regained interest in buying new clothes and caring once more about her appearance.

A change in Anne's approach to telling stories was in the way she reported chronology: in our early interviews, Anne's sense of time was mainly 'family-centric' – she recalled chronology in terms of when things had happened to family members. By the final interviews she was 'organisation-centric'.

She said she enjoyed taking part in the interviews and reading the transcripts and found they offered an important insight into herself and the changes she had experienced:

> I'm doing more for a starter. I'm completely different in what I do. I'm working now. More confident in myself as I was three years ago, and more knowledgeable in what I do as well. The different outlook on things, you know, in my work, because I'd only ever been, as I say I'd only ever been a hairdresser.
>
> (Interview 6, June 2007)

However, in the final interview Anne communicated some of her underlying anxieties about getting older and the personal costs that were involved in pursuing her job. She said it was a 'horrible feeling that I've no baby in the house anymore'. She was moving beyond her motherhood identity to becoming someone who enjoys being at work and sees it as necessary to fulfil herself as a 'people person'. At the same time she recognises the personal cost of being no longer available for her children in the way she was. Nevertheless her narrative justifies a *departure* from her established norms and patterns of belief (Bruner, 1990).

> I would have been a right miserable bugger or, you know, I don't know how I'd have been. So life takes you in such funny ways you never know what's there... so just go with it.
>
> (Interview 6, June 2007)

References

Alheit, P. and Dausien, B. (2002) 'The double face of lifelong learning: Two analytical perspectives on a "silent revolution".' *Studies in the Education of Adults*, Vol. 34, No. 1, pp. 3–22.

Biesta, G.J.J., Goodson, I., Tedder, M. and Adair, N. (2008) *Learning from life: The role of narrative*. Summative working paper 2 http://www.learninglives.org/Working_papers.html

Bruner, J. (1990) *Acts of meaning*. Cambridge, MA and London: Harvard University Press.

Goodson, I., Beista, G.J.J., Tedder, M. and Adair, N. (2010). *Narrative Learning*. London and New York: Routledge.

Part 2

Contexts for small-scale research

Understanding children's experiences and learning environments

Chapter 5

Knowledge exchange activities for home–school communication

Martin Hughes and Pamela Greenhough

One of the aims of Every Child Matters (DfES 2004) is that schools should 'build stronger relationships with parents and the wider community'. This enquiry explores two different approaches to home–school communication in four primary schools: two in Cardiff and two in Bristol. This enquiry conceptualises home–school communication as 'home–school knowledge exchange'. We have included this enquiry because it is a collaborative project involving school staff and outside researchers, and because it presents parents' perspectives.

The enquiry evaluates two approaches to home–school knowledge exchange. The first is a video activity designed to enhance communication from school to home, where parents view a literacy lesson in their child's class. The second approach is a bag or shoe-box activity designed to enhance communication from home to school, where children introduce themselves to their new teacher through objects and images collected over the summer holidays. In each of the four schools, six children in Key Stage 1 (5–7 year olds) participated as case studies and interviews were carried out with them, their parents and their teachers at regular intervals during the activities.

In each city, one school contained a high proportion of children eligible for free school meals (HFM) and one school contained a lower proportion (LFM). The LFM school in Cardiff was a Welsh medium school and all teaching was carried out in Welsh.

Research background

Despite the emphasis on two-way communication, in practice much communication between home and school takes the form of 'one-way traffic' (Marsh, 2003). While it is relatively common for schools to provide parents with information about school activities and events, it is much less common for schools to seek out parents' perspectives or knowledge. The idea of 'home–school knowledge exchange' is that families and their

Taylor & Francis Ltd. for permission to reprint extracts from 'Boxes, bags and videotape: enhancing home–school communication through knowledge exchange activities', Martin Hughes and Pamela Greenhough, *Educational Review*, 2006, Vol. 58, No. 4, 471–487, reprinted by permission of Taylor & Francis Ltd., http://www.tandf.co.uk/journals

communities contain rich and extensive 'funds of knowledge' which are the 'historically accumulated and culturally developed bodies of knowledge and skills essential for household or individual functioning and well-being' (Moll *et al.*, 1992, p. 133). In this project we extend the concept 'funds of knowledge' so that it applies to teachers as well as parents and families. By developing and evaluating a series of knowledge exchange activities between home and school, we aimed to draw out and make visible the different funds of knowledge possessed by parents, children and teachers, and for each to communicate them to the other party.

The video activity

One issue emerging from the four schools was that many parents felt they did not know enough about how literacy was currently taught in their children's schools. The introduction of the National Literacy Strategy in the late 1990s had led to major changes in English primary schools. Similar changes had taken place in many Welsh schools. Many parents felt that their children were now being taught literacy in ways which differed significantly from how they were taught. Teachers identified literacy as an area where they wanted to communicate their expertise to parents and one method chosen to do this was through making a video for them.

The video activity took a different form in each classroom, reflecting differences in the school and community contexts. In the Bristol HFM school the focus of the video was on writing. The class teacher wanted to show parents how writing was taught and in particular the structure of the literacy lesson. She also wanted to show parents how independent the children were, how hard they worked and how much was expected of them. More generally, the school was looking to improve home–school relationships.

In the Bristol LFM school the focus was also on writing. Home–school relationships were generally good: the parents were seen as being confident and vocal with clear ideas about what and how they wanted their children taught. The teacher wanted the video to encourage the children's writing at home and help parents to support their children. The parents wanted to find out exactly how writing was taught by this teacher.

In the Cardiff HFM school the focus was on reading. The teacher wanted to show how reading was taught in her class and the various elements of a reading lesson, with a mixture of whole class, small group and individual activities. Parents wanted to find out how reading was taught and how they might support their children at home. However the parents' interest in reading was overshadowed to some extent by a wider concern about high levels of teacher turnover in this class. Some parents reported that home–school communication about children's progress in reading had suffered as a result.

In the Cardiff LFM school the focus was again on reading. The teacher wanted to model the literacy session and show which strategies were used to support the children. As this was a Welsh medium school the teaching on the video was done in Welsh. However, as many of the parents were not Welsh-speaking the teacher explained some activities in English, hoping the parents would attempt these with their children. The video also provided parents with an opportunity to see how their child performed in a completely Welsh speaking environment.

Each school invited parents to watch the video at a special screening. In addition, all parents were given copies of the video to watch at home and an accompanying booklet providing ideas about how parents might support their children's reading or writing.

The teachers in all four schools considered that the video activity had been successful. The feedback from parents was generally supportive, and they reported a positive effect on home–school relationships. Other aims also appeared to have been met. For example, the teacher in the Bristol HFM school said that parents had seen how hard the children worked in class and that they were putting less pressure on the school to provide homework.

The children in all four schools appeared to enjoy the video activity. They seemed to be relaxed in front of the camera and behaved more or less naturally in the classroom. Many children accompanied their parents to the video screenings and/or watched themselves on video at home. At one screening, the teacher– researcher reported there was 'a buzz of excitement when they saw themselves on the screen'.

The parents also reported that they enjoyed the video activity. Their comments suggested that the most valuable aspect of the activity had been the opportunity to see their children in the school context. Many parents reported that they had little idea of how their child behaved in the classroom, and that the video had, in the words of one parent, 'opened up the world of school to us'.

Several parents commented positively on what the video had revealed about the teachers' classroom practice in general. They appreciated the way the teacher organised the class and managed to maintain the interest of 30 children at the same time. The parents' comments were not always positive, though, with some reporting that the video had confirmed their view that the work was not sufficiently challenging for their child or that their child appeared to be bored. Two parents thought that the children were not paying sufficient attention to the teacher, while one parent thought that the classroom was noisier than she expected.

Some of the things parents noticed were more idiosyncratic:

Parent: Me and his dad had a great laugh.
Interviewer: Why was that?
Parent: Well, he picked his nose and ate it!
(Parent of a boy, Bristol HFM)

The parents' primary focus then, was on their own children and how they were responding to the demands of the classroom. In contrast, the literacy content of the lessons was not a main concern in the parents' responses to the video, even though this had been the original rationale for the activity. Indeed, several parents found it hard to recall what, if anything, they had learnt about the teaching of literacy. For example, one mother who had commented positively about the way her son's teacher had got all the children in the class involved, said later, when asked about the literacy content:

> … …I can't remember what the specifics were now, but I did feel I did get something about literacy from it.
>
> (Parent of boy, Bristol HFM)

The mother whose son had picked his nose during the video seemed unaware that the lesson had been about literacy. Her son's teacher had chosen the growth of plants as a writing topic, and his mother assumed that plants, science topic, was the main focus of the lesson.

There was also little evidence that the video and the booklet had led to any significant changes in the ways parents supported their children's literacy at home. Some parents reported that the booklet had got lost, or that they hadn't managed to read it. One mother explained that as her daughter was doing 'okay' at school, supporting her at home was not a priority.

For one parent, however, the video had clearly changed her ideas about reading and how she might help her son. She explained that the video had started by comparing a child reading a book for the first time, with no expression, and one reading a book they knew well, with lots of expression:

> I learnt a lot because I never used to read a story first, I'd just open the book and start to read it, and that's where you get your 'no expression', but if you've read the book and you look through the pictures and you explain the story, by the time you get to read it then you're more into it, aren't you, because you know what you're looking at. It makes sense ... but you don't think to do it until you're actually shown yourself, do you? ... it sort of opened my eyes more to how they learn.

This parent suggested that she had tried to follow this approach when listening to her son read at home.

The shoebox activity

The shoebox activity grew out of discussions, between project teachers and the research team, centering on the desirability of an activity which allowed children to bring aspects of their out-of-school lives into school. Like the video activity, the shoebox activity took a different form in the four schools. In the Cardiff HFM school the children used shoeboxes to introduce themselves to their new Year 2 teacher. They were given empty shoeboxes to take home over the summer holidays, with a letter explaining the purpose of the box. Parents were asked to encourage their child to decorate the box and fill it with items such as photos, toys, postcards, a book or magazine, some writing or any pictures they had drawn, and anything else which might be 'special' to them. At the start of the school year, the children returned clutching their decorated shoeboxes filled with personal artefacts. The class teacher also took part by filling her own box, giving the children information about her 'out-of-school life'. She put in a key ring tennis racket and a pair of chopsticks (she played tennis and was very fond of Chinese food) together with other personal items.

The teacher used the contents of the children's shoeboxes across the curriculum. In a history lesson children were asked, 'What can you tell about this person from the contents of their box?' However the boxes were used most intensively within the literacy curriculum, with the teacher designing a full week of writing around them. The children also presented an assembly around the shoeboxes, to which parents were invited.

At the Cardiff LFM Welsh medium school the teacher used a variant of the shoebox activity giving a bag to each child to take home and bring back with a favourite toy.

She spent time talking with each child about their toy. Later they wrote about it. The teacher was interested in whether allowing the children to have some control over the topic (by choosing the toy) influenced their talking and writing.

All four schools successfully achieved the aims of the activity. The boxes and bags enabled the children to bring aspects of their home lives into school, and the teachers were able to use this knowledge within the curriculum. Moreover, the children found the activity enjoyable and highly motivating. Parents frequently commented on how involved the children had been, decorating and deciding which toys or artefacts to put inside the shoebox.

The teachers also commented positively on how much they had learned about the children. The teachers at the Cardiff HFM school were particularly struck by the diversity of the children's out-of-school lives. The class teacher said: 'If you look at these boxes you can see all the differences in just a small group of children'. Her colleagues commented that 'all too often this diversity is closed down in schools', and she herself wondered 'do we make them conform too much?'.

The teacher at the Bristol LFM school was struck by the impact of the shoeboxes on the children's creative writing. She talked about several children having 'literacy breakthroughs'. The shoebox activity enabled the children to share their out-of-school interests with their classmates. One boy placed photographs of his two pet budgerigars in his shoebox. Months later a fellow pupil could remember Douglas's presentation to the class in great detail:

> He has two, one called Harry and one called Potter [laughs] ... He said they're very funny. They fly on their side. And whenever Douglas says 'Come on', it goes the other way.

Douglas's teacher remarked on how animated he had become when talking about his birds in class:

> ... he's not one who does often contribute to class discussions, although he's very bright, and if you talk to him he's very interested in a lot of things, but he doesn't have a high profile within the class.

As a result of this activity Douglas became the class authority on birds, and the other children would consult him when they wanted to know something about birds.

Discussion

The two activities took different forms in each classroom. These differences reflect a number of factors, including the differing school and community contexts, the various purposes of the participants, and the history of home–school relationships in the four locations. These differences are important, as they remind us that innovation in education is not simply about identifying 'what works' and implementing it in a standard format across all schools and communities. Instead, new ideas need to be adapted to the particular characteristics of each individual context. In particular, if school staff are to play a key role in implementing new ideas, then they need to feel a degree of ownership over the ideas. It is worth noting that the shoebox idea emerged during a discussion between the teachers and the research team.

The two activities also provide insights into the nature of knowledge at home and at school, and allow us to examine some of the complexities of exchanging knowledge between home and school. Lave and Wenger (1991) and Wenger (1998) suggest that knowledge is essentially 'situated' within particular communities of practice. This view fits comfortably with Moll and Greenberg's perspective that: 'The key point is that *funds of knowledge are manifested (or visible) through events or activities.* That is, funds of knowledge are not possessions or traits of people in the family but characteristics of people-in-an-activity' (Moll and Greenberg, 1990, p. 326).

This raises the question of how the different types of knowledge at home and school can be communicated or exchanged. The two activities described provide contrasting but illuminating answers to this question. In the video activity, the teachers constructed a visual representation of their classroom practice which made it visible to outsiders. In the shoebox activity the children and their parents brought in artefacts such as toys or postcards providing concrete representations of their out-of-school activities. Both children and teachers had the opportunity to explain their representations and how they linked to lived experiences, practices or activities at home or school.

This process of knowledge representation is not by any means straightforward or unproblematic. In the video activity, the teachers had to make decisions about which aspects of their practice they wanted to represent and how they wanted to do this. This process was clearly influenced by their aims for the activity, such as the teacher who wanted parents to see 'how hard the children worked'. Similarly, the selection of artefacts for the shoeboxes was strongly influenced by how the children and their families wanted to represent themselves to the school.

The process of representing home and school knowledge in knowledge exchange activities, then, is influenced by a range of factors, including the purposes of the different parties and how they want to be seen by others. In turn, these various representations are not simply received in a passive way, but are actively interpreted in terms of particular agendas and concerns.

Issues of power and control in home–school communication are closely related to issues of risk and threat (MacLure and Walker, 1999). Both the activities described here contained a risk of participants being exposed in an unwelcome way. In the video activity, the teachers opened up their professional practice to the parents' scrutiny; the shoebox activity opened up the children's out-of-school lives to the scrutiny of their teachers and their peers. While some of the parents who saw the video activity were critical of the teachers' practice, a more common response was one of respect and appreciation of their classroom skills. And while some children may have been inhibited from bringing very personal artefacts into school, those who did found the responses of their teachers and classmates overwhelmingly positive.

This study has shown that more attention needs to be given to activities which allow elements of children's out-of-school lives to be brought into the classroom and linked to the curriculum. At the same time, the value of such activities may be limited unless they are accompanied by a more fundamental change in the power relationship between home and school.

References

Department for Education and Skills (DfES) (2004a) *Every child matters: Change for children* (London, DfES).

Lave, J. and Wenger, E. (1991) *Situated Learning*. Cambridge: Cambridge University Press.

MacLure, M. and Walker, B. (1999) *Secondary school parents' evenings*. End of award report to the ESRC.

Marsh, J. (2003) 'One way traffic? Connections between literacy practices at home and in the nursery'. *British Educational Research Journal*, 29(3), 369–382.

Moll, L. and Greenberg, J. (1990) Creating zones of possibilities: Combining social contexts for instruction. In: L. Moll (Ed.) *Vygotsky and education* (Cambridge, Cambridge University Press), 319–348.

Moll, L., Amanti, C., Neff, D. and Gonzalez, N. (1992) 'Funds of knowledge for teaching: Using a qualitative approach to connect homes and classrooms'. *Theory Into Practice*, 31, 132–141.

Wenger, E. (1998) *Communities of Practice*. Cambridge: Cambridge University Press.

Chapter 6

Children in transition from play to 'work'

Gabrielle White and Caroline Sharp

What does it means to 'get bigger' and do more 'work'? In this enquiry, we learn what children think about an important transition in their lives as they prepare to move from the Reception to Year 1. We included this chapter because it foregrounds children's voices: they discuss (and in some cases make drawings about) their understandings of work and play and how the classroom environment, the curriculum and approaches to teaching impact on their enjoyment of learning. A total of 70 children in 12 schools were interviewed informally on two occasions, in the Summer term of their Reception year and in the Autumn term of Year 1.

Findings

The findings from the study indicated that a majority of the children coped well with the transition to Year 1. However, the interviews with the children also highlighted the influence of the curriculum and teaching approaches on their enjoyment of learning. For many of the children the most positive element of moving to Year 1 was about 'getting bigger' or 'growing up', but this was counterbalanced by the experience of 'doing hard work' and having fewer opportunities for play-based learning.

Children's experiences in Reception

When asked about their experiences in Reception, the children in our sample gave detailed descriptions and drew pictures to illustrate the wide variety of activities they experienced at school. The children commonly used the word 'play' and rarely used the term 'work' to describe their experiences at school. Activities such as reading and writing were mentioned by some of the children but these were not labelled as either 'play' or 'work'. This is illustrated in the following extract:

Researcher: What sort of things do you do at school?

Girl: Read books, colouring, play on the computer, cut and stick, play with dominoes, play in the airport [role play area], play snap, drawing pictures.

Play activities were not the only activities children talked about when describing Reception class life, as the following account demonstrates:

Researcher: What sort of things do you do at school?
Girl: I love reading... I go to my house and say 'Mum can I read my reading book?'

Interestingly, when asked whether there was anything she did not like about school, the same girl said; 'I hate it when we do work. Every time we do work all we have to do is write and my hand gets tired.'

This particular girl equated the term 'work' with the writing element of her curriculum experiences in Reception. Writing was mentioned by several other children in answer to the question 'Is there anything that you don't like about school?' Number work (particularly if it involved recording in writing) was also unpopular, as illustrated by these comments from a girl and a boy:

Researcher: Is there anything you don't like about school?
Boy: Oh yeah, doing work like writing and numbers because it takes too long.
Girl: I don't like number work, because you have to write things.

In addition to identifying 'work' as an activity they disliked, several children said they disliked activities where they had to sit still for periods of time such as 'sitting on the carpet' and 'going to assemblies'. For example, one girl said: 'I don't like sitting for a long time because it's boring'.

The children were asked what they enjoyed doing most in Reception. In response to this question the children reported enjoying activities they described as 'play', particularly role-play, dressing-up and playing outside. Social interaction with their peer group was important for children: many talked about group play and drew pictures of themselves playing with their friends. For example, one girl said: 'I like playing with [the] tea set because you can share with other people.'

Anticipating life in Year 1

When asked what they thought it would be like in Year 1, children said that Year 1 would be quite different from Reception. They thought there would be fewer toys and terms such as 'work' and 'hard work' were common in their descriptions of Year 1:

Researcher: Do you think Year 1 will be different from Reception?
Girl: Yes.
Researcher: How will it be different?
Girl: Well you have to do hard work when you go to Year 1 because you are getting older. We will do all writing and stuff because they do more

work than us in Year 1. They don't have any toys, only some, not lots and they don't have dressing up things like here and I like dressing up.

Extracts from an interview with two boys at the same school revealed similar concerns:

Researcher: What do you think it will be like in Year 1?
Boy 1: Alright.
Researcher: Will it be different from Reception?
Boy 1: Yes.
Researcher: How will it be different?
Boy 1: All they have there is books. We have books and toys in Reception but all they have in Year 1 is books. Only Reception has the toys.
Boy 2: They don't have toys in Year 1 and sometimes we might go outside but sometimes we won't in Year 1. The work will be differenter because it will be harder because you are getting older. When you go in Year 1 you get older so you have to do harder work.

The children talked about having to do more and/or harder work in Year 1 because they were growing up. Some of the children were clearly worried about the workload increasing. Others said that there would be less opportunity to engage in the activities that they really enjoyed:

Researcher: Is there anything you are worried about?
Girl: Yes, not being able to play with my friends.

Although children's expectations of Year 1 were very consistent, there were some differences in the responses from children when comparing the data from different schools. For example, children from a school where the play-based, active learning approach was continued from the Early Years Foundation Stage into Year 1 were noticeably more positive about the move and tended not to use the term 'hard work' in their descriptions. They anticipated that there would be 'new things to do' when they moved up, such as model-making and 'doing new jobs'.

A minority of children (noticeably those who were younger) were confused about moving into Year 1, because they had not understood that the Year 1 children would be moving out. Some of them expressed anxiety about the prospect of being in a class with children who were older than them and they were worried they might get hurt or bullied as a result.

Most of the schools held a 'move up' day when all children spent time in their new class with their new teacher. This experience clearly helped the children to make sense of the transition process. Several children had already made a visit to their new class at the time of the first interviews. These children were able to base their ideas about what it would be like in Year 1 on their experiences during the visit:

Researcher: What do you think it will be like in Year 1?
Girl 1: I went there for a visit. We will do things like pictures when we go to Year 1.

Girl 2: I already know because I have been there because we had 'Change over classes'.

Boy: We went in their class already. Everybody moved up and I went in the Year 1 class.

One of the parents explained how the visit had helped her son to make sense of the impending transition:

> He said he had been to see the classroom and that he liked the classroom. It [the visit] was helpful and it focused his mind on it. He had been getting a bit confused because I had said to him that he would be moving up to X class after the holiday but he would say 'I don't know anyone in X class'. He hadn't realised that everyone would move up, so going to the classroom helped him realise what was happening.

In the course of their interviews, children frequently described physical features of their environment, such as the journey from the school entrance to their classroom, the way the classroom was laid out, the amount of space in the room, the pictures on the walls, the seating and the colour scheme. Most of the children who had visited their new classroom had noticed and remembered physical differences between their new classroom and the classroom they were currently occupying. For example, a girl in one school recounted the things she had noticed that were different in the Year 1 classroom:

Girl: It is very different. It has more stuff ... more chairs and tables and loads of carpet that is all joined up together. They don't have string for hanging the pictures on and they don't have our pictures on the wall, they have the other children's pictures there and they don't have any cupboards.

The children were asked whether they were looking forward to coming back to school after the summer holidays and if there was anything they were worried about. Although most children were positive about the move, a few were anxious about the changes. They were worried that the work would be 'difficult' in Year 1 or about being 'told off' by staff. This is illustrated in the following exchange:

Researcher: Is there anything you are worried about?

Boy: Yes, I might not know the words in the books because they have different books and the books in Year 1 are harder.

Girl: Being told off.

Children rarely mentioned their teachers during the interviews about life in Reception or Year 1. The research team asked children whether they had met their new teacher and the majority had. When asked what their new teacher was like, most said s/he was 'nice'. A few children said they were worried that their new teacher might get angry and shout at them.

Children's experiences in Year 1

The research team returned to the case study schools to interview the children a few weeks after the transition. It was evident that their descriptions of life in Year 1 mirrored their expectations in Reception. The phrases 'hard work', 'more work' and 'loads of work' featured frequently in their responses. Children commonly mentioned number work and writing in this context:

Researcher: What sort of things do you do in Year 1?
Girl: We do hard work. We have to count lots and we are trying to do some numbers.

Some of the children appeared to be adapting to the challenges posed by the changes in the curriculum and felt they were achieving well: 'I like doing hard work, I like doing lots of hard work'. However, many found life in Year 1 less enjoyable. In particular, children regretted the reduction in play activities and the loss of choice in their Year 1 curriculum:

Girl: It [Year 1] is different ... In Reception we used to dress up and we could play on the carpet with the dressing-up stuff. We *can* play in Year 1, but not lots of times any more.

The children also mentioned that they had fewer opportunities to work with friends, to move around freely and go outside.

When asked whether there was anything they did not like about being in Year 1, the most common response was that they disliked spending time sitting still, listening to the teacher during 'carpet time':

Researcher: Is there anything you don't like about being in Year 1?
Boy 1: Being on the carpet for a long time.
Boy 2: Neither do I, because it's very boring.
Boy 1: And it wastes our time playing.
Boy 2: It wastes your life.

A similar dialogue about carpet time took place between a boy and girl in a different school:

Boy: I don't like sitting on the carpet all the time.
Girl: Yeah we just sit, sit, sit.
Boy: Yes and it's boring.
Girl: Yeah and we could be playing outside and getting some exercise.

Similarly, two other children at the same school commented that they did not like sitting on the carpet in Year 1. Although they had experienced 'carpet time' when they were in Reception, they explained that they were sitting still more often in Year 1: 'Now we *always* have to sit on the carpet'.

Very few of the children interviewed in Year 1 identified opportunities to choose their activities. In 7 of the 12 schools, children's opportunities for choice in Year 1 were limited. Several schools had a period called 'Golden Time', usually on a Friday afternoon, when children could choose their activities. Some of the children identified these periods as a favourite part of their school life:

Researcher: What do you like doing best in Year 1?
Both children: Golden Time.
Boy: Because I like dressing up.
Girl: I like doing the art things.

In addition to identifying differences in their activities, children talked about differences in the geographies of their classrooms. They commented on what was different about the physical environment in Year 1 and how this impacted on their daily routine:

Researcher: What's different about this year compared to last year?
Boy: Well we have drawers now not a box for your book bag ... the lunch-boxes go under the craft tables now and we have to put our snacks in a different box.

Some children noted particular features of the classroom, including equipment and resources, that were different in Reception and Year 1. This is illustrated in the following dialogue:

Researcher: What's different about this year compared to last year?
Girl: We haven't got a pretend shop.
Boy: Or a house.
Girl: We have activities.
Boy: We have got Lego.

When comparing the data collected from different schools, one clear association emerged in relation to the children's descriptions. The children in schools where staff were continuing to provide play-based, practical learning opportunities in Year 1 tended not to use the phrase 'hard work' to describe their experiences. These children did identify some differences when comparing Year 1 with Reception but they also reported doing similar activities, as illustrated in the following dialogue:

Girl: We have the same toys, the Lego; we still play with the cars.
Boy: We still have the garage which is my favourite game.
Girl: Yes, and we have sand and water because we brought it with us.
Boy: We do choosing like we did in Reception.

Discussion

The analysis of children's views suggests that most children experienced a relatively smooth transition between the two stages of education. Children appeared to view the transition to Year 1 as a natural part of getting older and growing up. Their predictions

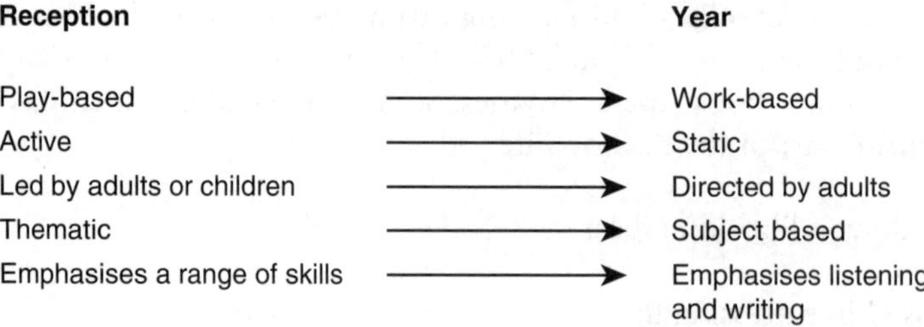

Reception
Year
Play-based
Work-based
Active
Static
Led by adults or children
Directed by adults
Thematic
Subject based
Emphasises a range of skills
Emphasises listening and writing

Figure 6.1 Changes experienced by children between Reception and Year 1

about Year 1 were largely confirmed by their experiences. A few had misconceptions about Year 1, but those who had visited the Year 1 class while in Reception had a clear and realistic picture of the new environment. Children in schools which used a similar curriculum approach in Reception and Year 1 noticed the similarities and were able to articulate these clearly to the research team.

The main differences experienced by children before and after the transition are summarised in Figure 6.1.

The interviews highlighted the influence of the curriculum and pedagogy on children's enjoyment of learning. Children valued their experiences in Reception and regretted the loss of opportunities to learn through play. They noted that they had fewer opportunities to choose their activities and to move around. While some enjoyed the new challenges and relished the chance to demonstrate their mastery of 'hard work', others were worried by their ability to cope with the workload in Year 1. Children disliked writing and were bored by sitting and listening to the teacher during 'carpet time' (which was particularly associated with the literacy mathematics lesson). These issues are clearly important in relation to children's enjoyment of learning.

The study could add to theoretical development in this area by identifying the features of transition that are connected with young children starting school and those that are connected with transition within school. For example, previous studies of the transition to school have drawn attention to children's concerns about making friends, understanding rules, adapting to routines and the balance between work and play. This study of children making a transition within school found that they were not particularly concerned about rules or making friends because these elements were unaffected by the transition in question. Children were aware of changes in their routine, although these were often relatively minor in nature. However, issues relating to the curriculum and pedagogy (i.e. the balance between work and play, the degree of choice and active learning) were very much to the fore. Children were also highly attuned to changes in their physical environment. In the course of their interviews, children frequently described features such as the journey from the school entrance to their classroom, access from the room to outside, the way the classroom was laid out, the amount of space in the room, the pictures on the walls, the seating and the colour scheme. These aspects demonstrate the importance of taking children's 'geographies' into account when considering their adaptation to a new environment.

In relation to policy, the study has clarified the nature of children's transition to Year 1 and has identified clear issues in relation to curriculum and pedagogy.

The research team therefore recommended that policy-makers consider providing more advice and training to teachers on how to ensure greater continuity of experience for children (especially continuing aspects of Reception practice in Year 1). The study identified 'carpet time' as problematic for young children and has suggested that teachers should be encouraged to provide opportunities for active, independent learning and learning through play.

This study provides encouragement for school managers and staff to adopt transition practices aimed at improving continuity, communication and induction. It was clear that time and effort expended on induction practices (such as ensuring continuity of experience and routine, visits to the new classroom and communication with children and their families) had a positive impact on children's understanding and experiences of the transition to Year 1.

Chapter 7

Children's experiences of domestic violence

Helen Buckley, Stephanie Holt and Sadhbh Whelan

This enquiry from the Republic of Ireland explores with sensitivity the experiences of children and young people who have lived with domestic violence. A total of 22 children and young people between the ages of 7 and 18 participated in this enquiry by sharing their experiences in discussion groups. In the groups, they describe the impact of domestic violence as having a sense of lost childhood. They discuss what they feel schools should know and could do which might help to alleviate their feelings of difference, fear, anxiety and isolation.

We have included this chapter because children who experience domestic violence tend to have 'low visibility' in schools, and because there is an irrefutable link between domestic violence and child abuse. This enquiry reminds us of the need and indeed the requirement for schools to support and protect vulnerable children and to share information across professions.

The children participated with the support of staff from a refuge centre and experienced health and social care professionals. Consent was obtained from children and parents, and the groups provided a safe peer environment which provided mutual support. Play-focused and 'ice-breaking' activities were organised before the group discussions. Like Chapter 15 by Jill Rutter on refugee children, this enquiry demonstrates how children respond in unique ways to traumatic experiences.

What children tell us about domestic violence

Children don't have to necessarily 'witness' violence directly in order to be aware that it is happening (Cunningham and Baker, 2004). Very few children, if any, will escape the experience of living with domestic violence unaffected and there is evidence to suggest that it affects children's emotional and mental health, their future relationships and sometimes their physical safety. The focus group discussions bore out these assertions with some very vivid illustrations. One of the impacts was on the children's sense of

John Wiley & Sons, Inc. for kind permission to reprint extracts from 'Listen to me! Children's experiences of domestic violence', Helen Buckley, Stephanie Holt and Sadhbh Whelan, 2007 in *Child Abuse Review* Vol. 16, 296–310.

their own safety and security and the fear and dread that it instilled in them. Although the older groups considered that their awareness of problems at home had developed in their early teens, it was clear from the contributions of the younger children that they too were conscious of fights and frightening occasions where they worried about their own, their siblings' and their mothers' safety as well as a general tension or uneasy atmosphere at home. A young child told us how she coped:

> I used to hide under my bed all week. I used to make a little place out of it with all my teddies. He ... always used to buy teddies for us ... and I used to store them under my bed, any time I felt sad or when they were screaming and roaring down in the kitchen ...

Not surprisingly, the children experienced considerable anxiety, not only when violence was occurring, but when they perceived certain triggers which signaled that it might be imminent. A teenager described the constant apprehension as 'spinning the whole time ... when it's not happening you're waiting for it again'. Another teenager compared his arrival home from school to 'walking into a nuclear war' and learned to anticipate trouble when his parents went out drinking. Another young person experienced the same sort of feelings of trepidation when her parents went drinking:

> The fear would start then and it didn't end until we knew they were in bed asleep. None of us slept at night when they went out ... we'd stay awake and try and intervene most of the time.

One of the most important needs that emerged was for the children to be able to feel safe.

Loss of confidence and self-esteem, stigma and secrecy

Research indicates that secretiveness about family problems is particularly characteristic of school age children (Alexander *et al.*, 2005) and the focus group findings in this study showed this to be a fairly universal trait among all age groups. Two young teenagers described how they would conceal what was going on at home for fear of being bullied and teased at school. Loss of self-confidence and self-esteem was also described by the older teenagers and young people, and an overwhelming feeling of 'being different', having 'a neon sign that told everyone what was going on', sticking out 'like a freak' were some of the feelings expressed by the older teenage group. Reluctance to trust, or fear of someone 'blabbing it out' also prevented some of the younger children from sharing their situation with friends. They shared a perception with the older ones that telling peers about what was happening at home would leave them open to being bullied, a point which will be developed later.

Relationships with classmates at school were affected. Children spoke of how wary they had been about becoming close to any of their peers in case their 'shameful' home circumstances were revealed. They also feared rejection, and tended to compound their own isolation by, for example, never inviting friends to their homes out of embarrassment in case of a potential row or 'shouting', thus separating themselves from the birthday party or sleepover circuit. The negative impact on their ability to make and retain friendships applied to all age groups, not just older teenagers and adolescents. Disruption of home circumstances by moving to refuges and re-settling elsewhere also meant that children were faced with the loss of their friends.

School experiences

Research indicates that academic and social success at school has an important impact on children's sense of self, with the school providing the opportunity for significant changes in the child's social life (Gilligan, 1998); their friends become more important as they develop relationships with people outside their families (Daniel *et al.*, 1999). One of the older teenagers interviewed saw school as his 'safe place' and saw it as a haven away from home for six or seven hours a day. However, for a number of the children involved in this study, school was or had not been a positive, or successful experience. As the research literature has shown, children witnessing domestic violence are nearly three times as likely to be involved in physical aggression at school (Dauvergne and Johnson, 2001).

Fear of being bullied in school was an issue for the younger children involved in this study who wanted to keep their home situations a secret. Difficulty in concentration was a problem for some, who were distracted by worry or lack of sleep. Sometimes, children found the strain of having to produce homework when things were chaotic at home to be intolerable, leading to conflict with teachers, which in turn acted as a disincentive for the children to engage with school. Some also gave examples of getting a 'rough time' from teachers who couldn't or didn't want to understand or intervene.

As already mentioned, the children feared that if information about their private lives leaked out in schools, they might be subject to bullying, and unfortunately this was something that many of them had experienced. Children said they would feel 'mortified' if their mothers or fathers spoke to teachers about their difficulties. Yet, one of the young people who had since left school expressed her regret that teachers had not reached out to her more:

> Personally, that time for me was horrible and if somebody just said it to me, 'Is there something you want to talk about?' I probably would have told everything. My god, somebody noticed ...

What children and young people want from schools and services

When asked about what services they felt would be helpful for children experiencing domestic violence, the young people, i.e. those over 17 years, focused strongly on school. Most considered that the problems they themselves had experienced there, particularly the bullying, would not have occurred if teachers had been more informed and understanding and open to talking to them about their situations. The older teenage group (14–17) supported the idea of a programme of information on domestic violence to inform teaching staff and other pupils and potentially to make extra provision, for example, a place to do homework for children who needed it, to encourage them to achieve good results in order to create 'an escape route'. They also felt that if schools demonstrated an awareness of domestic violence as a problem, children who were victims of it would not feel quite so isolated and different.

While the younger children (11–14) agreed that it would be beneficial for their teachers to know about their home situations, they considered discretion and privacy to be very important; for this reason they felt that attending the school counsellor might attract curiosity and that any visible contact between their parents and schools was a potential source of embarrassment for them.

The need for a place to talk and 'let it out' was identified by all the children's groups as a means of reassuring them that they were not alone and not different from everyone. Most of them felt it would have been hugely valuable if they had been able to share their feelings with someone, whether it was a teacher, a peer, or someone in a formal helping/caring capacity. Some of the young people favoured what they described as 'group therapy'. However, it was clear that not all children find it easy to reveal private events in their lives. Research has identified 'blocking' and embarrassment as features of adolescence (McGee, 2000; Mullender *et al.*, 2003; Cunningham and Baker, 2004) and this was particularly evident in the younger teenage group. As one 14 year old pointed out: 'people our age mightn't want to talk about it as much' and as another put it 'you'd feel weird about talking to someone you hardly know'. It was considered that, at least initially, any provision should be on a one-to-one basis rather than in a group. Some felt that having a mentor, possibly within their family, 'somebody you could look up to', might help and possibly be able to intervene with their parents. The younger teenage group in particular felt that choice was important and suggested a centre where opportunities would exist for them to talk about their problems but where other 'ordinary' activities would be available to them as well. Both the younger groups enjoyed youth club type projects but felt that they were not appropriate venues for talking about their situations at home, or their feelings.

When asked specifically what they would like for themselves in a refuge setting, the children and young people recommended a mix of activities 'so you won't notice what's going on' and people to talk to and 'know in the back of your mind they will always be there, whenever you feel like talking'. Some felt that it might have been useful to have someone talk to both themselves and their parents together. Being taken seriously and listened to in a way that was appropriate to their age was considered important by a member of one of the younger groups who commented that adults often assume that children are immature and 'not able to do anything'.

Implications for schools and services

The findings from this study confirmed that a specific service for children was required at different levels, including direct domestic violence related programmes as well as linkage with scools, community based agencies and organisations based on the children's needs, their developmental stages and their own perceptions of what would be helpful. The crucial element is co-ordination which must be in place to ensure that children do not slip through the net of fragmented services, and to effect as far as possible a fit between the children's different needs and the response being offered. Ideally, it would be co-ordinated by a dedicated agency or team, based in either a refuge or a mainstream children's service, who would take overall responsibility for its management and ideally would deliver on these three principal elements.

The children and young people's descriptions of the anxiety, fear and dread they endured in their childhood and teenage years, their experiences of being bullied at school, the burdens of responsibility they carried in relation to their parents and their siblings and their regrets about their lost childhoods and opportunities certainly belied any notion that situations and incidents of violence go unnoticed, or that parents can protect their children from its impact. One of the most striking aspects of the findings is the 'ordinariness' of the children's experiences, which on the surface disguises their detrimental impact. For example, it is developmentally normal for young children to show distress when parents are arguing, for teenagers to feel self-conscious about their families, to argue with parents and to present challenging behaviour in school. What is different here is that children who live with domestic violence are likely to experience these maturational processes in an acute and sometimes pathological manner. While some of the children's reactions had already attracted professional attention and concern, many of the others' went unnoticed, probably because they were mistaken for typical, exasperating, juvenile behaviours. Despite what we now know about the impact of domestic violence on children, lack of professional awareness in key services such as schools and police, combined with the children's wariness and tendency to conceal what was happening at home continue to contribute to the invisibility of this group. Given current pressures on mainstream child welfare services, it is unlikely that this situation will change unless a pro-active and co-ordinated approach is developed and targeted at these children.

References

Alexander, H., Macdonald, E. and Paton, S. (2005) 'Raising the issue of domestic abuse in schools'. *Children & Society* 19: 187–198.

Cunningham, A. and Baker, L. (2004) *What About Me! Seeking to Understand a Child's View of Violence in the Family*. Centre for Children & Families in the Justice System: London, Ontario.

Daniel, B., Wassell, S. and Gilligan, R. (1999) *Child Development for Child Care and Protection Workers*. Jessica Kingsley: London.

Dauvergne, M. and Johnson, H. (2001) *Children Witnessing Domestic Violence*. Juristat Cat No. 85-002 21, (6). Canadian Centre for Justice Statistics: Ottawa.

Gilligan, R. (1998) 'The Importance of Schools and Teachers in Child Welfare'. *Child and Family Social Work* 3: 13–25.

McGee, C. (2000) *Childhood Experiences of Domestic Violence*. Jessica Kingsley: London.

McGuigan, W.M. and Pratt, C.C. (2001) 'The Predictive Impact of Domestic Violence on Three Types of Child Maltreatment'. *Child Abuse & Neglect* 25: 869–883.

Mullender, A., Hague, G., Iman, U., Kelly, L., Malos, E. and Regan, L. (2003) *Children's Perspectives on Domestic Violence*. Sage: London.

Chapter 8

Walking and cycling to school

Joanna Kirby and Joanna Inchley

The benefits of participation in regular physical activity are well-documented as contributing to young peoples' physical, psychological and social well-being. In this chapter, Joanna Kirby and Joanna Inchley hear the views of Scottish children on walking or cycling to school in a semi-rural area and their thoughts on school-based strategies to promote active travel. We included this chapter because it is an enquiry which foregrounds children's voices and perspectives on policies which aim to promote their health.

A total of 66 children (29 boys and 37 girls) from four primary and three secondary schools participated in this enquiry; they ranged in age from 10 to 13 (in Scotland, 'P7' is the final year of primary school and 'S2' is the second year of secondary school). In 13 informal group discussions the children were invited to express their views as experts. They completed two short writing activities to prepare for the sessions: the first paper asked 'What might make walking or cycling to school easier?' and the second invited children to respond to the statement: 'Walking or cycling to school would be …' followed by a list of words to circle such as 'fun', 'uncomfortable', 'exciting', 'relaxing', 'stressful'. Children were also asked to describe their usual journeys to school.

Previous research has suggested that policies and programmes to promote physical activity will not be successful unless public views about safety and the benefits of walking and cycling are taken into account (Lorenc *et al.*, 2008). Asking children for their perspectives and what they would find encouraging may help to inform schools about the best ways to promote walking and cycling.

Perceived benefits of walking or cycling

Students were asked what they felt were the benefits of walking or cycling to school. Responses were varied, but three main themes emerged among both primary and secondary students. These were: health and fitness, environmental factors and social factors. Awareness of the health benefits of being active was high and there was

Emerald Group Publishing for permission to reprint extracts from 'Active travel to school: views of 10–13 year old schoolchildren in Scotland', Joanna Kirby and Joanna Inchley, 2009, in *Health Education* Vol. 109, No. 2, 169–183.

agreement among the majority of students that walking or cycling into school every day would help them to keep healthy and maintain fitness. Associations with physical appearance were suggested by one secondary girl who commented that exercise associated with active travel would help people to look better. Many students also commented on the physical and mental health benefits associated with being outdoors and getting fresh air, for example, several commented that active travel would help them feel more energised and more alert at school:

> It's good for our health. (Girl, S2)
>
> Well I find it exhilarating and an easy way of getting fit. (Boy, P7)
>
> [Active travel] wakes you up for school. (Boy, S1)

Students were generally very aware of environmental issues and expressed concern about the contribution of cars and pollution to global warming. Many discussed the links between active transportation and helping to alleviate environmental problems, including a reduction in both the use of fuels and the amount of pollution in the atmosphere:

> To help the environment because if you take the car to school, you use petrol and everything. (Girl, S1)
>
> You're not polluting the universe cos everyone's talking about global warming now ... you wouldn't be saving the universe, but it's like part of it. (Girl, S1)

Social benefits of active travel were also frequently reported. Students talked about the commute to school by foot or bicycle providing a good opportunity to meet and spend time with their friends. It gave them the chance to talk to their friends before arriving at school and, in some cases, an opportunity to make new friends:

> You get to spend more time with your friends if you are walking or cycling with them. (Boy, P7)
>
> If you do walk and you don't know people, on your first day if you meet people you can arrange to walk with them. (Boy, P7)

Indeed, spending time with friends was one of the main reasons for active travel being seen as an enjoyable activity. Almost all students who walked or cycled to school claimed to enjoy it. Apart from the social advantages, others talked about enjoying the sense of freedom it gave them. No students said they disliked active travel, although some were indifferent and said that they only travelled this way because they had to. To a lesser extent, some students reported that cost was another advantage of active travel, walking or cycling to school being cheaper than other forms of transport such as the car or bus: "It's a waste of money getting the bus everyday" (Boy, S1). Other benefits included greater road awareness, increased familiarity with their local area, less reliance on parents and a greater sense of independence.

Perceived barriers

Students were asked what prevented them from walking or cycling to and from school. The most common themes were personal safety, weather conditions, time and distance. Issues of safety related primarily to the amount of traffic or roads being too busy to cross, both of which impacted on the extent to which children felt safe and confident as pedestrians and/or cyclists. In some cases, the route to school was perceived as unsafe for other reasons such as unsuitable pathways. Stranger danger, commonly viewed as a major deterrent to young people being active outside the home, was not the primary safety concern among students in this study. However, it was discussed by some students for whom it added to safety fears in the area:

> Yeah, just worried about ... getting followed by some weirdo or something, which is sometimes quite ordinary in [town]. (Boy, S1)

Many students said that they would not walk or cycle to school if the weather was bad. Across all groups, children frequently cited this as a barrier to active commuting and reported that they would typically travel by car or bus if it was cold or raining. However, a number of students said they would actively commute irrespective of weather conditions. Often this was discussed in conjunction with the need for special clothing or equipment such as umbrellas or day-glow jackets:

> The weather [when walking], like you get right cold. It's horrible. (Girl, S1)
>
> If its really bad weather I would take the car. (Girl, P7)

Some students perceived active travel as being slower than other forms of transport and reported lack of time as a barrier to walking or cycling to school. These students expressed concern that they might be late for school or would have to get up very early in order to get there on time. Often, the issue of time was associated with the distance between home and school. Some students felt that they lived too far away for walking or cycling to be a feasible option. Undoubtedly, this is a real issue for many students, particularly in rural areas, and it is a challenge for schools to develop active travel programmes which do not exclude these students.

Three further, though less common, themes emerged relating to perceived barriers among both primary and secondary students. These were image, physical discomfort, and the physical environment. Students' main concern about image was in relation to wearing cycle helmets. Helmets were often viewed as "uncool" and were unpopular with some students because they would mess up their hair. Students talked about not being allowed, or not having time, to make themselves presentable once they arrived at school and therefore having to wear a helmet prevented some from cycling. Boys expressed more negative views about wearing helmets than girls, and this was reinforced by the girls themselves, who commented on their male peers not wanting to ruin their hairstyles:

> To be honest, people don't like wearing helmets on bikes and that is why they don't cycle. (Boy, P7)
>
> With all the gel in your hair, you can't wear a helmet. (Boy, P7)

Physical discomfort, particularly feelings of tiredness and having to carry heavy school bags, was also a deterrent to active travel. Several issues associated with the physical environment were discussed as barriers to active travel. These included, for example, a lack of cycle paths and poor street lighting. A number of barriers were identified by secondary school students but not mentioned by primary school students, suggesting that there may be some age-related differences in the factors which influence school travel. For example, many younger secondary school students said that they felt intimidated by the presence of older students hanging around in the streets and in some cases blocking the roads. This made them feel uncomfortable when walking or cycling in these areas especially if they had to travel past them. Bicycle safety was also an issue reported by secondary school students, relating to the provision of safe cycle storage within schools.

To a lesser extent, some secondary students were just "not bothered" and admitted that laziness prevented them from walking or cycling. Where other forms of transport were available these were seen as the easier option. This reflects a lack of motivation among these students, which was not apparent among primary school-aged children.

Social influences

A range of social influences on active travel were identified. In relation to travel choices, students were asked who made the decision about the way in which they travelled to and from school. Parental decisions were most common, although a number of students reported that they made the decision themselves. As described by students, parental attitudes towards active travel varied and parents could exert either a positive or negative influence over their child's behaviour. Students talked about parents being anxious when they went out on their bikes with friends, or concerned about the safety of the bike itself being left at school. Those students who made their own decisions regarding school travel tended to be in secondary rather than primary schools indicating increasing autonomy as children got older. Students were asked whom they travelled to and from school with. Those students who actively commuted to school tended to travel with friends, and this social side was a strong motivating factor. Many students also walked to school with siblings, often chaperoning a younger brother or sister:

> There might be seven or eight of us sometimes. Everyone just meets up at a place and we'll just go ... so we'll just cycle together really. (Boy, S2)
>
> I've got a wee sister and sometimes she wants to walk. (Girl, S1)

School support for active travel

The majority of students felt that their schools encouraged them to walk or cycle to school, and all students came from schools which were participating in active travel projects at the time of the research. Perceived support came mostly in the form of provision of facilities, for example, bicycle storage sheds and, more rarely, bikes. A number of schools provided cycle proficiency training which, in some cases, children were required to pass before being allowed to cycle to and from school. The students themselves suggested that the active travel projects were having a positive effect on their awareness and, along with posters about active travel around the school and other health promotion initiatives, they felt that the notion of healthy living was being addressed at school.

Students who thought that their school could do more to encourage active travel mainly recommended the provision of better facilities such as cycle storage:

> I think a lot more people would cycle to school if there was like somewhere safer to put their bike. (Girl, S1)

However, some students discussed additional things their school could do, for example, having more organised school walks and giving out rewards as incentives for active travel. In general, lessons relating to the health and environmental advantages of active travel were covered in school but teachers were not always seen as good role models. In some cases, students felt that their teachers did not put into practice what may have been emphasised in lessons:

> Basically all the teachers use their cars ... our teacher when she goes to [local shop], that's right over there, during school time she always takes the car. (Boys, P7)

Potential strategies to promote active travel

Primary and secondary students were asked "If it was up to you, how would you get more students to actively commute to school?" Students felt it was important to promote the fact that active travel would help to make people fit and healthy. A common theme in actually increasing the numbers of students walking or cycling to school involved offering an incentive or reward:

> You could have a competition where you have a prize, and if they [students] did it [active travel] and found out they liked it, they might do it more often. (Girl, P7)

Throughout the focus groups discussions, the idea of active travel being a social activity was often discussed. This theme continued to dominate in the promotion of active travel and students felt that encouraging people to walk or cycle into school together would be a positive promotion strategy. However, the most common suggestion was the inclusion of a physical element to the project, such as a group cycle or walk. For most students, it was clear that they did not enjoy sitting passively and listening to a lot of information about active travel. They were keen to have the opportunity to get on a bicycle or take part in an organised walk. For example, a number of schools had organised group walks or cycle rides for children in their final year of primary school to show them the route to their new secondary school and these were particularly well received.

One of the strengths of this study was the inclusion of students with a mix of travel patterns, thereby ensuring that a broad range of views about active travel was represented. The findings reflect the views of a sample of 10–13 year olds, and this has been identified as the age range where there is the largest decline in physical activity participation, and more specifically, in the number of students who actively commute to school (Inchley *et al.*, 2008); it is therefore an important age group to target in terms of active travel promotion strategies.

The journey to school and from school has the potential to increase physical activity levels thereby encouraging an active lifestyle and assisting disease prevention in later life. By addressing perceived barriers identified by children in a key age range, and concentrating on their perceived benefits as motivators for active travel, future policy and health promotion strategies will be better informed. More importantly, effective interventions could be enhanced through attention to student suggestions as to how active travel may best be promoted.

References

Inchley, J., Kirby, J. and Currie, C. (2008), Physical Activity among Adolescents in Scotland. Final Report of the PASS Study, Child and Adolescent Health Research Unit (CAHRU), The University of Edinburgh, Edinburgh.

Lorenc, T., Brunton, G., Oliver, S., Oliver, K. and Oakley, A. (2008), "Attitudes to walking and cycling among children, young people and parents: a systematic review", *Journal of Epidemiology and Community Health*, Vol. 62, pp. 852–7.

Chapter 9

Gender roles in children's television commercials

Jenny Lewin-Jones and Barbara Mitra

Our ability to interpret and 'read' the commercials that appear on television begins at a very early age and primary school children are considered an important market for advertisers, especially within children's programmes. Commercials, of course, are primarily about selling a product and this, rather than educational considerations, governs a maker's choice of content and the overall presentation. In this chapter, Jenny Lewin-Jones and Barbara Mitra report on their study of the content of advertisements selectively recorded from two British television channels (CiTV and Channel Five) during the period December 2006 to August 2007. They also discuss the findings of interviews carried out with 15 primary aged children (9 boys and 6 girls) who were shown a mixture of advertisements and asked to comment on gender roles and behaviour. Nine parents were asked about their own perceptions of gender roles and to reflect on the advertisements viewed by their children. The study gives reason to feel concern about the continued use of gender stereotyping in TV commercials in order to sell products to children and, moreover, the way in which such advertisements might result in children thinking and behaving in stereotypical ways.

The fifteen children interviewed in our study all watched television commercials, except one. They commonly watched television before and after school as well as at weekends. The children's awareness that advertisements targeted different genders was expressed in different ways.

First, the children interviewed associated certain product-types and colours with specific genders. For example, Harold (age 4) did not like the advertisements for Barbie dolls "because they are for girls", although he liked "the fighting ones" that were aimed at boys. Some children were unable to articulate just what made an advertisement "boyish" or "girlish" in some cases. Barbara (age 7) commented that some advertisements "just look boyish". Harold (age 4) again said that advertisements were "just boyish and just girlish". Another child Paul (age 9) commented about

Taylor & Francis for permission to reprint extracts from 'Gender roles in televisions commercials and primary school children in the UK', Jenny Lewin-Jones and Barbara Mitra, 2009, in *Journal of Children and Media* Vol. 3, No. 1, 35–50. Reprinted by permission of the publisher (Taylor & Francis Ltd., http://www.tandf.co.uk/journals).

a Barbie advertisement "it's just really girlie for me, I would say". In other cases, children were more able to articulate what made some advertisements more "girlish" and "boyish". For example, Tamsin (age 8) said that "for boys they just like cars and things and different colours like dark, dark colours", whereas girls "have things like make-up and flowers and hearts". Colours were seen as important: Joseph (age 10) noted "it's very pink for girls and quite dark colours for boys".

Second, some of the children saw the gender of the model or actors in the advertisement as important, and commented on the gender of the children playing with the product. For example, Joseph (age 10) observed when describing the Testube Aliens advertisement: "I think it's boys because there are boys talking and enjoying it ..." Paul (age 9) went further in his comment, saying: "When you see somebody playing with it when it's a girl, it's always for girls and when it's for boys it's always boys. In the things which can be for either people you usually see both."

Differentiation according to activity levels and type was commented on by some of the children. Joseph (age 10) noted "girls usually have jewellery and everything that are only worn by girls. Boys you have got footballing, rugby and cricket stuff for the boys." This indicates awareness of a link between physical activity and male advertisements. Paul (age 9) commented "Sometimes you see them building the Lego models really quickly and I like that"—he could imagine himself actively building Lego as well. The interview with Paul shows his awareness of the boys being active protagonists in the advertisements: "there are flying meteorites and boys trying to catch them. They are glowing when they are holding it in their hands."

A link between aggressive play being for boys was made by some of the children. Neil (age 9) commented on the advertisement for Playmobil as being for boys: "You can make people slaughter some others. Like I said just now it's mainly you think of blood and gore and stuff like that when you think of pirates."

The children interviewed make a distinction between the domestic images in the female advertisements and the outdoor or fantasy realm of the male commercials. When commenting on the Tiny Tears advertisement, Paul (age 9) noted "It's a girl holding a baby and the baby is a girl I noticed as well," Whereas for Testube Aliens he suggested that girls would not like the advertisement because "it's very *Star Wars* and shooting things really and aliens". Neil (age 9) noted that in the Frosties advertisement "It's a cereal ad so it would again be mixed, because it's animation. But if it was a real tiger it would be boys." So children, at one level, learn through television advertisements that boys can deal with tigers and girls play with baby dolls. Joseph (age 10) noted about Testube Aliens: "... and they are like Lego and girls don't really take interest in building things. ... I think boys like building things ... boys don't tend to like babies and younger things and it's a doll again and girls like playing with dolls most of the time. Babies and playing mothers and fathers and stuff like that." Joseph also talked about Barbie and the twelve dancing princesses: "I think it's aimed at girls again because it's got ballet and everything and I know there are a few boys who do ballet but it's pink and twirly." Joseph's comments are particularly interesting as he shows some caution in his observations—he uses the verb "tend" when talking about boys not liking babies, and he knows that some boys do ballet, so he avoids an over-simplification, but still sees a divide between what is generally appropriate behaviour for boys and girls.

The distinction between reality and fantasy was made even more explicit in some of the interviews. For example, Tamsin (age 8) commented on the Frosties advertisement: "It's silly because tigers don't crawl up ladders." One girl, Davina (age 4) liked the Tiny Tears advertisement "because it's like a mum", and hence related what she was seeing on television to the reality of her own mother.

Almost all of the children interviewed suggested that looking after a baby was a girl's role apart from the one child who did not watch television or television commercials. More children suggested that boys would drive tanks (thirteen said this and one child said both boys and girls would do this; one child did not participate in this activity). Similarly more children associated looking after a baby with girls (eleven children said this was an occupation for girls and three children said both boys and girls would do this). Driving a fork lift truck was more associated with boys (eleven said boys and three said both). Dancers tended to be associated more with girls (eleven said girls and three said both). Hairdressers and primary school teachers were associated with both boys and girls. It can be suggested that there is some kind of link between girls being shown more in domestic and caring roles and the types of occupations that children associate with specific genders advertisements because they are not "cool". Paul (age 9) commented "I might turn over if a really long girlie one [advert] was on." Boys tend to prefer to stick to their gender stereotypes, whereas some girls seem happier to deviate. This confirms the findings of Kolbe and Muehling (1995), who suggest that it is much less acceptable for boys to associate with female gendered behaviour.

Children's opinions of what the opposite gender would think of a particular advertisement tended to be accurate when they were discussing the male and female advertisements. But there were some discrepancies. The boys interviewed thought that the Frosties advertisement would appeal to both boys and girls. Joseph (age 10) said "It's ... funny type stuff so I think boys and girls would like that." Similarly, Neil (age 9) commented "I think boys and girls would like that ad because it's funny", and Paul (age 9) said "It's something that both boys and girls would have." However, the boys' expectations of how girls would feel were not borne out. Tamsin (age 8) summed this up when she remarked "It's silly. It's silly because tigers don't crawl up ladders and they don't eat breakfast cereals and they don't lose their stripes." What is intended as a neutral advertisement seems to appeal to boys to a greater extent than girls.

The narration and music of the advertisements were commented on by some children. Katherine (age 9) also noted with Testube Aliens that the voiceover used "a low voice" and she commented "I don't like it because it's too boyish." Joseph (age 10) noted that one Barbie advertisement is "quite high pitched and us boys can't sing very high unless you are an opera singer." Tamsin (age 8) noted that some voiceovers were really fast. She commented that in the advertisement for Playmobil "They speak really, really fast."

Conclusions

Television commercials are a factor in primary school children's perception of gender roles and behaviour. In many respects (such as activity levels and type, aggression, voiceover, setting and competitiveness) little seems to have changed in over thirty years. Commercials classified as male tend to show actors engaged in more physically active behaviour, with a greater element of aggressive behaviour. In contrast, commercials aimed at females tend to show domestic settings and more passive behaviour. The female advertisements feature reality-based scenarios, whereas the male advertisements depict fantasy and adventure.

The male advertisements usually feature what we have termed a "bullet-point" style of narration with a high degree of aggressive verbs and commands, whereas the female advertisements tend to feature more complex sentences and descriptive language focusing on the product rather than the child.

We note that supposedly neutral commercials use largely male production features, having on average fewer fades per minute and more dominant music than female advertisements. The content reflects a male style, with more action and aggression. The narration in the neutral advertisements is also closer to that in the male commercials, with a predominance of male voiceovers. This suggests that females may adjust to and accept the male production features and linguistic forms, but males are less willing or able to accept a different style. This indicates a subordination of the female styles.

The children interviewed showed themselves to be well aware of gender stereotyping from an early age, for example in terms of behavioural content and settings of commercials. This awareness is apparent even when their parents have made a conscious effort to challenge perceptions of gender associations with toys. There appears to be little room in advertisements for children who do not conform to their particular gender stereotype.

Although children were very confident in identifying which advertisements were aimed at girls and which at boys, they could not always articulate this. The use of adjectives such as "girly", "girlish" and "boyish" was common, indicating that children subconsciously recognised certain features as typifying a male or female advertisement despite their inability to articulate their reasoning.

When children did articulate reasons for their classification of specific advertisements as male or female, they tended to highlight product type and aspects of behaviour shown in the advertisements, and to voice their reasoning in generalisations about what "boys" or "girls" like doing.

The children's responses to the supposedly neutral advertisement for breakfast cereal were particularly revealing. The content analysis showed that this advertisement had features closer to a male advertisement than a female one, and it was the boys that expressed a liking for the advertisement.

Parents interviewed in this study were aware of their children's perceptions of gender differences and of the differentiation in advertising aimed at boys and girls, Some parents saw this as negative and had made a conscious effort to counteract it, although they tended to feel that their efforts did not have a lasting influence on their children's perception of gender roles. Other parents saw television advertising in a more positive light and an inevitable part of their children's world.

This exploratory study was conducted on a small scale with a small sample base. Further research needs to be conducted with a wider and more representative sample of children and parents. The question that arises is whether the "pink and blue market" of commercials (Buckingham, 2007) reinforces stereotyping to a greater extent in commercials than in television and social contexts in general. Further research could also examine other influences on children's perceptions including peer influences, online social networking and parental attitudes.

Reference

Buckingham, D. (2007). 'Selling childhood? Children and consumer culture'. *Journal of Children and Media*, 1(1), 15–24.

Chapter 10

Children's views on physical activity and healthy eating

Rachael Gosling, Debbi Stanistreet and Viren Swami

The rise of childhood obesity levels, concerns about the inactivity of some children, and worries about children's food preferences have resulted in social and educational initiatives that encourage children to adopt more healthy lifestyles. Rachael Gosling, Debbi Stanistreet and Viren Swami's study draws upon the perceptions of 32 Year Five children from two primary schools in the north west of England and uses focus groups to get a genuine sense of children's views and beliefs. Children are found to have important understandings related to healthy living and, for instance, able to distinguish between healthy and unhealthy food. However, the researchers note that children are provided with contradictory messages by the food industry which means children often mediate their understandings through social interactions with friends and adults.

Introduction

Obesity levels in England have almost tripled in the last 20 years (HAD, 2001) and the prevalence of obesity amongst children of all ages appears to be increasing. In 1998, the World Health Organization designated obesity as a global epidemic (WHO, 1998), and the rise in childhood obesity has more recently been referred to as a 'public health crisis' requiring a fundamental change in the social environment (Ebbelling *et al.*, 2002). In order to reduce levels of obesity, it is important to develop effective, preventive interventions among both children and their families.

Given the interest in childhood obesity as a public health issue, it is important to assess the perceptions of children concerning food choice, eating patterns and physical activity. Because habits learned in childhood typically persist into adult life (Lawson, 1992), it is important to understand how dietary habits and attitudes toward physical activity are formed in childhood, and the extent to which these can be modified through social and educational programmes. If we do not understand why children do things and their deep-felt beliefs, educators and health professionals will be unable to help them make healthy lifestyle choices.

Children's perception of physical activity

The children in our research focus groups clearly identified both the physical, emotional and social benefits of undertaking physical activity. In two of the groups, children specifically made links between physical activity and diet, suggesting that unfit children also had poor diets. Boys focused on the competitive aspect of physical activity and it was inherent in all the discussions that friends played an important part in their enjoyment of the activity. Negative perceptions of physical activity raised by both girls and boys included being injured, tired, smelly, getting thirsty and cheating.

Children's perception of food

The children were clear that fruit and vegetables could be categorized as 'healthy', while chocolate, sweets and fizzy drinks would be 'unhealthy'. The children created an 'in-between' category for foods they found difficult to categorize, when asked whether particular foods should go in a shopping basket marked 'healthy' or 'unhealthy'. This applied particularly to foods with several ingredients, as the following comments illustrate:

A1: Pepperoni pizza: Unhealthy. No, sometimes it's healthy 'cos it's got mushrooms on. Mushrooms are vegetables.
A2: Milkshake: It's healthy 'cos it's got milk in, but it's got chocolate in. It's got sugar in. Put it in the middle.

Their comments showed that they understood that the cooking method influenced the healthiness of the food. For instance:

B3: Chicken: It depends on the way you cook it. No, chicken nuggets can be unhealthy a bit, chicken nuggets with batter – but chicken, chicken that you have in a roast dinner, that's healthy because there's no batter, no fat on it ...
B4: That's unhealthy 'cos it's got fat in it. I think it's middle. It's healthy if you don't eat the skin. It's good for you as well because you have to have some chicken and some fish. It's healthy 'cos it's meat. It's protein.

Their discussions highlighted a range of factors underpinning their confusion, and a complex picture of external influences, personal beliefs, food likes and dislikes emerges as illustrated in the following discussion. The dialogue below shows the impact of a news story, the children's knowledge that fat and salt are 'unhealthy' and a discussion about the concept of 'balance':

C4: The chicken nuggets have got fat in them and the chips have got salt on.
C6: And the rest is OK – not bad for you.
C3: But people said on the news on the radio, that chicken nuggets have got bad things in.
C6: I don't care if they've got all that stuff in – I still like them.
C5: You know the chicken, when they're making them? They go on the floor and they pick 'em up and put them back on.

C4: It said on the news that in Iceland, they scrape all the fat off the floor and they put them inside the chicken nuggets.
C6: I don't have them from Iceland – I have McDonald's. They're too nice.
C3: McDonalds have got a good balance because they put salad on the burgers and they have the bread and the cheese with sesame seeds and everything like that and then it's got the McFlurries and the chips and that's fast food.

Influences on healthy eating and physical activity

The children identified a number of factors that influence their uptake of physical activity and healthy eating, acting as barriers or motivators. These were: parents, school, local environment, the food industry and the media, and peers.

(i) Parents

Not surprisingly, parents were deemed to be a major influence, seemingly more so on healthy eating than on physical activity. Many of the children identified that their parents, mostly mothers, made the decisions about where they eat and what they eat, though many saw this as a joint decision-making process. On the whole, children thought their mothers played a major role in preventing them from eating too much of their favourite 'unhealthy' foods. They described various strategies used in the home to serve these ends:

C7: If, like, I want to have a Kit-Kat, my mum says there's none left when there's two left.
C4: ... Yeah, my mum does that ... So does mine.

Mothers and aunts were clearly a source of knowledge and influence for children about food:

B9: My auntie Tina – she starts saying, 'This has got fibre in it, so you eat it'.
B7: My auntie Marie says, 'You better stop eating 'cos, like, you're getting too big'.

When some of the children were asked, 'How might children be helped to eat more healthily?' several of their suggestions were directed at the role of parents:

C7: You could do an advert, tell their mums to make sure their kids eat healthily.
C8: Tell their mums not to buy 'em [unhealthy foods].

(ii) School

The children participated in activities provided by the school, and the policies adopted by the school also had a direct impact on them. For instance, one school did not allow children to eat chocolates and sweets at break time, but provided toast as an alternative. The school had received a 'Healthy Tuck Award' about which the children seemed proud. The children identified school as a place where they learn about food and eating, in one case saying that 'hospital people' had come to talk to them. In one school, the children from both groups recounted what they had learned in a lesson in which they had read about 'couch potatoes'.

(iii) Local environment

Children's environment was an important influence on their uptake of physical activity, determining where and what they played. This applied to the leisure facilities available as well as having easily accessible, safe places and spaces to play with friends. Several boys described playing in the back alleys saying this was their only choice. A few children voiced their dislike of some facilities such as the swimming baths (dirty) and parks (boring). When children from all groups were asked, 'Why do some children seem to do more physical activity than others?' one suggestion was that they could not access places to play.

(iv) The food industry and the media

It was clear that the children incorporated news stories and other media messages into their everyday lives and conversations. They often referred to celebrity footballers, for example, when talking about their own games of football, or about being rich. The impact of the food industry's sophisticated marketing techniques could be seen by the way in which children referred to foods by their brand names. McDonald's symbolizes fast food, consumer culture. It has a powerful marketing strategy directed at children and was mentioned in every focus group. For the children, it was clearly the norm to eat and enjoy McDonald's food. Several children referred to the McDonald's play area as being a place where they were physically active, but pointed out that this could only be used once a meal had been bought. A child's confession to never having eaten a McFlurry ice-cream was met with shock and derision from his peers.

Advertising was only mentioned explicitly by one group of boys. In this case, the salient point was the contrasting ways in which different participants made sense of the advertisements they had seen:

C6: Lucozade is good, but that's the best fizzy drink because it's the healthiest.
C3: It's got sugar in it though. Lucozade says it gives you energy when you buy it, but it doesn't.
C6: Michael Owen has it.
C4: Michael Owen has it.
[Others: Yeah.]
C3: How do you know? So what?
C6: You see him on the advert.
C3: They're just doing that aren't they? [to RG] ... It's like Sunny D: they say it's healthy for you and it doesn't make your teeth rot, but when I went to the dentist, the dentist said I can't drink Sunny D ... 'cos it's got sugar in it.

(v) Peers

The influence of peers seemed to be important in two main areas: peers as play companions and peers as reflectors and creators of attitudes and self identity. The children's view of their physically inactive/overweight peers was complex, though many demonstrated negative views towards overweight people, reflecting prevalent social attitudes. A good example of this is a boy who took on the role of a doctor in the role-play exercise and exclaimed: 'You have got a disease of being lazy, you couch potato,' before going on to prescribe an exercise programme. Some children referred to physically inactive children as lazy or boring. Several children took the view that their physically inactive peers were making a lifestyle choice, preferring to watch television, or choosing other hobbies.

A5: They're boring ... I just think they're lazy and they can't be bothered and they're just on their own and they're no good at making friends.

However, some participants were empathetic and showed an awareness of how these children might be feeling: embarrassed, shy and unconfident about their ability.

For boys, the discussions about physical activity were closely associated with competition. For them, a peer who was not good at sport posed a threat to their winning the game. In addition, there was an expectation among boys that being able to handle pain was important.

Discussion

Tackling obesity requires primary prevention as well as treatment services, such as weight management services, that target whole communities, of which children are an integral part. The children interviewed in this study demonstrated that they understood the benefits of physical activity and could differentiate between healthy and unhealthy foods to an extent. They were aware of the influences that impact on their health behaviour, in particular, school, the media and the environment. Consistent with previous research, the role of parents was seen to be important, not just in the foods they give children but also in how they influence their views about food (Tilston *et al.*, 1991).

Children's worlds are not fragmented into the discrete topic areas of health strategies. They do not perceive physical activity as being something they 'should' do. They do it because it forms an important part of their social world, not least as it is an opportunity to spend time with peers. Similarly, their relationship to food is rarely tempered by self-restriction. Children are balancing their accumulating knowledge about diet against their own enjoyment of food. The children in this study demonstrated that they construct arguments that justify their food choices, so that they can continue to eat the foods they like. This parallels literature about lay health beliefs and smoking, which suggests 'being healthy' is not the prime motivator for changing behaviour (White, 2002).

Despite the influences that constrain children's choices and behaviour, these children felt they exercised control over many aspects of their lives. Their decisions appeared to be based on past experiences and what they learn from peers and adults. Some children found it easier than others to express their preferences, even if this went against the tide of peer pressure. While children identified the constraints on their lives, they also perceived themselves and their peers as making choices. Several children explained that one reason other children may not do physical activity was simply that they did not like it. Similarly, decisions about food ultimately were reduced to liking the taste and the social acceptability of food. Some girls seemed to be developing the notion of personal responsibility for health; for example, girls said they stop themselves from eating food that causes weight gain, showing a concern with body image. This contrasted with boys whose mothers took on the role of controlling their food intake and who believed that being overweight was beyond their control.

Public health practitioners need to work collaboratively with other agencies and the community in order to develop healthy public policy which tackles the broader societal and environmental issues associated with obesity. For instance, the children highlighted the lack of places and spaces available to them to engage in active play or physical activity. This emphasizes the need for health services to engage with other services, such as planning, housing and leisure services. Involving children early in the planning process, in thinking about ways to improve their access to leisure facilities and play areas, is important.

It has been argued that the medicalization of childhood is taking place in our society (for instance, Timimi, 2003). The medicalization of childhood obesity obscures the influence of the wider determinants of health and the social, psychological and cultural pressures on families and children. It is important that public health practitioners work with clinicians who are treating obesity, to ensure that clinical interventions form part of an integrated strategy, which has healthy public policy and primary prevention at its core.

In order for public health professionals to develop effective strategies to prevent the increase in obesity, it is essential that they attempt to understand the barriers and motivations faced and experienced by children. The challenge for public health practitioners is to position themselves where they can listen to, hear and respond to children's voices on obesity prevention and treatment.

References

Ebbelling, C.B., Pawlak, D.B. and Ludwig, D.S. (2002) 'Childhood obesity: Public health crisis, common sense cure'. *Lancet*, 360: 473–82.

HDA (Health Development Agency) (2001) *Obesity: A Growing Concern*. HDA: London.

Lawson, M. (1992) *Nutrition, Social Status and Health: Proceedings of a Conference*. National Dairy Council: London.

Tilston, C.H., Gregson, K., Neale, R.J. and Douglas, C.J. (1991) 'Dietary awareness of primary school children'. *British Food Journal*, 93: 25–9.

Timimi, S. (2003) 'The politics of attention deficit hyperactivity disorder'. *Health Matters*, 52: 14–15.

White, K. (2002) *An Introduction to the Sociology of Health and Illness*, London: Sage.

WHO (World Health Organization) (1998) *Obesity: Preventing and Managing the Global Epidemic*. WHO: Geneva.

Chapter 11

Children representing themselves through photographs

Michelle Newman, Andree Woodcock and Philip Dunham

Adults in schools now have a deeper understanding of the social life of school playgrounds. They are places where many children can freely enjoy their play pursuits but also places where some children can feel excluded and even very unhappy. Many schools now have policies and initiatives to help make playgrounds appropriate for all children's needs and more inclusive places, given the range of activities and interests that children take part in. Michelle Newman, Andree Woodcock and Philip Dunham invited Year Six children from one primary school to have photographs taken of themselves at school 'in a place of significance' and then followed this up with interviews about these photographic representations. Many children chose outside places, including the playground, and a major theme that emerged was gender related bullying.

This study provided opportunities for children, aged ten and eleven, to tell their own stories, albeit mediated through photography. It must be stressed that these photographs provide a glimpse at one version, or part, of the child's identity. It also should be said that the images have undergone a further process of mediation, or construction. It is always necessary to bear in mind that the researcher selects the images and the stories to be told, rewriting them in terms acceptable to a particular audience. The author is also involved in a web of relations with the children, staff at the school and discourses of education and schooling. It would therefore be an error to claim that this type of research provides a transparent 'objective' account of these children's lives. Rather it raises many questions about photography as a research method. More broadly it raises issues about conducting research whilst working as a teacher and the impact relationships have on the research process and vice-versa.

The aim of this study was not to establish an overall view of 'the child's' experience, but to give specific children the opportunity to tell a story of their choosing, based on one small slice of their experience of school.

Taylor & Francis for permission to reprint extracts from '"Playtime in the borderlands": children's representations of school, gender and bullying through photographs and interviews', Michelle Newman, Andree Woodcock and Philip Dunham, 2006 in *Children's Geographies* Vol. 4, No. 3, 289–302. Reprinted by permission of the publisher (Taylor & Francis Ltd., http://www.tandf.co.uk/journals).

Research methods

The children who took part in this study were my own [Michelle Newman's] year 6 class. After introducing the project I distanced myself from the photograph taking process, so the children would not feel inhibited by my presence, or try to please me. However it would be naïve as a researcher just to assume that my relationship with the class and certain children would not influence or be influenced by the activity.

The project started with a discussion of the nature of photographs. In order to introduce the problem of whether a photograph is 'real' I showed the children some images from magazines and brochures, clearly constructed for a specific purpose. We discussed how sometimes pictures of models in fashion magazines were airbrushed, and how holiday brochures only showed the pleasing aspects of a holiday resort. The children often demonstrated a sophisticated understanding of the ways in which photographs showed a partial reality. One group concentrated their discussion on holiday snaps, agreeing that photographs were often taken to show people back home what a great time they had, therefore only the good parts of their holiday were photographed. Daniel summed up the general consensus by saying 'They are true because they show something that happened, but they're not true, as well, because they don't show everything that happened'.

This established the context in which the children took their own photographs. They were asked to photograph a place of significance to them in the school and to think about their choice, and provide a caption for the photograph.

Findings: 'the unofficial story'

Anne had a photograph taken of her taking a penalty kick. She chose this image because although she loved football she did not have the opportunity to play under normal circumstances because the boys took over the playground and would not let her join in. She found the boys physically and verbally intimidating. Rebecca's photograph was of the sports equipment cupboard. She too said that she enjoyed football, but unlike Anne she was permitted to join in with the boys' game on the playground. When I asked her why she was able to do this when her friend could not, she explained that she was like the boys. She expanded by saying she was tall, and wore trousers. She did not 'act all girly, you know giggling and crying if the ball hits you and that'. She was accepted as one of the boys because of her physical appearance and her sporting ability. However she chose to be photographed with a mixed group of girls and boys, finding acceptance amongst both sexes. She refused to be defined by traditional gender roles and was able to find a place for herself. However despite being different from many of the girls, she was similar to the dominant boys. It was therefore less easy for them to conceptualise her as 'other'. Her acceptance came about by being like the boys.

Not all the images represented positive aspects of school life. The meanings given to seemingly 'pleasant' images demonstrated a darker side to school experiences. Michael called his picture 'Misery'. He deliberately chose an apparently innocuous photograph of himself on his own, sitting in a secluded part of the playground. When asked about the image he said that he did not want to be identified with a lot of the boys in his class and found playtime very difficult. He hated football and similar games played by the boys. He felt happier with the girls, although at the time that this photograph was taken he had been ostracised by some of his female friends due to outbursts of swearing and crying. Although usually he played with some of the girls on the edges of the playground, at this time his breaks were spent out of sight of both other children and staff, behind the 'maths hut', a temporary building occupying one corner of the playground. Recently some of the boys had noticed the way he identified with some of the girls and had begun a campaign of name-calling. He spent his time off the main playground hiding from the view of the other boys to avoid being bullied. Michael experienced how a certain type of masculinity is delineated by space/place in the school or playground context. Space within school is highly gendered (Renold, 2004) and clearly requires more attention in school design and organisation. The cultural importance placed on masculine physicality (such as footballing ability), within schools is clearly linked to the nature of the space. Most girls and some boys were pushed out of the playground into the margins.

After the bullying issues came to light I stepped out of the role of researcher and became the class teacher to discuss Michael's situation with other members of staff. Michael's experience, as it was revealed to me, met the criteria as defined by the DFES (2000) for a case of severe bullying. Despite this, Michael's situation was not dealt with entirely sympathetically. Although most of the female staff felt sorry for him several expressed the opinion that the bullying was partly his fault for not being a 'proper boy', meaning overtly masculine. One teacher stated that different masculinity must automatically mean homosexuality, and that it was a problem in so far as it was a deviation from the norm. Within the school culture the word 'gay' is used as an insult (Rigby, 2003). Although never explicitly stated by school authorities (Epstein, 1997), heterosexuality is the presumed norm in schools with 'gayness' an affront to school culture. School, even at primary level, is a highly sexualised environment (Epstein and Johnson, 1998). Difference is often considered unfavourably, as abnormal. Boys who adopted the more traditional macho role received a far greater level of tolerance than those who transgressed. Boys who meted out what was seen as instant justice in the form of a thump were often considered justified in their actions. When Michael complained of name calling to the male deputy head he was told that it was his fault because he needed to 'toughen up'.

As Michael's class teacher I dealt with his bullying on a day-to-day basis, expressing my intolerance of bullying and giving detentions to children who had called him names. We also had several class 'circle times' to discuss bullying, the different forms it may take, how it makes the victim feel and the damage name-calling can do. We also spent two literacy lessons writing and performing scenes depicting a bullying incident, to encourage empathy with the victim. The problem did decrease after this, but was never completely eradicated. The name-calling issue was never completely resolved, partly due to management in school not taking it as seriously as they might and with the perception of Michael as partially responsible for his bullying because he was a 'difficult child'.

When Michael was in his final year at this school, he was in trouble with the school authorities, and the police, for writing an expletive on the toilet wall. Interestingly his anger, as expressed through the graffiti, had not been directed towards the children who had bullied him, but towards the head teacher who had failed to protect him or to deal with the bullies effectively.

The complexities of power relations and the importance of 'playing the part', of performing identity, were shown in Jack's photographs. He was a rule breaker, and prided himself on that fact. The first photo he chose depicted him in detention. When asked why he had chosen this image he said, indignantly 'I'm always in detention, me ... even when Dan did it, I get the blame'. He followed this up with a huge smile and the comment, offered with an air of pride, 'I'm naughty aren't I Miss?' Through repeated rule defying acts, particularly those performed with humour, Jack consciously constructed the identity of the class 'joker' and 'lovable rogue'. This was who Jack was, through his own eyes, through those of other children and the adults in the school. However there was a pay off, a tension, which Jack recognised. The second photograph he chose depicted him in the wild area. When looking at the two photographs side by side Jack said 'I'm always in detention ... but I'd rather be here'. Through his performance in the role of defiant rule-breaker he knew that, ironically, he would have to sacrifice some of the freedom he craved.

Despite being a regular face in the detention hall, he remained popular amongst children and staff. The role of 'class clown' coupled with his footballing prowess and obvious masculinity meant that despite his apparent transgression of rules he was actually a conformist in many ways. Although a fairly low achiever academically he found success on the playground through his ability to form friendships with other boys, particularly through football. He was one of the football team and was therefore in a privileged position in the school, often rewarded through the receipt of certificates and praised for his 'team spirit', despite being one of Michael's tormentors. On one occasion it was suggested that Jack should not be allowed to play for the school team as a punishment for his persistent rule breaking, but the deputy head, saying that he was too good a footballer to be removed, vetoed this.

For children who do not achieve academically, school can be a place where they feel they do not fit in; they see themselves as out of place. This is especially so when achievement cannot be gained through physicality or sporting ability either. Oscar and John were regarded as 'low achievers'. Neither boy participated in sports, Oscar often forgetting his P.E. kit to avoid games lessons. Both chose to depict themselves in spaces reserved for younger children.

They both indicated that they were happier in the infants, where they could achieve through play, and where the differences felt through their lack of academic achievement were not so marked. When taking the photograph Oscar found to his delight that he could walk across a wooden bridge that he had been scared to play on as an infant. He was thrilled by a real sense of achievement denied to him by class work. In the junior playground there were no such facilities for the children to use. Instead, as indicated earlier, the playground was dominated by a large group of boys who played football, yet excluded children like Oscar and John, who did not fit into the normative roles carved out by other year six boys. However despite not conforming to type they were not subjected to the verbal and physical harassment that Michael suffered. One has to question why this should be. In fact several boys in the class were not overtly masculine, yet managed to maintain reasonable relationships with the footballers. Skelton (2001) suggests:

> While many, perhaps most, boys are not particularly happy inhabiting the space of the boy who is rough, tough and dangerous to know, the bullying of boys

> who present themselves as more thoughtful and gentle can be problematic in the extreme.
>
> (Skelton 2001, p. x)

However, this case study indicates that there is a group of quieter, more sensitive boys who avoid the bullying attentions of the more aggressive. Indeed Oscar and John were far quieter and more sensitive than Michael, who was prone to quite violent outbursts at times. It is too simplistic to say that sensitivity on its own attracts the attentions of bullies, or that an anti-academic stance is enough to fend them off. In this case many of the footballers were also 'high flyers' academically. It would seem that Oscar and John's quietness posed no threat to the masculinity of the dominant boys, whereas Michael's perceived effeminacy, did.

There seems to be a 'borderland' between the masculine qualities of the footballing type and those perceived as effeminate. Many boys inhabit this borderland, not a member of the overtly masculine group, yet not provoking conflict with this dominant group. The word 'borderland' is chosen deliberately to indicate both a metaphor for their social position and their actual place on the playground map. Not as marginalized either socially or spatially as Michael, who spent much of his time hiding away from the playground, yet not quite in the central position occupied by the full-time footballers.

Conclusions

This case study began as a small project intending to use the medium of photography to interrogate the uses of space within school by children. However gender related bullying emerged as a central theme when the context of the photographs was examined. The contrast with adult constructed images of school, for example those found in many official documents and websites, is striking. On face value the photographs denoted a well-equipped school with contented children. If they had been given different captions their meanings would have been quite different.

The construction of dominant masculinities in school, particularly as part of the playground culture and its role in bullying, has been well documented. Staff attitudes, both male and female, can contribute to this culture. However this research indicates a 'borderland', real and metaphorical, inhabited by less dominant boys, but ones who still maintain good social relationships with other children. This position may be gained through a humorous disregard for authority. Other 'borderlanders' may keep their identities as quiet, sensitive boys without posing a threat to, or attracting the bullying of, the boys who dominate the playground.

Photography is frequently used as a research method with children. However it would be a mistake to assume its transparency; its ability to 'speak for itself'. They are useful to research as prompts to a story. The pictures they present are always partial and skewed, as are the stories they serve to illustrate. They may conceal as much as they show. Photographs are a useful focus for children, enabling them to tell their stories. It also gave me as a researcher a way to open up a dialogue with the children. They were able to express themselves, through subsequent interviews, using the photographs as illustrations to a story, which led to a far deeper understanding than a simple conversation may have had.

References

Epstein, D. (1997) 'Boyz' own stories: masculinities and sexualities in school', *Gender and Education*, 9(1), 105–116.

Epstein, D. and Johnson, R. (1998) *Schooling Sexualities*, Buckingham: Open University Press.

Renold, E. (2004) ''Other' boys: negotiating non-hegemonic masculinities in the primary school', *Gender and Education*, 16(2), 247–265.

Rigby, K. (2003) Addressing bullying in schools: theory and practice, Australian Institute of Criminology: *Trends and Issues in Crime and Criminal Justice* No. 259.

Skelton, C. (2001) *Schooling the Boys: Masculinity and Primary Education*, Buckingham: Open University Press.

Part 3

Contexts for small-scale research

Understanding diversity, inclusion and barriers to learning

Chapter 12

The distinctive contribution of additional staff

Joan Stead, Gwynedd Lloyd, Pamela Munn, Sheila Riddell, Jean Kane and Gale Macleod

The deployment of teaching assistants to support children who find it difficult to conform to the behavioural expectations of schools has a long history. The rationale for this is that if close personalised support is provided to such children they are less likely (and have less opportunity) to misbehave. This chapter, by Joan Stead and colleagues, investigate the nature of the help provided by additional staff in three Scottish local authorities – two primary, one special and two secondary schools from each. Interviews were carried out with additional staff, teachers, parents/carers, education officers and children themselves. Although some additional staff were given low status in some schools, the study highlighted their important mediating role, particularly the value of their informal communications with parents and children. Additional staff can therefore be seen as offering a distinctive contribution of their own which, the researchers suggest, needs to be officially recognised.

There is increasing use of additional staff (teaching assistants, learning support assistants, behaviour support assistants, special educational needs auxiliaries, classroom assistants) to promote positive discipline and support pupils with behavioural difficulties in school in Scotland. We explore some findings from a Scottish Executive funded research project (Munn *et al.*, 2004), presenting some views of additional staff, pupils, parents and teaching staff on the diverse roles, professional and personal attributes and effectiveness of additional staff.

We will also comment on research that involved work at authority and school level. The questions explored with schools included:

- the nature and extent of additional staffing and how this was decided;
- the roles played by additional staff;
- perceptions of effectiveness of these staff in helping with discipline and the criteria of effectiveness being used;

Scottish Educational Review and the author for kind permission to reprint 'Supporting our most challenging pupils with our lowest status staff: can additional staff in Scottish schools offer a distinctive kind of help?' Stead *et al.* 2007 in *Educational Review* Vol. 39, No. 2.

- the effect of additional staff on school ethos;
- the availability of training and staff development;
- the sustainability of additional staffing.

Interviews with schools staff, pupils and parents allowed us to explore in some detail perceptions and understandings of the impact and role of additional staff. It was also important in this research that the voices of additional staff were included (O'Brien & Garner, 2001). In each of 3 authorities two secondary, two primary and one special school or unit for children identified with Social, Emotional and Behavioural Difficulties (SEBD), were identified and interviews and documentary analysis undertaken with a range of teachers (74), additional staff (30), parents/carers (40) and pupils (60 in total, some individual interviews and 11 focus groups). Interviews were also held with 11 key personnel in each authority. The interviews were semi-structured, specifying the general areas to be discussed but with no pre-determined order of questions, beyond a standard introduction and closure.

We cannot, of course, generalise from these local authorities to all local authorities in Scotland. We sampled only a small number of schools within each authority and within each school, talked with a small number of staff, pupils and parents. It is therefore likely that not all shades of perception have been captured.

The role of additional staff is very varied in that some are designated to help individual children who have a special identified need for additional support, others work to promote positive discipline with the generality of children through, for example, playground and lunchtime supervision duties, while a third group may have responsibilities for both individuals and the wider group at different times. The findings relating to the effectiveness of additional staff included:

- Additional staff were generally seen by teachers and local authority managers as effective in promoting positive behaviour. A key feature was that they were able to model different (from teachers) and more informal ways of working with young people and their parents or carers.
- Children, young people and their parents were generally very positive about the help they received from additional staff. Some felt that their children would not still be in their school without this help.
- Those described as classroom assistants as opposed to, for example, learning support assistants, behaviour support assistants, special educational needs auxiliaries, were accorded low status as an extra pair of hands and were not included in the staff lists of some schools.
- The presence of additional staff tended to reduce the teacher's direct involvement with all, or with identified pupils.
- Greater clarity about the role of different groups of additional staff would be welcomed.

Across the three local authorities, there was a wide variation in the description, training, support, title and remits of the additional staff in classrooms. This was reflected in the number of titles used to describe additional staff (teaching assistants, learning support assistants, behaviour support assistants, special educational needs auxiliaries, classroom assistants) and the overlap and diversity of roles in practice (though one authority was attempting to rationalise the roles of additional staff). It was also noticeable across the three authorities that many, if not all, additional staff in relation to discipline/behaviour support were generally not new recruits, as many had already held positions in the school (such as playground supervisors) and had an established reputation for working with pupils with challenging behaviour. This method of recruitment highlights the importance of personal skills and attributes above those of the purely academic. This method of recruitment may, however, have inadvertently led to further role and remit confusion as the skills of these staff would be known to a particular school.

The positive views of local authority managers and teachers towards Discipline Task Group (DTG) funded additional staff were based, in part, on the view that the model of the individual teacher keeping control of the class through strength of personality or fear was no longer appropriate, given the diversity of pupil characteristics and needs. Simply having another adult present offering a different type of engagement with pupils was, in itself, of great value:

> You only have to walk into a school and see the difference that learning assistants make, the difference that these approaches make ... The more integrated approach, support for learning [is beneficial]. (Education Officer)

> If the behaviour support assistant hadn't been there at lunchtimes and intervals, I feel I would have more problems to sort out which would have affected the atmosphere in the classroom and given me less teaching time with the children if I had been sorting out discipline and behaviour problems and I don't know that the children would have had such a successful year. I don't mean to talk myself down – you would do your best – but having support, having another adult there to take children out, to talk problems through, to reinforce positive behaviour .... (Primary teacher)

A key feature of the initiative, according to managers in the three authorities, was that the additional staff were able to model different and more informal ways of working and styles of interaction with parents/carers and children. This view was reinforced by staff and pupils in schools:

> [They work in a way] that makes behaving well and doing it in a real fun kind of way .... It just helps tremendously. (Primary teacher)

The flexibility of additional staff was also seen as important:

> We don't have them going off, getting paper ready when James in Primary 4 is having a bit of a shaky day. (Assistant Head Teacher, primary)

It was felt that aspects of the pupil/additional staff relationship, such as the use of first names rather than more formal forms of address, the opportunity for one-to-one support and conversations, and the opportunity to act as mediator or advocate for the young person, helped to re-engage some pupils with school. There were, however, a smaller number of counter examples where individual additional staff were perceived as being just as authoritarian as teachers. Children and young people who were supported were overall very positive about the help they received from additional staff and many parents were delighted with the additional support and believed that their child was only being maintained in school as a result of this support. One mother of a secondary school pupil said that having additional support made her son feel more positive about going to school when he knew this particular individual would be present in classes. Another parent commented:

> I think it's a good way of spending money, because it keeps them in their mainstream schooling ... they would just get taken out of the school and taken somewhere else ... it helps keep them in their own environment. (Parent)

Pupils generally felt positive about the support they received:

> It's stopped us (i.e. me) getting into trouble and getting kicked out of class. (Secondary school pupil)
>
> ... If they know I'm going to get mental, they calm us down. ... If they weren't there I'd just get into total trouble – and end up getting excluded again. (Secondary school pupil)

The following comment suggests that pupils not directly targeted with support were generally aware and appreciative of extra support in the classroom:

> If there is troublesome members of the class, they concentrate on those and keep them quiet and the actual teacher can get on with the teaching without having to worry about keeping people quiet as well. (Secondary pupil in a focus group)

However, despite the fact that additional staff were generally regarded as making a positive contribution to classroom ethos and learning, there were some issues with regard to their status. A few parents in one authority believed that additional staff were a rather poor substitute for extra teachers. Parents in this authority had strong concerns about confidentiality issues when people from the local community (who were employed as additional staff) may have access to information about sensitive family matters.

Across the authorities, however, teachers tended to regard additional staff described as special educational needs auxiliaries and behaviour support assistants as fellow professionals. Those described as classroom assistants, on the other hand, were seen as 'an extra pair of hands' rather than colleagues or fellow professionals – even if there was considerable overlap in the tasks undertaken. The low status accorded to the 'descriptor' of classroom assistant was also evidenced by a failure in some schools to include them in staff lists.

In many schools, a lack of clarity about the specific remit of additional staff, which was further complicated by the many different job titles and overlapping job descriptions. There were examples of additional staff allocated to class which included a pupil with SEBD, though working with the class in general; as part of behaviour support, with responsibility to help develop behaviour control management; providing general support for class/subject teacher; providing a mixture of behaviour support, administration support and general educational support. There were also examples of some additional staff having their role clearly negotiated in advance, and those who were allocated tasks on the day.

A general view across sectors and authorities was that greater clarity in the role of different groups of workers would be welcomed. It was suggested that there was a need for training for class and subject teachers in how to work efficiently with additional staff and that further improvements in the training, pay, conditions of service and career structure of additional staff were required.

Additional staff were almost all women, often from local areas; some had qualifications well beyond those required for the post and which could have been associated with more highly paid work. Some staff were willing to work at this level because of the hours that fitted with family life, others enjoyed the work. Many respondents acknowledged that many additional staff offered skills and qualities well beyond their level of employment and pay.

There was concern that some schools need to address the problem of the low status assigned to additional staff, which may be conveyed to pupils and parents and is likely to limit the possibilities for effective action. Important issues of confidentiality were also identified, as many additional staff working in the school could be close neighbours and/or members of the local community and they may have access sensitive family information.

In summary the issues raised by the research were those of: the importance of personal skills and attributes; different and informal working practices; flexibility; maintaining some pupils in mainstream; confidentiality; roles and responsibilities; and low status.

Discussion and conclusion

From the perspectives of education officers, senior school managers, teachers, parents and pupils this research indicated overwhelming support for the role of additional staff in the classroom. However, the range of reasons given for this – contributing to classroom discipline, supporting individual pupils, supporting the teacher, keeping a pupil in school – do give an indication of the complexity of the role and expectations of these staff. The range of roles and expectations is now reflected in the UK-wide *National Occupational Standards* (2001) for teaching/classroom assistants, which places emphasis on responsibilities rather than listing specific tasks or duties:

- Working in partnership with the teacher
- Working within statutory and organisational frameworks
- Supporting inclusion
- Equality of opportunity
- Anti discrimination
- Celebrating diversity
- Promoting independence.

The above is a very far step from that of being 'an extra pair of hands' in the classroom and presents particular challenges both for additional staff and teachers in the management of roles and responsibilities.

The role of additional staff in Scotland is clearly to support and to be directed by the teacher in charge of the class (GTCS, 2003). But there has been widespread concern regarding additional staff who are used to help manage pupils with challenging behaviour. Indeed O'Brien and Garner (2001) suggest that this situation is particularly problematic when viewed in terms of these most vulnerable pupils being supported by the least trained staff. The ability and flexibility of additional staff to accompany a pupil with challenging behaviour out of the classroom could, and often does, remove the immediate responsibility for the child from the teacher. This may result in teachers advertently, or inadvertently, avoiding dealing with behaviour or the circumstances that may have prompted it.

There needs to be recognition of the confusion between the role of additional staff and that of the teacher (Calder and Grieve, 2004), especially when the role of additional staff may be seen to encroach upon that of the teacher in terms of additional staff increasingly providing learning support (Wilson *et al.*, 2003). There is also a further tension between providing clear definitions of roles and responsibilities while maintaining the valued flexibility of the role (Schlapp and Davidson, 2001). The increasingly prominent profile of additional staff highlights the lack of training and career structures currently available to them (Wilson *et al.*, 2003). Although the recruitment of additional staff is dependent upon personal qualities above those of academic qualifications and formal training (Groom and Rose, 2005), this should not prevent or hinder the professional development opportunities for additional staff. However, although training and qualifications for additional staff are being developed locally and nationally, it would be detrimental if such training inadvertently resulted in more rigid working practices and a diminishing of the informal nature of these relationships in schools.

Although professional status and training are important, for most pupils and their families this was less important than the interpersonal qualities and skills of the individual. Despite the complexity of the issues affecting young people and their relationships, it is possible to identify some characteristics of effective helping (Lloyd *et al.*, 2001b). In earlier research a parent was asked who, out of the several professionals involved with the family had been the most helpful, answered 'some woman came round' (Lloyd *et al.*, 2001a). The impact of this anonymous individual (who had visited the family only once) had remained with this parent because they had engaged with them empathetically and with concern and understanding. There were also some examples (in the research) of the person described as most trusted and supportive (by both parents and pupils) being an assistant head teacher or principle teacher. The approach modelled by these individuals is similar to those modelled by additional staff in schools and reflects moves to encourage communication and understandings between pupils, parents and school. These models of working can promote levels of equity and participation between those involved, and it may also be that additional staff can offer the kind of informal support valued by some parents who are intimidated by teachers and aware of their own negative experiences of schooling. In the context of multi agency working in schools (Lloyd *et al.*, 2001b), support was valued when it was perceived as non-judgemental, genuine and equitable. Although this way of working was often found among those such as youth workers, and the semi specialist 'children in trouble' workers, it was often the case that others, such as additional staff or mental health workers, were not regularly included in these meetings. So if, as we are arguing, the effectiveness of additional staff is partly located in their relationship with the young person, their exclusion from forums such as inter agency meetings is of concern, as these staff could play an important role as mediators and advocates for young people.

The effectiveness of additional staff has been discussed in terms of their ability to offer different and more informal ways of working and styles of interaction with parents/carers and children; offering non-judgemental, genuine and equitable support (both educational and emotional). The value of having additional staff in our schools is now widely accepted, but this research suggests that their role within schools needs to be recognised and clarified; this is most likely to be achieved when concerns over low pay, low status, short term contracts and of feeling undervalued, can be more satisfactorily addressed. Paradoxically, however, there remains the question as to whether the ambiguous and more informal status of classroom assistants in itself contributes to the positive relationships that many have with pupils and parents; making it important that, if we are to further professionalise this role it does not acquire those characteristics of defensive distance, sometimes seen to be inherent in other educational professionals.

References

Calder, I. and Grieve, A. (2004) Working with other adults; what teachers need to know *Educational Studies*, 30(2), 113–126.

General Teaching Council of Scotland (GTCS) (2003) Classroom Assistants: A GTC Scotland Position Paper. Online at http://www.gtcs.org.uk/gtcs-content/docs/classroom%20Assistants%20Position%20paper.pdf.

Groom, B. and Rose, R. (2005) Supporting the inclusion of pupils with social emotional and behavioural difficulties in the primary school: the role of teaching assistant, *Journal of Research in Special Educational Needs*, 5(1), 20–30.

Lloyd, G., Kendrick, A. and Stead, J. (2001a) 'Some woman came round': inter-agency work in preventing school exclusion. In S. Riddell and L. Tett (eds) *Education, social justice and inter-agency working. Joined up or fractured policy?* Routledge: London.

Lloyd, G., Stead, J. and Kendrick, A. (2001b) *'Hanging on in there': A study of interagency work to prevent school exclusion in three local authorities.* Published for Joseph Rowntree Foundation by The National Children Bureau: London.

Munn, P., Riddell, S., Lloyd, G., Macleod, G., Stead, J., Kane, J. and Fairley, J. (2004) Evaluation of the Discipline Task Group recommendations: the deployment of additional staff to promote positive school discipline. Report to the Scottish Executive.

National Occupational Standards (2001) Teaching/Classroom Assistants. Online at: http://www.skills4schools.org.uk/downloaddoc.asp?id=86

O'Brien, T. and Garner, P. (eds) (2001) *Untold Stories. Learning Support Assistants and their work*, Stoke-on-Trent: Trentham Books.

Schlapp, U. and Davidson, J. (2001) Classroom Assistants in Scottish Primary Schools. Online at: http://www.scre.ac.uk/spotlight/spotlight85.html

Wilson, V., Schlapp, U., Robertson, R., Elliot, K., Campbell, C. and Whitty, G. (2003) An 'extra pair of hands', *Educational Management and Administration*, 31(2), 189–205.

Chapter 13

Breakfast clubs and school lunches

Their impact on children

The School Food Trust

The quality of food provided for children in schools has recently received a great deal of attention due, in part, to the high profile campaign of celebrity chef Jamie Oliver. After a period, which saw little intervention in relation to the food served in English schools, the School Food Trust was established in 2005 with the remit of improving the quality of food in schools and promoting the education and health of children and young people. In the same year, the government announced new standards for school food, which were phased into all local-authority maintained schools in England in 2009.

Although many teachers have a vast array of anecdotal evidence that suggests a link between eating and behaviour, there has been little robust or scientific evidence to support these claims. To help address this gap, as well as evaluating any intervention designed to improve the school meal experience, the School Food Trust has undertaken studies with the specific aim of investigating whether an improved diet, eaten at school, is associated with improved behaviour or attainment. This chapter includes two such studies. The first describes a randomised controlled trial (i.e. randomly allocating schools to either a control or an intervention group) which used systematic observations of children in the classroom after changes were made in the dining room. Results between the two groups were compared over time. The second presents results from a case-control study which compared academic attainment and attendance rates in schools with and without breakfast clubs.

The impact of primary school breakfast clubs in deprived areas of London

Key findings

Key Stage 2 results were better in primary schools in deprived areas of London one year after introducing breakfast clubs compared with the results of a comparable group of schools without breakfast clubs.

The School Food Trust for kind permission to reprint 'The impact of breakfast clubs in a deprived neighbourhood' (2008) and 'School lunches and behaviour' (2008): These are web-publications www.schoolfoodtrust.org.uk

- Average KS2 results were statistically significantly higher by 0.72 point in the year after the introduction of a breakfast club in 13 primary schools in deprived areas of London compared with a non-significant 0.27 point increase in 9 control schools matched for area deprivation, percentage Free School Meal eligibility, and percentage of minority ethnic groups.
- Schools started breakfast clubs to address problems relating to children being hungry on arrival at school and by mid-morning showing signs of tiredness, lack of concentration, and poor behaviour or learning.
- Pupils most likely to attend the breakfast clubs were those who had been arriving early because their parents needed to be at work or college. Children who reportedly arrived at school having had no breakfast, were frequently late, had behavioural or learning issues, or who came from a family in crisis were also encouraged to attend.
- Amongst the control schools, the main reason for *not* wanting to start a breakfast club was that it was morally wrong to provide children with breakfast as this was the domain and responsibility of the family. There were also concerns about additional demands placed on staff, the cost of staffing, and the ability to maintain the programme indefinitely.
- There was a real perception that the many facets of a club added value to the school through a variety of channels and benefits. The present study adds to the growing bank of evidence that breakfast clubs can have a beneficial impact, specifically on academic performance and punctuality. It will require a larger study in more representative samples and with better assessment of potential confounders to confirm the findings presented here and the role of food *per se*.

Background

There has been a trend over the last ten years for schools to introduce breakfast clubs, especially primary schools. This has mainly been driven by concerns that a substantial proportion of pupils are not eating breakfast and arriving at school hungry, which may impact negatively on learning and behaviour. The main aims of many breakfast clubs fit into four categories:

- provision of food at the start of the day
- improving pupils' education
- meeting the social needs of children and improving social skills
- improving school relations with parents.[1]

The role of breakfast clubs is wider than the provision of food; they also provide a calm and safe environment before school, help develop social skills and provide the opportunity for additional learning through 'play' activities, or provide time to complete homework. Attending a breakfast club may also assist pupils to arrive at school on time (or even encourage them to attend at all), and be ready to learn when classes begin.

Aims

The three aims of the study were to:

- assess whether the introduction of a breakfast club in primary schools was associated at the school level with improved academic performance, punctuality and reduced absences compared with schools with no breakfast club
- describe the perceived benefits of breakfast clubs to individual pupils and to the school community
- establish which aspects of the breakfast club contribute to any perceived benefits.

Methods

Selection of schools

In February 2007, 53 primary schools (including junior schools) were identified in Lambeth, Haringey and Camden (all areas of similar deprivation)[2] with 30% or greater known eligibility of free school meals (FSM) and more than 50 pupils on roll. In addition, 17 schools known to operate a breakfast club in other London Boroughs were contacted. Six clubs were set up by Magic Breakfast, three by Greggs Bakery, and the remainder by the school, parents, or other group. Schools were selected to take part in the study if they had either run a breakfast club for between 1 and 5 years (breakfast club schools) prior to recruitment or they had never run a breakfast club (control schools). Control schools were matched for area deprivation, percentage Free School Meal eligibility, and percentage of minority ethnic groups. Of those eligible, 13 (29%) with breakfast clubs and 9 (41%) without took part in the study.

Data collection

Key Stage 2 average point scores were obtained from the Department for Education and Skills (DfES) Achievement and Attainment Tables[3] for the academic year preceding the introduction of a breakfast club, for the year in which the breakfast club was introduced, and for each subsequent academic year through to 2005–2006. (DfES is now Department for Children, Schools and Families (DCSF).) For each of the nine control schools, information was obtained for the same time period as for the corresponding breakfast club school with the most similar characteristics. Percentages of both authorized absence and unauthorized absence were also obtained from the Achievement and Attainment Tables for each time-point. Breakfast club schools were asked about attendance at the breakfast club, the food served and the activities on offer at the breakfast club. In April and May 2007, an in-depth qualitative interview was carried out in every school They were asked about the reasons for starting the breakfast club, how the club was run and the perceived benefits. Control schools were asked their views about breakfast clubs and why they currently did not have one.

Results

Approximately 13% of pupils on the school rolls attended the breakfast clubs, with 10% of pupils attending the breakfast clubs regularly (three or more days a week).

Quantitative results

Breakfast clubs were introduced between September 2001 and February 2006 inclusive. The end of the academic year prior to the start of clubs therefore ranged from July 2001 to July 2005. Compared with the year prior to the start of the breakfast club, breakfast club schools showed a statistically significant 0.72 point increase in the Key Stage 2 average point score in the year immediately after the introduction of breakfast clubs (Table 13.1). This difference was sustained in subsequent years, although there was no further increase in average Key Stage 2 scores. There was no corresponding change in the control schools (Table 13.1). There was no difference in average point scores at either time point between the two groups (unpaired t-test).

Authorised and unauthorised absence rates were also compared. Although there was a greater decline in authorized absences in the breakfast club compared with the control schools in the year after the breakfast clubs were introduced, the difference between time points or between groups did not reach statistical significance.

Qualitative results

Schools had started breakfast clubs because they were aware that some children were coming to school having not eaten. Some pupils appeared to suffer from tiredness, lack of concentration, poor behaviour or learning issues by mid-morning. In addition, some pupils were arriving at the school gate very early (raising issues of pastoral care and safety) or regularly arriving late.

The children most likely to attend were those who had been arriving at school early because their parents needed to be at work or college. Children known to arrive at school having had no breakfast, be frequently late, have behavioural and learning issues, or come from a family in crisis, were targeted to attend.

Table 13.1 Key Stage 2 average point scores (mean, sd) before and after the start of breakfast clubs or corresponding period in control schools, by type of school

Key stage 2 average point scores	*Type of school* Breakfast club		*Control*	
n	*13*		*9*	
	Mean	*sd*	*Mean*	*sd*
One year before* start of breakfast club (or corresponding period in control school)	26.1	1.74	27.3	1.19
One year after* start of breakfast club (or corresponding period in control school)	26.8	1.58	27.5	1.94
Mean difference (95% CI)	0.72	(0.06, 1.38)	0.27	(−0.81, 1.34)
P	*0.03*		*0.58*	

* Refers to the Key Stage 2 results in the three terms immediately preceeding the introduction of a breakfast club or in the three terms following its introduction. In the control schools, results for the corresponding terms were used.

Schools believed that they had reaped significant benefit through the introduction of breakfast clubs especially in the case of the most socially deprived children. The benefits fell into four categories:

- improving children's social skills
- promoting links between parents and school and children and class teachers
- improving the punctuality of children who were frequently late
- improving children's health and concentration levels.

Furthermore, the introduction of a breakfast club was seen as a welcome addition and benefit, having a positive and synergistic impact on other activities in the school.

There were some concerns about running breakfast clubs: extending the school day for staff; using volunteers; having poor facilities for running the club; and the club being used as cheap childcare. Most importantly, there was concern about the long-term effects of schools taking on the role of parents at a time of day which encroaches on family time. There were also concerns about the costs (extended staff time, breakfast ingredients) and continuation of the breakfast club if support from charitable organizations ceased. Amongst the control schools, these same concerns were expressed as reasons for *not* wanting to start a breakfast club.

Discussion

The many perceived benefits of breakfast clubs reported by schools included a strong sense that: children were less hungry; were mixing with a greater range of pupils (in particular different ages); were more focused in their work; and punctuality improved.

This study is unique, however, in suggesting that over the longer term (i.e. one year or more), the introduction of a breakfast club in schools in deprived neighbourhoods was associated with an improvement in pupils' Key Stage 2 average point score. Of further importance is that the observed improvement was sustained over time. Control schools did not show significant improvements in attainment over equivalent periods.

The two main limitations to this study were sample selection bias and limited quantitative data to allow control of confounders in the analysis. The greater improvement in the Key Stage 2 average scores in the breakfast club schools compared with the control schools may be accounted for by the presence of head teachers in the breakfast club schools who were more keen than those in the control schools to introduce changes in the environment generally that were likely to improve pupils' performance. There were a number of potential confounders of the improvement in Key Stage 2 average point score for which it was not possible to control, such as other initiatives that may have been introduced in the school at the same time as the breakfast clubs, or changes in or addition to key school personnel. This is consistent with the finding that on average only about 10% of pupils in the schools with breakfast clubs could be described as 'regular' attenders, and it is unlikely that the changes in Key Stage 2 outcomes could be attributed to this 10% alone. Importantly, head teachers themselves perceived that improved attainment was as a result of the introduction of a number of related initiatives associated in part with the introduction of the breakfast clubs.

Conclusions

In this group of schools with breakfast clubs, there was a real perception that the many facets of a club added value to the school through a variety of channels and benefits. The present study adds to the growing bank of evidence that breakfast clubs can have a beneficial impact, specifically on academic performance and punctuality. It will require a larger study in more representative samples and with better assessment of potential confounders to confirm the findings presented here.

References

1 Harrop, A. and Palmer, G. (2002) Improving breakfast clubs lessons from the best. London: New Policy Institute.
2 DfES (2007). Schools and pupils in England: January 2007 (Provisional).
3 Department for Children, Schools and Families (2007) School and college achievement and attainment tables. London: Department for Children, Schools and Families. www.dfes.gov.uk/performancetables

School lunch and behaviour: systematic observation of classroom behaviour following a school dining room intervention

Summary

- *Aim* Evidence that improvements in school food benefit pupils' behaviour is patchy and anecdotal, The aim of this study was to determine whether a) improvements in school food provision at lunchtime to meet the new food-based standards and b) changes to the school lunchtime dining room environment to meet best practice, improved pupils' concentration and made them more alert and calm in the classroom in the learning period after lunch.
- *Methods* Six primary schools in Sheffield were matched in triplets by school and neighbourhood characteristics. The intervention was in two six-week phases: in two of the matched schools, changes in food provision were followed by changes in the dining room environment; in two schools, changes in environment were followed by changes in food provision; and two schools acted as controls (no intervention). Observers blinded to the type of intervention made objective measurements of learning-related behaviours in the classroom during the teaching session immediately after lunch at three time points (baseline (pre-intervention), after 4–6 weeks, and after 10–12 weeks) in 146 randomly selected pupils aged 8–10. In total, 25,750 10-second observations of behaviour were made. Outcomes were assessed over the 12-week period as a whole, and by phase (nutrition or environment), taking into account school characteristics, class size, presence of additional adults in the classroom, English as an additional language, FSM eligibility, SEN status ethnicity, and lunch type (school meal or packed lunch).
- *Results*
    - 90% of the study pupils were White British, 97% spoke English as a first language, 26% were eligible for free school meals (FSM), 29% had special educational needs (SEN).

  - 'On-task' behaviours (measure of concentration) and 'off-task' behaviours (measure of disengagement (disruption)) were observed within three settings (pupil–teacher interaction, pupil–pupil interaction, working alone). Overall levels of on-task were high (80%) and levels of overall off-task were low (11%).
  - When the 12-week intervention was assessed as a whole, pupils in the intervention schools were 3.4 times more likely to be on-task in the teacher–pupil setting compared with pupils in the control schools. However, in the pupil–pupil setting, pupils in the intervention schools were 2.3 times more likely to be off-task than those in the control schools.
  - When the effect of the intervention was compared group by group (nutrition first vs. environment first vs. control), pupils in the nutrition first group were 5.4 times as likely to be on-task in the teacher–pupil setting compared with the control schools. They were also 3.6 times as likely to be off-task in the pupil–pupil setting in the nutrition first intervention schools compared with the control schools.

- *Conclusion* A combined nutrition-environment intervention in primary schools had a beneficial impact on pupils' behaviour in the teacher–pupil setting, but was associated with increased off-task behaviours when pupils were being asked to work together without direct teacher supervision. The nutrition-first intervention was more powerfully associated with this effect than the environment-first intervention. The findings are consistent with the more subjective anecdotal evidence from teachers that pupils are more on-task following a healthier lunch in school.

Background

The role of school food in promoting children's nutrition, growth and development, and health, is clear.[1] The re-introduction of standards for school food, and significant government investment into this policy area in recent years has therefore been warranted.[2–4] The wider educational benefits of improved school food in terms of readiness to learn, pupil mood, behaviour, and thus learning and attainment, are also of key interest. However, there is little robust research in this area. Anecdotes from teachers and parents describe dramatic improvements in children's concentration, behaviour, learning and academic performance when healthier school food is introduced. Case studies and best practice guidance also support improving the school dining environment to support children's behaviour, well being and learning.[5] However, a recent systematic review[6] concluded that no firm inferences can be drawn on the relationship between nutrition, including school food, and educational outcomes due to a lack of clear evidence.

Only two previous studies have explored school lunches and educational outcomes.[6] Other studies in schools have focused on breakfast, snacking, single foods, nutrients or nutrient supplementation, food insufficiency, or general dietary advice. Few studies on nutrition and educational have accounted for key confounders such as family circumstance, habitual diet, physical activity levels and school lunch environment. Outcomes relevant to the classroom setting (i.e. learning behaviours and mood) that can be assessed in a valid, consistent and comparable manner have also not been measured.

Studies have also focused on the benefits for children in special circumstances or with special needs (e.g. ADHD, nutritionally at risk), limiting generalisability of study results to all school children. Finally, much of the existing research focuses on the role of nutrition *per se* (e.g. individual nutrients, meal composition, or nutrition promotion) in mediating educational improvements. It has failed to address the way in which nutrition interventions themselves alter the environment in which children's behaviour is being evaluated, and the potential interactions between nutritional and environmental interventions. The environmental changes and interactions with nutrition may also influence children's behaviour, mood and readiness to learn, and their possible impact needs careful evaluation.

Methods

Study design: A two-phased controlled intervention trial involving six primary schools which were matched in triplets and randomly assigned to three groups:

- *Nutrition first*: introduction of healthier school food at lunchtime over six weeks followed by changes in the school dining environment over six weeks;
- *Environment first*: changes in the school dining environment over six weeks followed by introduction of healthier school food at lunchtime over six weeks;
- *Control*: wait-listed control schools in which there was no intervention for 12 weeks (but which had support with nutrition and dining room changes at the end of the study).

The school-based intervention aimed to ensure (a) that the food provided in school at lunchtime met the new food-based standards,[4] and (b) that the dining room environment in which food was served promoted best practice.[7] Behaviour related to learning outcomes was measured objectively by observers in the classroom during the afternoon teaching session in randomly selected individual pupils at baseline (pre-intervention), after 4–6 weeks, and after 10–12 weeks. Parents and pupils provided a detailed study information sheet. Pupils whose parents did not want them to participate in the study, or who had anaemia, acute or chronic illness were not included in the pupil selection process.

Six primary schools in Sheffield were matched in triplets by school and neighbourhood characteristics (meal environment scores, catering provider, school roll, free school meal eligibility, Healthy School status, participation in the Social and Emotional Aspects of Learning (SEAL) program, and school lunch take up). Observers blinded to the type of intervention made objective measurements of learning-related behaviours in the classroom during the teaching session immediately after lunch at three time points in 2007 (baseline (pre-intervention), January/February, prior to spring half term; after 4–6 weeks, in March, prior to the Easter holiday; and after 10–12 weeks in May, prior to the summer half term) in 146 randomly selected pupils aged 8–10, In total, 25,750 10-second observations of behaviour were made. Outcomes were assessed over the 12-week period as a whole, and by phase (nutrition or environment), controlling either for school group ('unadjusted') or taking into account school characteristics including class size, presence of additional adults in the classroom, English as an additional language (EAL), FSM eligibility, SEN status ethnicity, and lunch type (school meal or packed lunch) ('adjusted').

Results

The three groups of schools (nutrition first, environment first, and control) were similar in relation to size (average 435 pupils), EAL (98%), and SEN (30%), but differed in relation to FSM eligibility (7% in control schools vs. 24%–27% in the intervention schools). The characteristics of the pupils taking part, however, were very similar: 90% (± 5%) White British, 97% (± 2%) EAL, 26% (± 12%) FSM, and 29% (± 0.6%) SEN.

The relative occurrence (Odds Ratios (OR)) of on-task behaviours in the intervention schools versus the control schools in the adjusted model (Table 13.2) shows that overall, there were apparently no statistically significant differences (total on-task OR = 1.14, p = 0.86; total off-task OR = 0.83, p = 0.31). When broken down by setting, however, pupils were over three times more likely to be on-task with the teacher in the intervention schools than in the control schools. Surprisingly, pupils engaged with other pupils were less likely to be on-task (OR = 0.45) and more likely to be off-task (OR = 2.28) in the intervention schools compared with the control schools.

When assessed by intervention groups separately (nutrition-first vs. control and environment-first vs. control), the nutrition-first group showed greater individual on-task (OR = 2.04) and teacher–pupil (OR = 5.37) on-task behaviour compared with the control group. Again, pupil–pupil on-task behaviour was less likely in the intervention group (OR = 0.34) and off-task behaviour was more likely (OR = 3.57). The environment-first school showed no statistically significant differences from the control group, although the on-task behaviour showed trends similar to the nutrition-first group.

Discussion

A combined nutrition-environment intervention in primary schools had a beneficial impact on pupils' behaviour in the setting in which teachers are directly engaged with

Table 13.2 Occurrence of on-task and off-task behaviour overall and for each setting separately for the intervention schools combined relative to the control schools

	Intervention vs. control		
	*Odds ratio**	*95% CI*	*p*
Total on-task (concentration)	1.14	0.87, 1.49	0.86
On-task by setting:			
Individual on-task	1.27	0.94, 1.74	0.14
Pupil–pupil on-task	**0.45**	**0.28, 0.70**	<**0.001**
Teacher–pupil on-task	**3.40**	**1.56, 7.36**	**0.009**
Total off-task (disengagement)	0.83	0.74, 1.19	0.31
Off-task by setting:			
Individual off-task	0.71	0.37, 1.35	0.29
Pupil–pupil off-task	**2.28**	**1.25, 4.17**	**0.007**
Teacher–pupil off-task	1.09	0.35, 3.45	0.89

* Model adjusted for class size, presence of additional adults in the classroom, English as an additional language (EAL), FSM eligibility, SEN status ethnicity, and lunch type (school meal or packed lunch).

Table 13.3 Occurrence of on-task and off-task behaviour overall and for each setting separately for the nutrition-first vs. control schools and environment-first vs. control schools

	Nutrition-first vs control			*Environment-first vs control*		
	*Odds ratio**	*95% CI*	*p*	*Odds ratio**	*95% CI*	*p*
Total on-task (concentration)	1.22	0.89, 1.67	0.21	1.06	0.78, 1.45	0.69
On-task by setting:						
Individual on-task	**2.04**	**1.04, 4.01**	**0.04**	1.02	0.56, 1.85	0.62
Pupil–pupil on-task	**0.34**	**0.20, 0.58**	**<0.001**	0.59	0.35, 1.01	0.06
Teacher–pupil on-task	**5.37**	**3.70, 12.0**	**<0.001**	1.86	0.82, 4.23	0.14
Total off-task (disengagement)	0.94	0.64, 1.39	0.76	0.71	0.47, 1.08	0.11
Off-task by setting:						
Individual off-task	0.53	0.25, 1.12	0.10	0.93	0.43, 1.98	0.84
Pupil–pupil off-task	**3.57**	**1.84, 6.92**	**<0.001**	1.08	0.53, 2.21	0.82
Teacher–pupil off-task	0.77	0.24, 2.50	0.67	2.07	0.61, 7.05	0.25

* Model adjusted for class size, presence of additional adults in the classroom, English as an additional language (EAL), FSM eligibility, SEN status ethnicity, and lunch type (school meal or packed lunch).

pupils in a learning activity. When analysed according to whether the intervention was nutrition-first or environment first, the nutrition first intervention was more powerfully associated with the observed differences in behaviour compared with the control schools. This is consistent with the more subjective anecdotal evidence from teachers that pupils are more on-task following a healthier lunch in school.

Generally increased arousal in pupils who have eaten a healthier lunch may help to explain the increased off-task behaviours when pupils were being asked to work together without direct teacher supervision. When pupils were working on their own in the nutrition-first group, they were significantly more likely to be on-task than pupils in the control schools (OR = 2.04), but no more likely to be off-task.

Conclusion

This is the first time that improvements in learning-related behaviour in school children in a developed country have been objectively assessed following a well-controlled nutrition and dining environment intervention. The underlying causes of the improvements and their associated mechanisms need to be further evaluated. It is likely that the interventions *per se* rather than changes in nutritional status are responsible for the observed changes. A study in secondary school pupils to be started in 2008 will address these issues.

References

1 School Meals Review Panel (2005). Turning the Tables – Transforming School Food: The Development and implementation of nutritional standards for school lunches. www.schoolfoodtrust.org.uk/UploadDocs/Library/Documents/SMRP Report FINAL.pdf

2 Statutory Instrument 2000 No. 1777. *Education (nutritional standards for School Lunches) (England) Regulations 2000.* London: TSO.

3 Statutory Instrument 2007 No. 2359. *The Education (Nutritional Standards and Requirements for School Food) (England) Regulations 2007*. London: TSO.
4 Statutory Instrument 2006 No. 2381. *The Education (Nutritional Standards for School Lunches) (England) Regulations 2006*. London: TSO.
5 *North Yorkshire Business & Education Partnership, Business & Education South Yorkshire. (2004)*. The Dining Room Environment Project. Food in Schools Programme (DfES, DH).
6 Centre for Food, Physical Activity and Obesity Research. A systematic review of the effect of nutrition, diet and dietary change on learning, education and performance of children of relevance to UK schools. www.food.gov.uk/multimedia/pdfs/systemreview.pdf
7 Meal experience guide.

Chapter 14

What languages do you speak?

Linguistic journeys in school

Raymonde Sneddon

In this chapter, Raymonde Sneddon revisits her enquiry of 1997 where she asked: what does it mean to a child to be bilingual? It is a question as relevant in primary schools now as it was then. Raymonde's original enquiry set out to discover, through interviews and observations, the ways in which children and parents in 40 families used Gujerati, English and Urdu at home, in school, at the community centre, at the mosque, at work, shopping and at leisure.

Since 1997, Raymonde's enquiry has continued and expanded to include children and their families from a wide range of language backgrounds: Somali, Albanian, Czech and Polish to name but a few. We have included this chapter for several reasons: it is an enquiry which draws upon local expertise and networks to link school, home and community; it reflects change and continuity over time around a key issue in primary education (support for children at various stages of using English); and it suggests a practical way of discovering children's language competences which enables adults to provide more effective support in schools.

Working with the community (1997)

As a new teacher in the late 1970s I was anxious to build relationships with parents who, through lack of confidence in their communication skills in English, were reluctant to visit the school. At the time I found the most effective strategy was though work in school that valued children's home languages. We made books with photographs of the children which they persuaded their parents to come and see. We soon had parents coming regularly to tell stories in Punjabi, Urdu, Gujerati and Greek. They helped us to choose dual language books and other language resources for the school. They also helped us plan assemblies, make costumes and teach the children traditional dances. We ran bilingual parent-child writing groups and together made books in fourteen languages.

Centre for Literacy in Primary Education for permission to reprint extracts from 'What language do you speak at home? Linguistic journeys in school', Raymonde Sneddon, 1997 in *Language Matters* CLPE: 1996–1997 with a 2009 update from the author.

I also discovered the potential of community organizations such as the Turkish Education Group and the Asian Women's Support Group to help us as teachers to get to know our children's communities better. Community education workers came into school to talk to us, and they convened meetings with parents where we learned about hopes and anxieties which we would never otherwise have known about. They helped us to set targets for children's achievement by working more closely with parents. At the request of a group of Sylheti speaking mothers, the school set up a Bengali Saturday class.

All of this work led me in the 1990s to carry out research with five linguistic communities (Punjabi, Gujerati, Urdu, Turkish and Bengali) to explore the extent of the support children receive at home for their bilingualism, through story-telling, reading, language and religion classes. This initial enquiry revealed how committed parents were for their children to achieve literacy in their first and home languages as well as being successful in English at school.

In this project, with Gujerati-speaking research assistant Sakina Hafeski, we are attempting to get closer to the complex realities of bilingual and multilingual children's language and literacy experiences, and the effect of these experiences children's school achievement. We were looking at the way children use Gujerati, English and Urdu at home, in school, at the community centre, at the mosque and how their parents use languages at home, at work, shopping and at leisure. We were also investigating media (at the time of writing, newspapers, radio and television) in the home, how stories are told and read, who helps with homework from school and mosque, and how parents see their role in developing children's language and literacy. Forty families with amazing good grace helped with this enquiry – answering endless questions, reading dual language books with their 3½, 7 and 11 year old children and allowing us to observe and tape-record them doing so. The project made me aware of how very little we know as teachers about the richness of children's linguistic lives.

What does it mean to be bilingual?

Many teachers are dissatisfied with the term 'children who speak English as a second language' because it seems to focus on what the child lacks and functions mainly from the perspective of the monolingual English speaker. Adoption of the term 'bilingual' focuses more on the child's linguistic skills and encourages adults to value and develop these. But when we talk about a child being bilingual, what exactly do we mean?

The term 'bilingual' is commonly used to refer to children who speak two languages interchangeably and are equally proficient in both, but this particular notion of 'balanced bilingualism' is rather rare. It can be a very narrow definition which leads to comments such as 'This child is not bilingual, she doesn't speak either language properly'. I have also come across 'bilingual' being used negatively to refer to children who speak little or no English and I have been told, in an obviously multilingual school, 'You won't find any bilingual children here – they all speak English'. The majority of people in the world use two or more languages in their everyday lives: if this broad definition of bilingualism is adopted, it enables us to begin (for those of us who are monolingual) to investigate how children, like bilingual adults the world over, use their languages in different contexts determined by people, places and topics. Context tends to trigger the choice and variety of language (standard or non-standard) and whether children mix the languages they speak. Helping children to investigate their language use is a valuable way of developing reflection and language awareness for children, teachers and teaching assistants.

How do you find out about children's languages?

Well, of course, you can ask. And you may get the answer that children think you expect: 'I speak English.' 'I speak Gujerati.' And even, if they think you are very ignorant, 'I speak African.' The child of course may not know the English name for the language they speak, and that may be another reason for answers like the last one. If you ask 'Do you speak English at home?' and the answer is 'Yes'. You may assume, as a number of teachers do, that that is the whole answer when in fact English is only one of several languages used.

How else can you ask? You can describe your own language use and invite children to talk about the languages they use: how we mix languages when talking amongst friends, how we may answer in a language other than the question addressed to us, and how it is easier to talk about certain things in a particular language (for example, things that happen at the mosque in Urdu and things that happen at school in English).

If you introduce an activity which allows children to visually represent their language networks and to estimate or measure their language use, this usually sparks a lively and intense debate. You can invite children to diagram and colour code their languages, estimating much of which language they think they speak, and to whom. This sometimes reveals imbalances and can create a discussion about how and why this happens. Children's graphic diagrams and networks often reveal a 'three generation model', where children speak to grandparents exclusively in the home language, a mixture of home languages and English to parents, and mainly English with siblings.

What Rehana speaks

Rehana drew images of her language networks. The diagrams she devised – with circles and arrows indicating which languages the members of her family speak and to whom – show that she speaks mainly English with her brothers and sisters, both English and Gujerati with her parents, Gujerati with her grandparents and a little Urdu with her grandfather. Rehana's drawings show that her mother and she use roughly the same balance of English and Gujerati when speaking together, and that her father speaks to her primarily in Gujerati with Rehana speaking to him mainly in English. At school, Rehana uses a little Gujerati in the playground and in the classroom, and a little at lunch time 'because my auntie is a dinner lady'. At the mosque, Rehana speaks Gujerati, reads and writes in Urdu, and is learning to read the Koran in Arabic. Rehana also listens to music and watches films in Hindi.

Children's language networks

Although the process of children estimating their own language use is imprecise, we have discovered through separate interviews with parents that children's diagrams correspond to what parents report. Children use English much more than their parents do. They speak almost exclusively in a home language to grandparents, and a surprisingly large number of children speak only a home language with parents. There is an interesting finding that twice as many children use only a home language with their fathers than with their mothers. In school, children who have access to other children who speak their home languages will mix these languages and English; they will use home languages occasionally in the playground and in the classroom because 'Sometimes you want to explain something and it's easier in Gujerati'. Significantly, only a few children report having an opportunity to use their home languages with an adult in school. Children aged 7 and 11 have the greatest freedom of language use with their siblings: they are competent in English and at least one other language, and they are not constrained by teachers or other family members.

The reservoir of language knowledge that children bring to school can be tapped by teachers and teaching assistants and used creatively to encourage in all children an interest in and enthusiasm for language learning.

Linguistic journeys revisited (2009)

Since the publication in 1997 of 'Linguistic journeys in school' I have continued to study children's language use at home, at school and in their communities. Twelve years later, I have in front of me a diagram of how Elina uses language in her family

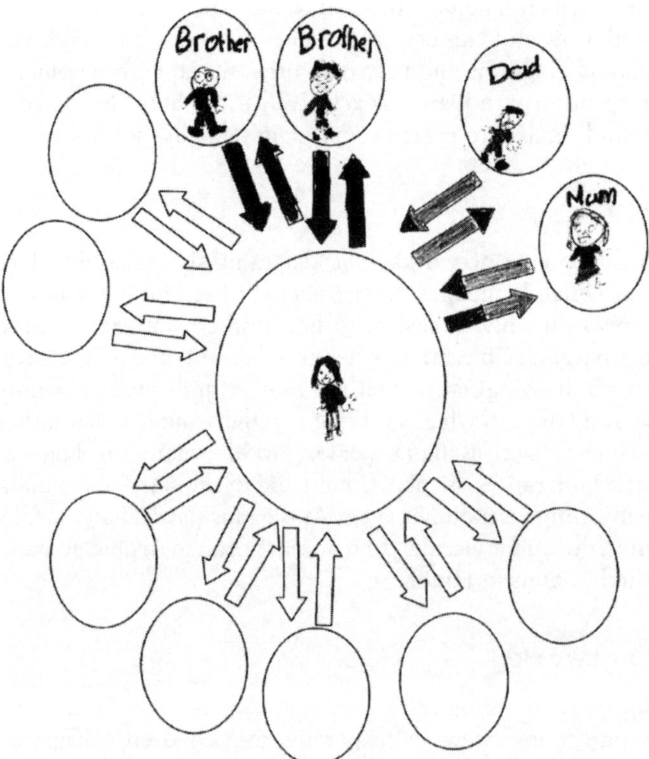

Figure 14.1 How Elina uses languages

(Figure 14.1): she uses grey to signify Albanian and black to signify English. She is using a modification of the diagrams devised by Rehana all those years ago:

Elina is seven years old. She was born in London of Albanian parents who arrived as asylum seekers in 1999. As part of the ongoing study I have interviewed her about her attendance at Albanian classes. I have also spoken to her mother. As part of the interviews I have asked them both about their use of Albanian and English in the home. Elina has drawn portraits of herself and her immediate family and coloured the arrows to indicate which language she speaks to members of her family and which language they speak to her. She has used black for English and grey for Albanian. Her drawing confirms what she and her mother have told me: that her parents are very keen that she should retain the use of Albanian, so they speak to her almost entirely in that language. She understands them well and responds mostly in Albanian, with some English, more to her mother than to her father. The diagram also indicates that Elina and her brothers speak entirely in English to each other. This was one of the reasons her parents enrolled her in an after-school Albanian class. They hope that, by mixing with other children in an Albanian-speaking environment, Elina will get into the habit of using the language more with her siblings. Elina loves the Albanian classes, especially the opportunity to learn some traditional dancing after the literacy work.

Finding out what skills children have in their languages, and how and when they use them, is an essential starting point for all adults who support the learning of bilingual and multilingual children, and the template for Elina's diagram is reproduced at the end of this chapter.

Reading in two languages

In the 1997 research, the ways in which children made use of dual language books led me to analyse children's retelling of the traditional tale *The Raja's Big Ears* in Gujerati. The children's recorded narratives demonstrated how they transformed the rather formal language of the story into the form of Gujerati that they use with their family and friends and made it their own. In the same way as my original study attempted to get closer to multilingual children's language and literacy experiences, I have gone on to explore what children actually do when they read from two languages on the same page. In my study of how children learn to read in the language of the home, with their mothers or with each other using dual language books, one of the most significant findings is how excited and motivated children are by the challenge of reading from two languages and how and proud they are of their achievement.

As part of this study, parents were encouraged to use dual language books at home to read in both languages with their children and to teach them to read in the language of the home if they were interested. A number of parents allowed me to observe and record them with their children. Transcribing and analysing the observations revealed the many different strategies that parents used: teaching children the phonics, supporting them to de-code the home language text, reading several times, checking with the English version, and posing questions which they discussed in both languages. Several parents invited their children to retell the story in their own words in both languages. Not all parents were totally fluent in English and several reported that working together with their child helped their English as well as developing the child's home language.

My study would suggest that in primary schools, in addition to sending dual language books home, there is considerable scope for bilingual adults to carry out such reading activities with children who share the same language, individually or in groups. For example, I observed Lek and Durkan, two Turkish speaking children in Year 2, help each other to read in Turkish from a dual language version of *The Giant Turnip*. They explored the way in which Turkish sentences are structured differently from English ones and enjoyed explaining this to me:

> You add –an and it makes it bigger. If you spell zürafada, that's just a giraffe, but if you add –an, it makes it like, more popular, it's like there's more giraffes.

His friend Durkan intervenes to suggest that this addition means bigger and Lek expands:

> If you have, like, connectives and stuff, it makes the word bigger.

Practitioners who do not share the children's language can encourage children, like Lek and Durkan, to help each other and to teach the teacher.

Personal book-making, as I described it in 1997, is as popular as ever with bilingual children. What has changed is how much easier it is and how much more professional the results look. Fonts for all languages are readily available, as is book-making software that allows for two languages, some of which includes the option of sound files for children to record their narratives. As a bonus children's personal books can be shared with a wider audience over the internet.

Since 1997 classrooms have become ever more linguistically diverse: children have arrived as refugees from conflict zones and contributed new languages such as Somali and Albanian to the classroom; the enlargement of the European Union has brought languages such as Lithuanian, Czech and Polish. Not only has the number of bilingual children risen and the range of languages spoken increased, but the patterns of language use are increasingly varied. The same classroom is likely to have children from second or third generations of well-established local communities who are much more fluent in English than in the original language of the home, and new arrivals just coming to terms with a new country and a new language.

As classrooms become ever more linguistically rich and varied, it is important for practitioners who support children's learning to explore the language diversity of their classes as well as the very individual pattern of each child's interaction with languages in their everyday environments. The strategies I described in 1997 are as relevant now as they were then. The language use diagram (Figure 14.2) is best introduced with children working in pairs or small groups, preferably with an adult who can initiate a discussion about how people who speak more than one language use them with different people and in different places. The diagrams can be enlarged, and they can be displayed as posters. Their use provides a starting point for exploring, sharing and building on children's language experience and skills.

Activity sheet:

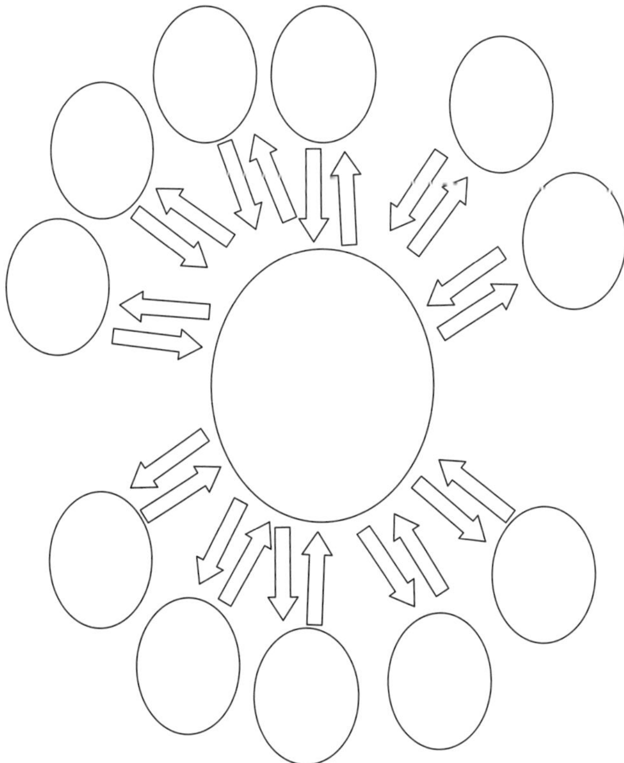

What languages do you speak with your family?

Key:

Colour	Language

Figure 14.2 Language use diagram

References

Barkow, H. (2001) *The Giant Turnip*. London: Mantra Lingua.
Desai, N. (1989) *The Raja's Big Ears*. London: Mantra Lingua.
Sneddon, R. (2000) 'Language and Literacy: Children's Experiences in Multilingual Environments'. *International Journal of Bilingual Education and Bilingualism*. Vol. 3: 4. pp. 265–282.

Sneddon, R. and Patel, K. (2003) 'The Raja's Big Ears, the journey of a story across cultures'. *Language and Education* 17(5): pp. 371–384.
Sneddon, R. (2009) *Bilingual Books, Biliterate Children*. Stoke-on-Trent: Trentham Books.

Website

www.uel.ac.uk/education/research/duallanguagebooks

Chapter 15

Achieving successful home–school links with refugees

Jill Rutter

Jill Rutter's chapter is an overview of her extensive research into the experiences of refugee children and families, focusing in particular on Somali and Congolese communities. She draws together key findings from research into refugee experiences, and discusses how an understanding of resilience and risk factors can help adults support refugee children in schools. Like Chapter 7, this enquiry examines how children cope with traumatic experiences.

Who are refugees and asylum-seekers?

The term *refugee* is generally used to describe persons who have had an experience of forced migration. However, the term refugee is an immigration status and has a precise legal meaning. A person with refugee status is defined as someone who has fled from his or her home country or is unable to return to it '*owing to a well founded fear of being persecuted for reasons of race, religion, nationality, membership of a particular social group or political opinion*'. An *asylum-seeker* is a person who has crossed an international border in search of safety, and refugee status, in another country. In the UK asylum-seekers are people who are awaiting a Home Office decision as to whether they can remain. The definition of refugees is taken from the 1951 UN Convention Relating to the Status of Refugees and its 1967 Protocol, an international law now signed by 137 states including the UK. These two legal instruments enshrine the rights of asylum-seekers and refugees, preventing them being returned to countries where they fear persecution. Families described as refugees seek to regularise their immigration status by applying for political asylum, and the period while an asylum application is being determined is often stressful. Asylum issues are often the priority, and issues such as supporting a child's schooling may be of lesser importance.

Multiverse for kind permission to reprint extracts from 'Achieving successful home–school links with refugees', Jill Rutter (2006). This is a web-publication www.multiverse.ac.uk

Research, refugee children and schools

Research about refugee children is dominated by literature about trauma and Post Traumatic Stress Disorder (PTSD). Many research studies that examine the psychological consequences of war and persecution conclude that refugee children manifest high levels of mental illness, meaning their ability to function in normal social settings is severely and adversely affected.

The research literature about the traumatic experiences of refugee children has had a major impact on how they are viewed by staff in schools (Rutter, 2006). Refugee children's background and needs are framed by educationalists largely in terms of trauma; an understanding of pre-exile experiences, other than the 'trauma', is neglected. The post-exile experiences of refugees in the UK, which may include material deprivation, loss of social status, as well as racial attack, appear to be deemed less significant by schools, where refugee children tend to be viewed as a homogenous group and labelled as universally traumatized; this obscures the role of refugee parents in promoting their child's well-being. Refugee children's problems in schools are largely viewed as mental health problems that require a medicalised response, most usually provided by the health service. At the same time, theories of PTSD have been critiqued for failing to fully recognise the social worlds of refugees, and refugee families may have other complex educational and social needs which limit their capacity to form successful links with their children's school.

Risk and resilience

Recent psychological literature on refugee children has suggested a different framework for understanding their experiences and adaptation: that of risk and resilience. The concept of resilience draws on work with physically and sexually abused children and observations that some children survive abuse without manifesting severe psychological distress (Rutter, 1985). This work has identified protective factors and resilience on one hand, and risk factors and vulnerability on the other hand, in children's lives. Protective factors are attributes or conditions that make it more likely a child will achieve some degree of resilience, and less likely that a child will manifest distress severe enough to become dysfunctional. Risk factors are attributes or conditions that make it less likely for a child to achieve some degree of resilience. These concepts of resilience and risk draw on a holistic model where refugee children's development is influenced by a number of factors, such as:

1 the personal characteristics and personal world of the child;
2 the home country and flight, repeated exposure to stress (war, famine);
3 the situation in exile, quality of parenting or secure housing;
4 the external environment, including the school.

The quality of parental care is probably the most important factor in determining the resilience of refugee children. A study of Cambodian refugee children concluded that those with the best mental health were those with intact families (Kinzie *et al.*, 1986). Research undertaken in London schools concluded that refugee children who were not coping experienced greater family upheaval, including changes of carer (Massoud and Dowling, 1997).

The concept of resilience is very relevant for educationalists. By asking a key question – What makes some refugee children resilient and others not? – schools and educational support workers can consider what they can do to minimise children's vulnerability and maximise children's resilience. Clearly, interventions to support refugee parents will promote their children's resilience.

Much research about home–school links among refugee children assumes homogeneity among refugee populations. While there are many commonalities among refugee populations of different national origins, my own research argues that sometimes factors specific to certain refugee groups can influence home–school relations. Such factors can include different understandings of home–school relationships, different levels of English language competencies and parental employment patterns. Drawing on my own research, the following section analyses factors influencing home–school relationships among Congolese and Somali refugee groups (Rutter, 2006).

The Congolese in the UK

The 2001 Census showed that 81 per cent of the UK's Congolese live in Greater London. Significant proportions of Congolese children have experienced changes to household structure as a result of flight and exile. In the four case study schools in which my research was undertaken, some 34 per cent of all Congolese children had experienced a change of carer, mostly living with 'aunts and uncles' in private foster-care arrangements that did not seem to be known to social services or to the children's teachers. There were also children who had been orphaned in the UK by AIDS and later fostered by relatives. Schools and teachers need to be aware that many refugee children experience changes in care arrangements and this may affect their learning in school, as well as the home–school relationship.

Two studies of Congolese refugees have been undertaken in the UK (Haringey, 1997; Healthy Islington, 2000). Both surveys identify issues relevant to children's education and welfare, including home–school liaison, namely:

- The Congolese in Haringey fell into two groups: the well-educated and those who have had little or no education. Some 47.8 per cent of those interviewed had started a university course, a proportion much higher than any other group surveyed. But 17.39 per cent had no education at all (a proportion also higher than many of the other refugee groups surveyed).
- Some 23 per cent of Congolese surveyed could not read and write French and 45 per cent could not read and write Lingala.
- Congolese community informants described the stigma of illiteracy, as well as the status associated with speaking French; there are very few English language courses targeted at those who are not literate in their home language.
- There was considerable diversity in class and educational background among the Congolese. Schools need to be aware that some Congolese parents may lack literacy in French or Lingala. This will mean that written communication may not be understood. As in all communities, illiteracy is a condition associated with shame

and may also mean that parents and carers do not want to form positive links with their children's schools.

The home–school relationship

Concerns about the underachievement of Congolese children prompted one London local authority to fund research into this issue. Poor home school links emerged as a major theme in the research, both from the perspective of the parents and the school (Rutter, 2004). Both schools and parents seemed very unclear of what comprised a good home school relationship. A number of parents felt that schools in the UK wanted too much from parents – they were expected to attend too many meetings. Despite this complaint, school records indicated that most Congolese parents did manage to attend parents meetings.

Congolese parents talked about five issues that prevented successful home school relationships:

1 lack of parental knowledge about the UK education system
2 lack of parental confidence in liaising with schools
3 parents and carers' lack of fluent English
4 children withholding information from parents
5 parents working long hours.

The pressures of sorting out immigration status and appeals, housing and work often had to take priority over forging successful home school relationships. The need to earn money – to survive – often took priority over issues concerning children's schooling.

Parental work patterns also acted to prevent good home–school links. Parents often worked as cleaners on early morning shifts necessitating leaving home before dawn and often not returning until mid-morning. By late afternoon, parents were too tired to help with homework. Work patterns of Congolese parents resulted in some children being continually late for school, because parents were going out early in the morning, leaving quite young children with the responsibility of getting themselves and siblings to school on time.

Many teachers felt they had a very incomplete picture of the home circumstances of the Congolese children. However, in one school (despite high turnover of staff and pupils) many teachers knew about children's family circumstances because the school implemented a system where all teachers had access to brief records about each child's background. Securing knowledge about children was also embedded within the ethos of the school; staff asked questions where they did not know about children's backgrounds.

In other schools, staff talked of messages to meet parents which were not acted upon and parents/carers being unwilling to talk to class teachers. Indeed, a few teachers appeared to view Congolese parents as secretive or difficult, and as parents who appeared to frustrate the best efforts of teachers. Conversely, some teachers in all schools were able to cite examples of Congolese parents who were very supportive of their children's schooling. Despite both sides acknowledging that home–school liaison was problematic, both school and home appear to blame each other for this. This 'barrier of blame' acted to prevent interventions to improve the relationship.

Somalis in the UK

Somalis are the largest refugee community in the UK, as well as being the most well-researched (Harris, 2004). London hosts the largest Somali community. Outside London the largest communities are in Liverpool, Manchester, Sheffield, Cardiff, Leicester and Birmingham.

The Somalis form one of the most ethnically and linguistically homogenous populations in Africa and over 80 per cent identify themselves as ethnic Somalis. But in other ways they are divided. Despite their strong sense of linguistic and cultural unity, clan affiliation has proved to be an increasingly divisive factor. Clan identity affects settlement patterns in London and this means that schools may well have quite different populations of Somali children, with very different prior experiences. Although it is difficult to discuss clan with many Somalis, it does impact on community life in the UK. Memories of war and atrocities scar social relations between Somalis in the UK. Within a school Somali parents may well not want to socialise with other Somalis, or may be suspicious of interpreters assigned to them. Differences in prior occupation and social class also manifest themselves in the UK. Somali refugees who arrived in 1989–1991 were predominately urban and middle class.

Much recent writing about Somali children highlights their educational underachievement (DfES, 2005; Rutter, 2006). This is attributed to a number of factors, including interrupted or non-existent prior education, traumatic experiences in the home country, bullying, poor school attendance, poverty, parental illiteracy and poor home school links.

Like the Congolese, key social factors within the Somali community influence the quality of home school relations. Parents and community informants stated that the quality of the home–school relationship was affected by:

- parental illiteracy
- lack of fluency in English
- larger family size with consequent time pressures.

Parental illiteracy impacted on the home school relationship. Unlike the Congolese, many Somali adults also lack fluency in spoken English. One cause of this was the isolation of many adults. Few were in work and unemployment among Somali refugees remains very high. Mothers reported how they felt they could not help their children with homework. They also felt the stigma of being illiterate. Indeed, many Somali children did have difficulty in completing homework: teacher interviews and an examination of homework diaries indicated that that most Somali children had severe problems completing homework.

Family size among in Somali households tends to be larger than the UK average, with five or six children common. There are also a disproportionate number of single female heads of household as a result of men being killed in Somalia, families being split up (some men are working in the Gulf states) and also divorce. Family separation has been identified as an issue in a number of studies, and the psychological consequences for those separated from their spouses, children and support networks. Both family size and loss of extended family emerged as a factor that prevented a number of Somali families achieving good relationships with their children's schools. There were a number of Somali parents, all single mothers who faced such time pressures that they were unable to engage with their children's schools.

> I have seven children, the youngest is four and the oldest is seventeen. When they were smaller, it was really hard just getting them to school. At that time we lived on the fifth floor of a block of flats with no lift. Getting them to the top and bottom was so hard, crossing the road was very hard.... I did not have enough time to help them all with their reading and homework. But now things are easier. My oldest son is at college and the older children help. (Somali mother, South London)

Schools may view Somali parents, like the Congolese, as lacking in knowledge, skills and resources when it comes to choosing schools and establishing relationships with teachers. In interviews however many Somali parents discussed choosing schools, debating nearness and convenience in relation to how supportive and welcoming the school might be to Somali parents, and there was no evidence to suggest that Somali parents attend school meetings and events less than other populations. As with the Congolese community, many teachers were unaware of the Somali children's backgrounds and origins (for example, that a child's mother held a post-graduate qualification and had a successful career came as a surprise to teachers in one school).

The way forward

The research conducted among the Congolese and Somali communities revealed a number of factors which prevent successful home school relationships. These were:

- A low level of understanding among teachers of the social background of Congolese and Somali children, coupled with a lack of appreciation of diversity within these communities and little attempt to understand the social worlds of children and families.
- High staff and pupil mobility.
- Schools problematising refugee communities and feeling that refugee parents had little to offer.
- A lack of clear consensus from the perspective of both parents and schools as to what constitutes a good relationship between home and school.
- Failure to communicate to parents what is expected of them in their relationship with the school.
- A lack of parental familiarity with the structures and culture of the UK education system having come from countries where there is little parental participation in schools and events such as parents' evenings are unfamiliar.
- Past experiences in their countries of origin making parents suspicious of authority and wary of contact with schools. An insecure position in the UK may also make them nervous in unfamiliar institutions.
- Parental illiteracy.
- Lack of fluency in English.
- The pressures of finding work, housing and a secure immigration status, making engaging with their children's schooling a low priority.

There are also examples of good home–school liaison practice in many schools. These included:

- Translating essential information and school information 'welcome booklets' into refugees' languages and booking trained interpreters for school admission interviews and any assessments of the child's background.
- Showing parents and carers around the school and encouraging teachers to talk about the possible differences in learning methods between the UK and the child's home country.
- Organising social events such as a coffee morning for parents who are new to the locality.
- Auditing parents' skills, including their language skills.
- Securing funds for projects to support refugee parents and carers, including statutory funds for parental literacy or English as an additional language.
- Using computer suites for an after-school computer club for parents, encouraging parents to come on a designated evening to access news on the internet in their home languages; providing a crèche and, at the same time, teachers dropping in to talk to parents about their children's education.
- Putting together a mini-library of books and tapes in home languages.
- Translating details of GCSE coursework demands and deadlines.

All these initiatives had factors in common. The schools spent time getting to know refugee families and their backgrounds and had appreciated the diversity within communities. They attempted to understand the barriers that acted to prevent good home school relationships. There was a recognition that refugee communities are not homogeneous and are many differences in pre-migration and post-migration experiences. Home–school liaison initiatives, therefore, were flexible and not 'one size fits all', and aimed to build resilience among parents and children.

Bibliography

Department for Education and Skills (DfES) (2005) *Ethnicity and Education: the evidence on minority ethnic pupils*, London: DfES.

Haringey, London Borough of (1997) Refugees and Asylum-Seekers in Haringey, London: London Borough of Haringey.

Harris, H. (2004) *The Somali Community in the UK*, London: Information Centre about Asylum and Refugees, available on www.icar.org.uk

Healthy Islington (2000) The Islington Zairean Refugee Survey Report. London: Healthy Islington unpublished report.

Kinzie, J., Sack, W., Angell, R., Manson, S. and Rath, B. (1986) The psychiatric effects of massive trauma on Cambodian children, 1. The Children in *Journal of the American Academy of Child Psychiatry*, Vol 25: 370–376.

Massoud, R. and Dowling, J. (1997) A Report on a Study into the Needs of Refugee Pupils at North Westminster Community School and Arrangements to Meet These Needs. Unpublished report, Westminster Educational Psychology Service.

Rousseau, C. and Drapeau, A. (2003) 'Are refugee children an at-risk group: a longitudinal study of Cambodian adolescents' in *Journal of Refugee Studies* Vol. 16 (1): 67–81.

Rutter, M. (1985) 'Resilience in the Face of Adversity – Protective Factors and Resistance to Psychiatric Disorder', in *British Journal of Psychiatry*, Vol. 147: 598–611.

Rutter, J. (2004) Congolese children in Camden, London: London Borough of Camden, unpublished report.

Rutter, J. (2006) *Refugee children in the UK: their migration, urban ecologies and education policy*, Buckingham: Open University Press.

Chapter 16

Support for children with physical disabilities

Snaefridur Thora Egilson and Rannveig Traustadottir

Like Chapter 17 which examines the experiences of disabled children in mainstream primary school playgrounds, this enquiry from Iceland offers an international perspective on support for children with physical disabilities in 'regular' schools (as mainstream schools are called in that country). We included this enquiry because it looks in particular at the role of teaching assistants, a relatively recent role in Icelandic schools.

Two questions guided this enquiry in 11 schools: What are the characteristics of the assistance provided to children with physical disabilities? and What are the factors which affect this assistance? The qualitative methods involved observations, informal discussions with 14 children between the ages of 6 and 12 (9 boys and 5 girls), and semi-structured interviews with 17 parents and 18 school staff. All of the children had physical disabilities related to medical conditions such as cerebral palsy, myelomeningocele, or neuro-muscular disorders.

Assistant roles and responsibilities

One of the most notable findings was the variation in the roles and responsibilities of the teaching assistants. It was generally unclear what their role should be and no formal definition existed as to what their duties were and under which conditions they should work. Most received limited supervision from teachers or other professionals. Although many assistants worked under teacher direction and were available to all classroom pupils, at least two provided the primary instructions for the pupil with physical disability. On occasion the pupil was not meant to take directions from the class teacher and the assistant was responsible for deciding when it was appropriate to do so. Anna's teacher said:

> I am so lucky when I am giving out assignments that Helga [the assistant] hears immediately when I am addressing the class but maybe not Anna [the child with physical disability].

Taylor & Francis for permission to reprint extracts from 'Assistance to pupils with physical disabilities in regular schools: promoting inclusion or creating dependency?', Snaefridur Thora Egilson and Rannveig Traustadottir, 2009 in *European Journal of Special Needs Education* Vol. 24, No. 1, 21–36. Reprinted by permission of the publisher (Taylor & Francis Ltd., http://www.tandf.co.uk/journals).

Sigrun's teacher stated:

> You have to count on the assistant to do his job, listen to me [in class] and follow things through [with the pupil with the disability].

In both of these and several other cases there were few formal meetings between the teacher and the assistant, so the latter had an immense responsibility in figuring out the appropriate action each time, and thus, make essential decisions about the education of the pupil with the physical disability.

The relationship between the pupils' educational needs and the roles and responsibilities of their assistants was not always clear. Rather, the teacher's decisions and teaching style, traditions, or simply coincidence appeared to be the decisive factors. The interviews with the teachers revealed that often the responsibilities of the teacher assistant had not been explicitly considered, laid out or discussed.

Quantity and content of support

The assistance provided was first and foremost arranged to facilitate academic learning within the classroom. The pupils typically received assistance in completing educational assignments and during examinations. They also received support in practical activities, such as eating, toileting, dressing, and transfers within and between classrooms, and in practical subjects such as art, crafts, and physical education. However, despite the obvious challenges experienced by the pupils in these practical matters, often there was not enough help available. Limited flexibility was apparent; at times, either 100% assistance was offered or very little. As an example, Simon received full-time assistance during his first years at school. The set-up was discontinued in sixth grade. As a result he received no assistance in challenging situations and occasionally ran into problems with practical issues.

The pupils had no control over the amount or content of the assistance they received, and most frequently the support appeared to be provided on the teachers' or the assistant's own initiative. Although some pupils were satisfied, a few claimed they would like to decide where and when assistance was provided. They even named strategies that would enable them to work more independently in class. Kristin in fifth grade said:

> I would like to get less support and I would like to decide who supports me ... and in which parts of my schedule ... If I were allowed to use the computer more I wouldn't need so much help at school. It's not much fun having all these old ladies hanging around me all the time.

Snorri in fourth grade, who needed help with all personal care claimed his various assistants acted differently, and that new assistants always needed time to adjust to him – rather than he needed time to adjust to these different people.

Numerous positive incidents were observed where the assistants enabled the pupils to participate in educational activities. There is, however, a fine line between support that facilitates participation and support that restrains child interaction and the development of autonomy. Too much assistance can result in limited use of the children's skills and potential, and possibly create unnecessary dependencies and helplessness, as witnessed during a visit to Daniel's class. Daniel required assistance to go up to the board, to access books from shelves, or to distribute assignments. His assistant also helped him get in and out of the chair and to the bathroom during breaks. Other than that, the assistant had no specific role in class and sat passively close to Daniel most of the time. Daniel's teacher and parents said he was able to complete almost all his educational assignments without help although he was a slow writer. Daniel's mother was concerned that her son was getting too much support. She believed it was important for him to develop independence and not have to rely on assistance all the time. Yet she was hesitant to discontinue the services as she thought Daniel might run into problems.

The characteristics of the pupils, such as their physical or educational capacities, did not necessarily affect the content or amount of assistance they received. As an example, Daniel and Simon had similar functional abilities. While Daniel received full-time assistance, Simon was without assistance at the time of the study. Neither did the physical accessibility within school, use of assistive devices, nor the number of pupils in the class appear to be decisive factors.

Proximity to the pupil with physical disability

The assistant's proximity to the pupil with physical disability varied. Five assistants kept regular contact with the pupil they supported but did not sit next to them throughout lessons unless necessary. Six were situated by the pupils' side most of the time, even when the pupils could work independently on assignments. As a result, a few pupils did not take directions from the teachers but rather from the assistants. In addition, they were not as active as their peers in general classroom work. The assistant's proximity sometimes resulted in the pupils feeling stigmatised. Maria's mother reported:

> Maria is so independent and she has been very annoyed with having an adult constantly at her side. She wants to do everything just like the other kids.

Many parents and teachers mentioned that they preferred 'invisible' assistance: someone to keep up the pupils' pace and attention in class and ensure they were safe in crowded areas such as the playground, the hallways, and the cafeteria. Thor's teacher illustrated her thoughts regarding the complexities inherent in the assistant role:

> Not everyone can stay beside a child all day and it is quite easy to become passive as an assistant. But you have to be aware of everything ... People [i.e. assistants] have to know what to do but at the same time let him [Thor] decide and not manipulate too much. But you always have to intervene when necessary. It is a fine line, to control but to let him feel that he is in control.

Some assistants solved this dilemma well, while others helped much more than needed. It can be hard to go about 'doing nothing' and it requires insight, knowledge, and skill to recognise when and how to intervene. With unclear definition of their roles, responsibilities, and limited supervision, the success was often up to each assistant.

School priorities

The assistance provided was mainly in the academic aspects of the school day but most pupils and parents prioritised social participation and acceptance in the pupil group. Frequently there was a lack of assistance during recess when the assistant had her or his coffee break. Even though a pupil had been assigned an assistant, the support was not always prioritised. In the distribution of scarce school resources, the pupil sometimes remained unserved or underserved when other important issues were at stake.

For example, Jon had full-time assistance for all his school hours. Once, the class was scheduled to go on a fieldtrip in a hilly area that Jon could not manage. The day before the trip his parents received a message from the school to keep their son at home, as his assistant was needed for the other pupils on the trip. Lack of assistance during fieldtrips was noted by one-half of the teachers and parents.

Some of the strategies utilised by the schools to 'survive' in challenging situations were problematic for the child with disability and his or her family. To minimise what was seen as a burden on staff, three pupils had a number of assistants, even up to 10 individuals in a given school year. Accordingly, it was difficult to coordinate expectations and procedures; for example, regarding behaviour or the use of assistive devices. As Robert's teacher reported:

> One person knew how to position him in the chair but another one didn't and so on. And several people didn't know how to help him to the toilet. Even Robert was trying to instruct them what to do.

Usually parents were not consulted on the number of assistants, which sometimes strained the collaboration between the home and school. At the time of the study Simon was without assistance. In the interview, his teacher Nina said she had insisted that someone would help the 12-year-old boy travel to and from the school gym, 'because I had to take him to the gym and help him. And afterwards it changed, they [the school authorities] realised it couldn't go on like this. Since then Karl [the janitor] takes him to the gym'. Later on in the interview Nina said, however:

> But there is always someone sick and then they move people around to other tasks. Like Karl who is supposed to help him [Simon] to the gym. I hardly see him these days. We do it [help Simon to the gym], me and the boys in class. We haven't seen Karl for a long time.

In both of these cases the needs of the disabled children were considered inferior to other pressing priorities within the school. If the assistant was sick, the pupils commonly missed out on sessions such as physical education or swimming as no one could help out with the practical matters. Six parents reported being contacted and asked to pick up their child from school in such instances, especially during the first few years of the child's schooling when the system appeared to be learning how to accommodate his or her needs. This hardly occurred in the upper grades.

Independence and autonomy of the child

Although the children at times objected to the presence of the assistant, they tended to consider the assistant as their 'possession' and thus sometimes complained if he or she attended to their classmates. Other issues regarding power balance and boundaries were observed. Magnus carefully dictated a spelling assignment to his assistant, but when it came back with corrections Magnus blamed his assistant for the errors although they were all his own. Apparently, the boy did not perceive that he was accountable for the results, reflecting a lack of perception of control and responsibility for his actions. Nina described Simon's development of independence and autonomy in school after his assistant left and he had to manage more by himself, and the positive effect on social relations when Simon suddenly needed help with various practical matters and a group of boys stepped in to assist, and then became friends with him:

> Originally, they [the boys] were just looking for something to do, I think. But now they find Simon fun to be with. It isn't only Petur and Bjarni, it is Emil and many others who have joined the group. They join him during recess and they run and turn him around and I am just scared stiff. But it is all just very enjoyable.

When left without adult assistance Simon demonstrated skills and abilities that enabled him to be socially integrated and an active participant in the peer group. Thus he was using and developing important strategies essential for future challenges.

Relationship between the teacher and the assistant

Although a majority of the teachers who had an assistant in class claimed his or her presence was a prerequisite for a successful integration of the pupil with physical disability, many found the high turnover stressful and said it was a challenge to constantly have to relate to different people of dissimilar character and competence. Limited time for collaboration complicated matters considerably, especially when the teacher and assistant differed in their expectations, ideologies, and styles of interaction with the children. A few assistants assumed an important role in the classroom in collaboration with the teacher. Occasionally they took on parts of the teachers' role for the pupil with physical disability and helped his or her classmates on various matters.

Not all teachers like the idea of having another person in their classroom, and some find it challenging to assume a supervisory role over another adult. On one occasion the presence of an assistant was a burden too large to overcome. Lisa's class was about to have a new teacher. The newly graduated professional claimed he did not object to having a child with disability in class but disapproved of the presence of another adult. School authorities then arranged to move Lisa to a different class and contacted the family only when matters were fully arranged. The parents and Lisa herself objected loudly and eventually the issue was resolved with another teacher instead of moving Lisa. Conversely, the assistant was sometimes the constant factor, such as when there was high teacher turnover. Then it was the assistant who knew the child best and often was able to provide valuable information on aspects regarding his or her educational or on practical issues.

Discussion

The pupils with physical disabilities had difficulty keeping up with their peers in various contexts. The school playground and practical subjects, such as physical education, art, and crafts, were a particular challenge as they demand a great degree of physical performance. Overall, least assistance was provided in these settings compared with the general classroom. This is noteworthy as the children's barriers to participation in physical activity are so apparent given the limitations imposed by their impairments. The assistance provided appeared to be mostly focused on the academic aspects of the school day, such as the educational tasks in the main classroom. Although one of the main functions of school is to contribute to pupils' social development, measures to promote active involvement in break activities and other non-academic tasks were not a priority, reflecting a disregard for the importance of the social aspects outside the classroom. The pupil and parent interviews revealed, however, that most respondents prioritised social participation, meaning that the pupils were accepted in the group and not excluded from specific activities and settings. Thus, an over-reliance on adult support was found for some contexts and pupils, while this support appeared to be under-utilised or ineffectively delivered in other situations, especially in practical subjects and break activities. Dependency on assistants by the pupils was commonly reported, and on several occasions the children received more assistance in the classroom than strictly needed just because an assistant was available.

The parents in this study expressed conflicting concerns regarding the assistance provided to their child. Because of their concerns about how their child would be accepted and instructed in school, some parents agreed to or even requested individual support for their child although experiencing ambivalence about whether the assistance was really needed. The patterns of assistance provided changed over time, for example with a different teacher or assistant or increased educational demands. Thus, the situation was often erratic and fluid, depending on the transaction between many aspects. Factors affecting content and amount of support were inconsistent and no direct relationship was found between the pupils' educational needs and the content or amount of assistance provided. Neither did type or severity of disability affect the utilisation of assistance.

It is reasonable to expect that use of adaptive equipment and environmental modifications will support the participation of pupils with physical disabilities, and minimise their need for support. Interestingly, physical accessibility within school or use of adaptive devices did not consistently affect the content or amount of assistance the pupil received. Neither did the number of pupils in class have a great impact. The interaction between various aspects influenced the adult support provided each time, but the attitudes and abilities of individual teachers to modify the curriculum, instructions, or educational activities appeared to be the most important factors. Often these matters had not been fully considered or discussed within the school. Thus, individual teacher's views and teaching style, traditions within school, or simply coincidence had the most influence on the characteristics and amount of support.

Self-determination, independence, and autonomy are considered to be important outcomes of the education system. Yet, lack of perception of control in one's life is commonly experienced by pupils with disabilities. Teacher assistants can make valuable contributions in promoting participation and learning among pupils with disabilities, as observed in this study. Nevertheless, there is a fine line between support that facilitates social inclusion and support that inhibits interaction and autonomy. The constant presence of an adult may increase children's need for help and make them less socially competent. Too much assistance can result in limited use of the children's strengths, and may possibly create unnecessary or unhealthy dependencies. It may also affect and impede the development of important life skills, such as will, self-esteem, and resilience.

The findings of this study reveal that most pupils and parents prioritise assistance to promote social inclusion, engagement, and interactions with peers, while schools emphasise the use of assistants to support academic learning. It is imperative that schools listen to the views of students and parents and align with them to identify alternative ways to promote participation and learning of pupils with disabilities in regular schools.

Chapter 17

Including children with disabilities in the playground

Helen Woolley, Marc Armitage, Julia Bishop, Mavis Curtis and Jane Ginsborg

A national survey of school play-times which studied changes from 1991 to 1996[1] revealed that 26% of junior schools had shortened the length of the lunch-time play period, and that 12% of infant schools and 26% of junior schools had abolished afternoon play-time entirely.

If mainstream primary school children are having fewer opportunities to play, provision and access to play for disabled children is further limited.[2] This chapter reports on some of the findings of an enquiry into the inclusion of disabled children in six mainstream primary school playgrounds in Yorkshire. The authors discuss social factors (such as the relations children have with peers and school staff) and organisational factors (such as school routines, staff experience and training) and identify good practice.

Across the six schools, 18 children in Key Stages 1 and 2 participated in the enquiry. The children had a wide range of impairments including autism, muscular dystrophy, epilepsy, Down's Syndrome, hearing and sight impairments, cerebral palsy, congenital heart disease, spastic quadriplegia, impaired growth, development delay, communication difficulties and spina bifida.

On maps of their playgrounds the children showed researchers where they played, and they took researchers into the playgrounds to show them exactly where different play took place. Researchers observed children during play times and recorded their observations in written field notes and with still and video cameras. Semi-structured interviews were organised with children in their friendship groups, and all 18 children participated in a discussion session. Each school provided policy and procedures relevant to disabled children and play. Interviews were also carried out with head teachers, class teachers, special educational needs co-ordinators, lunchtime supervisors, personal support assistants (PSAs) and school caretakers. This chapter is an interesting comparison to Chapter 16 which also examines support in mainstream schools for children with disabilities.

Taylor & Francis for permission to reprint extracts from 'Going outside together: good practice with respect to the inclusion of disabled children in primary school playgrounds', Helen Woolley, Marc Armitage, Julia Bishop, Mavis Curtis and Jane Ginsborg, 2006 in *Children's Geographies* Vol. 4, No. 3, 303–318. Reprinted by permission of the publisher (Taylor & Francis Ltd., http://www.tandf.co.uk/journals).

Social factors

There were two areas of good social practice, with respect to the inclusion of the focus children in the playground, which are worth some discussion. These are the relationships the focus children had with their peers and the relationships that the focus children had with staff. Although what goes on in a primary school playground can seem to be chaotic to adults research has developed classifications of play observed in these spaces. The play observed and discussed in this project was classified, building upon a previous classification (see Bishop and Curtis, 2001) as: play with high verbal content; play with high imaginative content; play with high physical content; and less structured play including walking, talking, sitting and watching.

The focus children were observed to be included in all these categories of play. The inclusion in play for the focus children was found to be determined by strategies used—consciously or not—by both the focus children and their peers. These strategies have been identified as being as a result of: the focus children themselves; the use of the focus children's equipment; and the adaptation of play by peers. In addition it became clear that sometimes the focus children created their own opportunities for play, either amongst themselves or with peers.

An example of one of the focus children who was not only fully involved in the play, but controlling it—revealing a strong personality and leadership trait—was Helen. She played something which she called Mission Girls, which she described thus: "I'm a computer and when I go beep-beep-beep, it means that there's a mission for them (her friends) to solve. And on this tree they've got to press what the problem is and then they go and solve the problem. When they come back, they switch me off and go to bed." This strength of character was acknowledged by one of the lunchtime supervisors who stated that: 'She knows what she wants' and 'She likes to tell people what to do'.

Sally was a focus child who used her equipment to good advantage in play. During an invented game called Tiggy Off Ground where different colours or objects were 'safe', Sally would avoid being 'caught' when the safe colour was blue by sitting on the back of her blue walking frame. Joe also joined in this game: while his friends moved around him he wheeled his chair around and the friends held their hands out to be 'Tigged' by him.

A very positive example of inclusion facilitated by friends was found when Sally and her friends played Bouncing up on the Bridge. The bridge was a wooden construction with a series of logs which were joined together and suspended close to the ground between two fixed, vertical supports. The play involved one child jumping, from one of the end supports, onto the logs with the result that whoever was on the bridge would get bounced up when the one person jumped. Helped by her friends, Sally would sit on the bridge while her friends took it in turns to bounce her. It was clear from Sally's expression and response that she really enjoyed this.

Sometimes the facilitation of the involvement of a focus child, by their peers, might not be how the focus child would wish it to be, and they would assert how they wanted to be involved. This was found to be the case with a game of Farmer, Farmer Can I Cross Your Golden Field which was described by Helen: "There's a person that's on and these other people at the other side. The people have to say, 'Farmer, farmer can I cross your golden field?' And the person that's on has to say 'Only if' and they can say anything—like, 'Only if you've got blonde hair' ." Now Helen liked to be the person who was 'on' but was often thwarted in this desire by the fact that the children she played with, apparently in an effort to favour her, often chose things which only she had. Thus Helen was able to cross to the other side rather than be among those who were chased. On one occasion Helen had had enough of this and simply said, 'I want to be on' and so the others let her be on.

The role of support staff

There were examples of good practice where a PSA would encourage a focus child to try things that at first the child thought they might not be able to do. In these situations the staff were encouraging confidence and ability in the child. One example of this was Joe who felt very secure in his wheelchair and when his PSA suggested anything different he tended to say 'no' straight away. However, the PSA encouraged him to go onto the grass and he found that he could go over the edge between the path and the grass: 'Now he's found he can play like everyone else on the grass'. The PSA encouraged Joe to be 'the same as everybody else apart from the equipment for his physical needs'. Joe's PSA also recalled how she tried to get the children to talk directly to Joe and not to talk to him through her, because she felt that this would help to build up Joe's confidence and the confidence of the other children in their interactions with him.

In another school, the PSA who was responsible for Jessica had, over a period of time, encouraged her in the playground. The PSA and class teacher took a joint decision that, as her confidence grew, Jessica need not be accompanied in the playground. The decision was made upon observing Jessica's maturity and feeling that she was able to cope 'without disappearing' and after they had 'made sure she was happy'. The school staff realised that Jessica needed the PSA less and was actually coming to the PSA less. They commented that 'We felt it was time she was doing things on her own'.

Some Personal Support Assistants (PSAs) felt a great deal of job satisfaction from their job, despite it being financially unrewarding. This appeared to be because the PSAs were appreciated by the teaching staff and specialists, such as physiotherapists and speech therapists, and by the children's parents. In one school this resulted in PSAs remaining in the school for many years, allowing them to build up a high level of skill. In other schools it was the custom to move the PSAs round from one child to another, thus increasing the PSAs breadth of experience and giving them new challenges.

Training for work and encouraging/facilitating play with particular children and understanding of their impairments was patchy across the schools. Any such training which staff had received usually related to health and safety issues, such as lifting or manual handling. At one school support assistants were encouraged to go on training courses, and they were encouraged to remain at the school and pass on their expertise to other staff in the school. In another school support staff experienced a training session where they began to understand something of what it was like to have a visual impairment and this had resulted in an increased respect for the way one particular focus child was coping. It also led to a greater awareness of how to help visually impaired children join in ball games. The staff particularly found this to be helpful when playing French cricket with Akram because they were able to teach the children to bowl more slowly than they would have done, so that Akram could respond to the movement of the ball.

Some of the PSAs revealed a good understanding of the benefits of being outside for the focus children for whom they had responsibility, to the extent that they would take the child outside, even during class time if they felt that the child would benefit from this. There were two situations where we became aware of this happening. One PSA stated that she took the focus child she was responsible for outside to play on the equipment when the child lost concentration or became noisy in the classroom. They played together in the playground and sometimes on the fixed play equipment. The PSA stated that, 'We go out more than the other kids really'. This approach could be seen as excluding the child from the classroom, thus missing some formal teaching time, but it could also be seen as responding to the individual child's needs by taking her outside to her benefit.

Organisational factors

A variety of organisational good practice was identified but there was no consistency across the schools, with each one apparently working towards inclusion in the playground in their own way. There appears to be no framework, even of an indicative nature, or guidelines for schools to work with, with respect to play—and access to or inclusion in play—for disabled children in primary school playgrounds.

The existence, or lack, of playtimes obviously affects all the children in a school, either providing opportunity for the benefits of play or not. Three of the six schools had no afternoon playtime while two had afternoon playtimes for Key Stage One children only, while only one school had an afternoon playtime for both Key Stage One and Two children. One school had two morning playtimes of mixed age groups, in an attempt to allow play to happen between family members, if they so desired. Another school had a rolling lunchtime, thus enabling children of different ages to be in the playground at the same time as each other.

It was observed, and confirmed in discussions, that it is important for disabled children to be out in the playground at the beginning of play time because it is difficult to join in a game once it had started. This was confirmed by one ten-year-old girl who said: "If they want to play a game and you've only just started, they could wait until you've finished the game but if they say, 'Can I join in?' and they say yes, the game will get complicated and they'll have to start, they'll have to wait ... If it's a game of Bulldogs Charge or My Grandfather's Chest even, you could do a round and they could join in".

Some of the disabled children had routines for playtimes and lunchtimes which were different from the routines of the non-disabled children. These routines could result in the disabled children arriving in the playground later than other children, thus putting them at a disadvantage with respect to joining in play at the beginning of playtime. One example of good practice in an individual child's routine was identified with Susie. She was allowed to participate in playtime because her physiotherapy took place during some assembly times or quiet reading times. Although such an approach might be perceived as negative with respect to these other learning activities, there was a benefit that Susie could be in the playground at the same time as the other children, and as already mentioned this could have an impact on whether a child could be included in the play and the consequential socialisation which this allowed for.

In the good practice examples it was clear that disabled children were treated as individuals and this was expressed by the timing of any support activities required, such as physiotherapy, and by routines for getting to the playground at break and lunch times. These children were able to be in the playground at the beginning of playtime and therefore had a better chance of being included in the play. In situations where best practice was not undertaken children were not treated as individuals, and in one example the disabled children were always gathered together in one group at break and lunch times, often with the result that they were not in the playground at the beginning of playtime, therefore missing out on the benefits associated with this timing.

In this overview of the research we have not discussed physical good practice because very little was found, with the exception of the provision of ramps to allow access into playgrounds.

Notes

1 Blatchford and Sumpner, 1998.
2 The 1995 Disability Discrimination Act outlaws a 'lower standard of service' for disabled people and requires that 'reasonable adjustments' should be made so that they can enjoy services and facilities in the same manner as non-disabled people. In schools this is often expressed by the provision of disabled toilets, ramps into buildings, access around buildings and access to desks and computer terminals, but with little attention (if any) being paid to the playground.

References

Bishop, J. and Curtis, M. (eds) (2001) *Play Today in The Primary School Playground*, Buckingham: Open University Press.

Blatchford, P. and Sumpner, C. (1998) 'What do we know about break-time?: Results from a national survey of break-time and lunch-time in primary and secondary schools', *British Educational Research Journal*, 24, 79–94.

Chapter 18

The inclusion of children with attention difficulties

Neil Humphrey

The great majority of children with attention difficulties are educated in mainstream schools. The difficulties relating to inattention, impulsivity and hyperactivity experienced by many of these children present teachers and teaching assistants with a unique set of challenges but also opportunities. In this chapter, Neil Humphrey discusses approaches to facilitate the inclusion of children who are seen to be experiencing 'attention deficit/hyperactivity disorder'. He suggests, in particular, there is a need to reframe our thinking about this disorder, to better understand the role and implications of medication and to seek ways of providing predictability, structure and routine for these children.

AD/HD is characterised by *inattention* (for example, difficulty in sustaining attention in tasks, easily distracted, seeming not to listen when spoken to), *hyperactivity* (for example, often fidgeting with hands or feet, talking excessively, difficulty in playing or engaging in leisure activities quietly) and *impulsivity* (for example, often having difficulty awaiting their turn, often interrupting) (APA, 2000).

Ideas about what causes AD/HD and how it is best managed have also changed over time (and continue to be debated). AD/HD can be seen as a medical condition caused by dysfunction in the developing frontal lobes (Wilding, 2005). This is a radically different view from the idea that it is a socially and culturally engineered phenomenon (Breggin, 2000). The former provides a 'within-person' explanation, while the latter does just the opposite. These two polarized views affect the management of AD/HD. Some advocate the use of psycho-stimulant medication (MTA Co-operative Group, 1999) and others argue for strongly non-pharmacological interventions alongside changes in the way we view discipline and challenge behaviour in the classroom (Doggett, 2004). In reality, a more eclectic, moderate position is often taken.

Although most people consider AD/HD to be a medical condition, there is (as yet) no 'litmus test' for it; that is, there has been no biological marker identified that can reliably distinguish between children with and without the condition.

Wiley Blackwell for kind permission to reprint extracts from 'Including students with ADHD in mainstream schools', *British Journal of Special Education*, Vol. 36, No. 1.

Estimates suggest that between 2% and 6% of students are affected by AD/HD (Cooper, 2005). Around three times more boys than girls receive a diagnosis of AD/HD (although the ratio may be as high as 9:1; Phares, 2003). Up to 75% of students with AD/HD are prescribed stimulant medication, with methylphenidate (Ritalin) being the most commonly used drug (Department of Health, 2003).

What do we mean by 'inclusive education' in relation to students with AD/HD?

Terms such as 'inclusion' and 'inclusive education' are by no means universally agreed upon, and it is therefore worth considering how their meaning is construed. To a certain extent, the development of definitions of 'inclusion' has paralleled educational reforms in this area. For instance, prior to the time of Excellence for All Children (DfEE, 1997) in the UK, and, at the international level, the Salamanca Statement (UNESCO, 1994), the term 'inclusion' was still used primarily to refer to the question of where a student with special educational needs was to be educated (that is, in a mainstream or special school). Furthermore, inclusion was still almost exclusively used with reference to special educational needs. More recent reforms (for example, DfES, 2004; Individuals with Disabilities Education Improvement Act, 2004; UNESCO, 2005) broaden the term to include the promotion of *all* students' *presence* (that is, without the use of withdrawal classes or other forms of 'integrated segregation'), *participation* (that is, the quality of students' educational experiences), *acceptance* (for example, by teachers and peers) and *achievement* (for example, greater academic progress, better social and emotional skills) in mainstream schools, where possible (Booth and Ainscow, 2002). However, this whole area is still hotly debated among policy-makers, academics and practitioners alike, with some authors arguing that the push for inclusion as a human rights issue has meant that considerations of 'what works' for certain groups of students have been given a lower priority (Norwich, 2005).

The four-pronged definition of inclusion (presence, participation, acceptance and achievement) provides stimulus for teachers to think of inclusion as an ongoing process. This is preferable to the earlier, more rudimentary 'inclusion as the placement of students with special educational needs in mainstream schools' definition, which, although much easier to 'achieve' (in the sense that, theoretically, all a mainstream school has to do in order to be considered 'inclusive' is to enrol students with special educational needs), does not necessarily imply high-quality education for such students.

Starting with the more rudimentary definition of inclusion, research by Reid *et al.* (1994) suggested that up to 80% of children diagnosed with AD/HD are educated in mainstream settings, although this is dependent upon a number of factors, including whether they are on medication and whether they also have learning difficulties. Children with AD/HD certainly appear to be over-represented in certain sectors of the special education system; for instance, Place *et al.* (2000) found a prevalence rate of 70% in special schools for children with emotional and behavioural difficulties.

With the more progressive definition of inclusion (presence, participation, acceptance and achievement), the picture becomes even more opaque. Cooper (2005) suggests that teachers in mainstream schools may be prone to 'typing' students with AD/HD; that is, placing students into ready-made categories relating to perceived ability, behaviour, motivation and so on, on the basis of limited interactions and observations. This practice, of course, may turn out to be a self-fulfilling prophecy.[2] It is generally accepted that students with AD/HD are considered among the most difficult to include effectively.

Students with AD/HD are more likely than others to experience social isolation, with fewer reported friendships and greater levels of peer rejection (Bagwell *et al.*, 2001). They are considered to be at 'a higher than average risk' of being excluded. (Watling, 2004). Students themselves suggests that many experience 'confusion, anxiety, blame, [and] guilt' (Hughes, 2007) in relation to their education.

Is there a distinct pedagogy for learners with AD/HD?

In considering strategies and approaches to facilitate the inclusion of students with AD/HD, we are faced with a key question: are there distinct pedagogies for such learners? Expressed another way, we might ask, 'Just how specialised is the teaching of students with special educational needs?' As Norwich and Lewis (2005) explain:

> If inclusion is about increasing the participation of all learners in mainstream schools, then it must go beyond general questions of the presence of children with special educational needs in such schools ... We need to address questions of classroom teaching and curriculum in considering inclusion and inclusive practices.
>
> (p. 2)

Of course, arguing for a 'distinct pedagogy' position in relation to students with special educational needs is not the same as saying that they require distinct provision or curriculum objectives; rather, it is suggesting that the needs of such learners dictate that they require distinct kinds of teaching in order to learn the same content as those without special educational needs.

This question is the subject of a great deal of interest currently, and also a fair degree of contention.

However, Norwich and Lewis (2005) provide a useful conceptual framework for thinking about these students' needs. They argue that pedagogic needs can be addressed in three ways; first, by thinking about those needs that are common to all; second, by thinking about those needs that are specific to a certain group (such as students with AD/HD); and third, by thinking about those needs that are unique to individuals. They describe the combination of all three of these considerations as the *general differences position*. Practice is informed primarily by specific group needs, with common and unique individual needs being addressed in the background.

Strategies and approaches to facilitate the inclusion of students with AD/HD

The ideas and strategies that follow take account of research and professional knowledge in this area and are based upon the principle that by creating a better fit between the school environment and the student, we are creating opportunities for him or her to succeed. Students with AD/HD often experience difficulties in mainstream classrooms and schools because the emphasis on meeting common needs means that their specific group needs are not addressed (Cooper, 2005).

Reframing 'AD/HD'

Cooper (2005) suggests that a useful strategy to aid the development of inclusive practice for students with AD/HD is to 'reframe' the way in which we view the concept of AD/HD itself. In particular, he suggests that if we view it as a particular cognitive style rather than a 'deficit', then we begin to develop strategies that exploit, rather than inhibit, the common characteristics of such students. For instance, students with AD/HD are reported to be somewhat verbose, talking at inappropriate times. This aspect of AD/HD can be exploited by designing lessons that allow increased opportunities for verbal participation. The need to keep such verbal participation. 'on-task' can be facilitated by adapting seating arrangements within the classroom, such as by seating students in a semicircle around a teacher or in small groups. Furthermore, the fact that students with AD/HD struggle to sustain their attention over time, more so than other students, can be used as an opportunity to restructure lessons such that 'seatwork' is punctuated by frequent periods of other, different activities. Research has shown that this kind of approach can lead to decreases in disruptive behaviour and increases in 'on task' behaviour. If sustained periods of 'seatwork' are unavoidable, physical activities that can be carried out at the student's desk (such as squeezing a ball) are reported to be beneficial in helping to maintain focus (Levine, 2002a).

Another result of reframing AD/HD is that the practice of 'typing' (Cooper, 2005), although still evident, is much more likely to relate to positive expectations regarding ability, behaviour, motivation and so on. This in turn will result in better staff-student relationships and a positive classroom ethos. Such a change in focus may be difficult to achieve. Recent research by Ghanizadeh *et al.* (2006) demonstrated that more tolerant and positive attitudes towards students with AD/HD are associated with levels of knowledge of AD/HD among teachers. This suggests that training to increase teachers' and teaching assistant's knowledge of AD/HD may need to be a priority if subsequent shifts in attitudes and practice are to occur.

Understanding the role of medication

Since up to 75% of students with AD/HD are prescribed stimulant medication (Department of Health, 2003), it is important for their teachers to develop an understanding of the role it plays in their students' lives, and the subsequent implications for education. Indeed, teachers can play at least two pivotal roles in relation to medication. First, they can provide detailed information that will help in the assessment that leads up to the prescription of medication. Second, they should take an active role in monitoring the effects of medication observed in the classroom (Cooper and Ideus, 1996). Over and above these roles, a better understanding of the effects of stimulant medication – what it can and cannot do, how it is likely to impact upon a given student's behaviour and so on – will enable the teacher to plan in a way that takes these factors into account.

Medication should never be used as the sole means of intervention for a student with AD/HD. Thus, the fact that Ritalin is being prescribed for a student does not relieve teachers of the responsibility of adapting their approaches to better meet that student's needs. Stimulant medication takes effect very quickly, but its influence may not last throughout the school day. A range of factors – including the individual student, type of stimulant and dosage – will influence the effects of the medication, but it is important to note that it will typically have differential effects. For instance, its effects on behaviour (in terms of activity level) typically last longer than its effects on cognition (in terms of attention). As such, even though medicated students may not be up and out of their seats or blurting out answers as much as usual, they may still not be accessing the curriculum because they are struggling to maintain their focus on the material presented. Furthermore, medication may cause side effects (such as increased anxiety) that provide further barriers to learning and participation (Cooper and Ideus, 1996). Finally, although medication may be effective in managing the core difficulties experienced by those with AD/HD (inattention, hyperactivity and impulsivity), it is less useful in alleviating 'secondary' problems, such as social isolation and academic underachievement (Doggett, 2004).

Minimising distractions

Students with AD/HD have a lower threshold for distraction than other students. As such, it is important to create a classroom environment that accommodates this difference whenever possible. The student may need to be given preferential seating in a place that is as free from distraction as possible – for instance, away from doors and windows, and in an area of the classroom with a direct line of sight to the teacher (although not necessarily directly in front of the teacher's desk, since this may be considered a punitive measure by other students and could therefore draw further unnecessary attention to the student's differences) (Levine, 2002a). This will mean that the teacher can easily monitor and reinforce a student's on-task behaviour (Department of Education, 2006).

Although students with AD/HD may have a greater need for quietness than other students to help them maintain their attention, it is important to note that having a classroom that is devoid of any sensory stimulation can also create difficulties. In such circumstances, students with AD/HD can become distracted by their own thoughts (Cooper and Ideus, 1996). What needs to be achieved, therefore, is what might be referred to as an 'optimal' level of stimulation, wherein unnecessary distractions are removed, but the tasks and activities provided are still varied and rousing enough to maintain students' interest (Levine, 2002b).

Providing predictability, structure and routine

Students with AD/HD will benefit from being provided with a clear structure to each day, lesson and task. This is particularly crucial in the light of recent research evidence that suggests that a core underlying difficulty in AD/HD may be related to temporal perception (Smith *et al.*, 2002). At the level of the school day, dividing into broad units of time will make it seem more manageable to the student. At the level of each lesson, the US Department of Education (2006) suggests that teachers need to provide a consistent structure that involves a routine of introducing the lesson, conducting the lesson and concluding the lesson. When introducing lessons, it is useful to:

- review the previous lesson (remind them of what the key topics and concepts were, and explain how they link to the current lesson);
- provide an advance outline/schedule (talk students through the order of the various activities planned for the current lesson) (Levine, 2002a);
- set learning expectations (make clear what and how they will learn);
- set behavioural expectations (explain what is and is not acceptable, and how and when this could change during the lesson – for example, that talking with other students is acceptable during a group activity, but not during a test at the end of a lesson);
- state needed materials and resources (explain what students will need to complete the various activities and where they can find these materials);
- simplify instructions and choices (ensure that these are communicated in a clear, uncomplicated manner) (Department of Education, 2006).

Research regarding the typical learning styles of students with AD/HD suggests that they learn more effectively when they are able actively to experiment and are presented with concrete examples that are visual in nature (Cooper and Ideus, 1996). Learning technologies that facilitate this style of learning, such as the use of overhead projectors and computers, should therefore be an integral part of lessons. Any directions given to the class should be followed up (either orally, or in writing on a whiteboard) and clarified in order to ensure that the student has understood what he/she is required to do. Lessons with frequent but short breaks between activities are also to be encouraged.

In relation to concluding a lesson, the US Department of Education (2006) suggests that teachers of students with AD/HD need to provide advance warnings (five or ten minutes prior to the end) of how much time remains in a lesson; check assignments and work; and preview the next lesson (that is, give students a brief overview of the topic and any resources they will need). Such practices will help to circumvent the difficulties with transitioning that many students with AD/HD experience.

Although the nature of tasks and activities within lessons inevitably varies according to a wide range of factors (such as subject and available resources), there are some key 'design principles' that can be applied in order to facilitate the learning of students with AD/HD. First, all tasks need to be broken down into small, manageable chunks. This helps to accommodate the shorter attention span of such students. It may also be useful to provide models of completed work as a visual prompt for a task. Key information should be highlighted (for example, key words or instructions on a worksheet presented in bold, or in a different colour) wherever possible. This will help students who experience difficulties in selective attention (that is, knowing what information to select for 'processing') (Levine, 2002a). Over time, students can be taught to practise drawing focus to key information themselves.

Applying cognitive and behavioural strategies

Behavioural strategies use principles of reinforcement and punishment to reduce maladaptive behaviours and increase adaptive behaviours. Once a dominant force in education, some of these strategies have fallen out of favour recently, but key techniques based on their principles, do have a convincing evidence base that such approaches can be successful in establishing behaviours conducive to classroom learning for students with AD/HD (Fiore *et al.*, 1993). Within the range of specific approaches that are underpinned by behavioural principles, the authors concluded that there were three (*positive reinforcement*, where appropriate behaviour is immediately rewarded; *behaviour reduction strategies*, such as reprimands and redirection; and *response cost*, a form of punishment in which something important is taken away after an undesired behaviour takes place) that appeared to be the most effective. However, Purdie *et al.* (2002) caution that:

> Consequences or contingencies for ADHD children generally need to be more immediate, powerful, tangible, and frequent than those that teachers often use in their everyday work with other children in the classroom.
>
> (p. 67)

Cognitive-behavioural approaches emphasise the use of reinforcement principles to alter thoughts or cognitions related to AD/HD behaviours. In particular, they focus on the way internalised speech serves to regulate behaviour. Students are taught to use self-talk, self-instruction, self-monitoring and self-reinforcement to develop self-control of their attention and impulsive behaviour problems. Simple examples of the application of such techniques in the classroom include teaching children to subvocalise (repeating a piece of key information under their breath to help them maintain their focus on it), use self-testing strategies (for example, when reading, students are encouraged to stop at key points and ask themselves questions about what they have just read) and use self-reinforcement (giving themselves praise for achieving targets, such as staying on task for a specified period of time).

Conclusion

The overall aim of this article was to provide an up-to-date overview of evidence-based strategies that can be used by teachers to facilitate the inclusion of students with AD/HD. Yet it should be noted that this article is not intended to be completely comprehensive (is this at all possible in such an ever-changing field?), but rather a starting point that hopefully provides a stimulus for discussion and development.

References

APA (American Psychiatric Association) (2000) *Diagnostic and Statistical Manual of Mental Disorders* (fourth revised edition). Washington, DC: APA.

Bagwell, C. L., Molina, B. S. G., Pelham, W. E. and Hoza, B. (2001) 'ADHD and problems in peer relations: predictions from childhood to adolescence', *Journal of the American Academy of Child and Adolescent Psychiatry*, 40, 1285–1292.

Booth, T. and Ainscow, M. (2002) *Index for Inclusion.* Bristol: Centre for Studies in Inclusive Education.

Breggin, P. R. (2000) 'What psychologists and therapists need to know about ADHD and stimulants', *Changes: An International Journal of Psychology and Psychotherapy*, 18, 13–23.

Cooper, P. (2001) 'Understanding AD/HD: a brief critical review of the literature', *Children and Society*, 15, 387–395.

Cooper, P. (2005) 'AD/HD', in A. Lewis and B. Norwich (eds) *Special Teaching for Special Children?* Buckingham: Open University Press.

Cooper, P. and Ideus, K. (1996) *AD/HD: a practical guide for teachers*. London: David Fulton.

Department of Education (2006) *Teaching Children with ADHD: instructional strategies and practices*. Washington, DC: Department of Education.

Department of Health (2003) *The Prevalence of Methylphenidate and Amphetamine Prescriptions in the Commonwealth*. Richmond, VI: Department of Health.

DfEE (Department for Education and Employment) (1997) *Excellence for All Children*. Nottingham: DfEE Publications.

DfES (Department for Education and Skills) (2004) *Removing Barriers to Achievement*. Nottingham: DfES Publications.

Doggett, A. M. (2004) 'ADHD and drug therapy: is it still a valid treatment?' *Journal of Child Health Care*, 8, 69–81.

Hughes, L. (2007) 'The reality of living with ADHD: children's concern about educational and medical support', *Emotional and Behavioural Difficulties*, 12, 69–80.

Levine, M. (2002a) *Developing Minds: attention*. Boston, MA: WGBH/All Kinds of Minds.

Levine, M. (2002b) *A Mind at a Time*. New York: Simon & Schuster.

MTA (Multimodal Treatment of ADHD) Cooperative Group (1999) 'A 14-month randomized clinical trial of treatment strategies for ADHD', *Archives of General Psychiatry*, 56, 1073–1086.

Norwich, B. (2005) 'Inclusion: is it a matter of evidence about what works or about values and rights?' *Education 3–13*, 33, 51–56.

Norwich, B. and Lewis, A. (2001) 'Mapping a pedagogy for special educational needs', *British Educational Research Journal*, 27, 313–330.

Phares, V. (2003) *Understanding Abnormal Child Psychology*. Hoboken, NJ: Wiley & Sons.

Place, M., Wilson, J., Martin, E. and Hulsmeier, J. (2000) 'The frequency of emotional and behavioural disturbance in an EBD school', *Child Psychology and Psychiatry Review*, 5, 76–80.

Purdie, N., Hattie, J. and Carroll, A. (2002) 'A review of research on interventions for ADHD: what works best?' *Review of Educational Research*, 72, 61–69.

Smith, A., Taylor, E., Rogers, J. W., Newman, S. and Rubia, K. (2002) 'Evidence for a pure time perception deficit in children with ADHD', *Journal of Child Psychology, and Psychiatry*, 43, 529–542.

UNESCO (United Nations Educational, Scientific and Cultural Organization) (1994) *The Salamanca Statement and Framework for Action on Special Needs Education*. Spain: Ministry of Education and Science.

UNESCO (United Nations Educational, Scientific and Cultural Organization) (2005) *Guidelines for Inclusion: ensuring access to education for all*. Paris: UNESCO.

Watling, R. (2004) 'Helping them out: the role of teachers and healthcare professionals in the exclusion of students with special educational needs', *Emotional and Behavioural Difficulties*, 9, 8–27.

Wilding, J. (2005) 'Is attention impaired in ADHD?' *British Journal of Developmental Psychology*, 23, 487–505.

Chapter 19

Using objects and touch cues to communicate

Anna Kilberg and Ros How

Spoken language is the main medium for communication and learning in the great majority of schools. However, some children and the adults who teach them need to develop specific ways of making meaning together. St Margaret's Residential School, Tadworth, Surrey, educates children and young people with profound and multiple learning difficulties and complex medical needs. This chapter, by teachers Anna Kilberg and Ros How, describes how adults at the school draw upon gesture and objects to enable communication to be established.

St Margaret's is a purpose-built residential school for children and young people between 5 to 19 years with profound and multiple learning difficulties who are cognitively functioning up to the age of 12 months. We provide a holistic service embracing education, therapy and care. The school has six classes, each staffed by a multi professional team.

Some years ago the headteacher introduced a system of self-review and this takes place each term. Sometimes the topic suggests itself and sometimes it is selected by the teachers or headteacher. Each review has an appointed leader that gives every teacher a chance to lead and formulate a report. This collaborative process enables us to reflect on the quality of our work and the provision for our pupils. It gives us the tools for development. This is an ongoing process because we collect evidence, implement changes and after a while go back and review them again.

The pupils' complex educational needs mean most of them are at a pre-intentional level of communication. They say something or have an experience without the intention of communicating with others. Many pupils have severe physical disabilities that affect the way they are able to communicate. We feel it is very important to prepare our pupils for whatever is happening to them: We use a variety of methods to help them understand and we use verbal cues, music cues and touch cues as well as objects of reference to support our communication.

British Institute of Learning Disabilities for permission to reprint extracts from 'Improving our use of objects of reference and touch cues', Anna Kilberg and Ros How. Reproduced from *The SLD Experience*, Spring 2007, Issue 47, 11–14, with permission of the British Institute of Learning Disabilities.

Touch cues

Touch cues are a form of touch signals that have been developed by our speech and language therapists at the school and are used both in school and residential houses. Touch cues are intended to supplement the existing signals and cues that the child/student may be deriving meaning from already. At meal times, for example, we give the touch signal 'time to eat' by stroking the corner of the student's mouth and this reinforces cues they are getting from smelling, feeling, seeing and tasting the food. The cues are designed to give the student advanced warning of an action and this increases the opportunity for two-way communication to take place between the student and the adult. They also have the benefit of reducing startling the pupil. We take every opportunity to encourage our students actively to participate in what we are doing: helping our students to anticipate our actions leads to a greater participation in and understanding of everyday activities and language.

Objects of reference

Objects of reference were developed originally for use with people who are deafblind. They were later found to be a useful tool for students with learning disabilities. Speech and language therapists and educational staff at the school worked together to devise objects of reference that are appropriate for our pupils. The objects of reference are used alongside touch cues to give our students advanced warning of an activity and to encourage anticipation and understanding of these activities. With the help of objects of reference some of our students are able further to develop their communication skills. The students can be encouraged to make choices and understand a sequence of events.

Each class has its own set of objects of reference to cover the students' core activities. These include bells to introduce music sessions; a torch for visits to the multi-sensory room; a cup for drinking; and a book to introduce story time. We feel some of our pupils benefit from their own personalised set of objects if they engage in a different set of activities and these are kept in a bag on the back of the pupil's chair so that they are always with them.

Touch cues and objects of reference introduce activities that our students are likely regularly to take part in during the day. In order for the students to derive meaning from the cues it is important that they are used consistently throughout the day in all situations.

Although we all believe strongly in the importance of giving touch cues and objects of reference, we felt we could improve on how consistently they were being used. It was decided therefore that this would be an ideal topic for our self-review. Our aim was: To find out about the use of objects of reference and touch cues throughout the school.

In particular, the review was to identify:

- the understanding by the school staff teams of the pupil/student communication systems
- the consistent implementation of pupil/student communication systems
- recommendations for future practice.

Use of touch cues

For assessing the use of touch cues we made a series of 30-minute observations. Staff took it in turns to visit other classrooms. They tried to be as unobtrusive as possible while observing the class and recording which touch cues were used and when opportunities were missed. We wanted to find out how frequently touch cues were being used and how they were used in various contexts during the school day. Therefore the observations were made before school, during group sessions and at lunch and drinks time. We also observed one session when a group was preparing to go on an out on a school visit.

Use of objects of reference

Reference objects are used in a different way from touch cues. Whereas touch cues are used throughout a session, objects of reference are given to students at the start of a session and so we chose a more appropriate method to collect data about them. We asked staff in each class to record which objects of reference had been used over a period of three days.

Collating the information

When we examined the information from the observations we found that touch cues were used during all the observed activities but there was a variation in the frequency of use. The ones used most often were 'well done' 'look', 'listen' and 'stop'. We compared the number of times each touch cue was used with the number of opportunities for using them and found that staff had used these touch cues consistently well. 'Toilet', '(gastro) feed' and 'walk' also scored highly. The touch cues that were not used so consistently were 'eat', 'drink', 'lift/hoist' and 'go'.

To find out how touch cues were used in different contexts, we compared the use of touch cues in structured groups – like 'Good Morning Group' – with their use in less structured sessions, such as topic work. We also included lunch and drinks times as these are more social events and we wondered if this would influence the outcome.

As we had suspected we found that the formality of the session affected the use of touch cues. Touch cues scored highest during the more structured sessions: six out of eight of the cues used scored 90 per cent or more. Scores were slightly lower during less structured sessions and there was more variation in their use during lunch and drinks times when only seven out of the 13 cues observed scored 90 per cent or above.

We noticed some variation in the way that people used touch cues. The touch cue 'ear', for example, was sometimes used several times during a meal but on other occasions only at the start. The cue to 'hoist' was sometimes given before being moved by the hoist and at other times as the sling straps were being attached. We also found that touch cues were sometimes used together with objects of reference but at other times only an object of reference was used.

When we looked at the evidence about objects of reference we found that in each class all of the objects of reference had been used during the three days. However, there was a lot of variation in the frequency of use. One factor affecting this was the variation in the level of opportunity for their use. On the one hand, the opportunity may have arisen only once during the three days, for example, the swimming suit for hydrotherapy. On the other, giving a pupil a cup to prepare them for having a drink is likely to take place at least twice a day and this needed to be reflected in our conclusions. We found that the cup, glove and book were used the most whereas the torch and flannel were used the least.

Improving our practice

From all the evidence we collected it was clear that the use of both touch cues and objects of reference are part of our daily routines but there was room for improvement. The touch cues that were most frequently used such as 'look' and 'listen' scored the fewest missed opportunities.

Looking particularly at the use of touch cues in different contexts during the day, we decided that one reason why touch cues were used more consistently during the structured sessions was that they are an integral part of the sessions. At the start of 'Good Morning' groups, for example, all staff give the touch cue 'listen' to pupils sitting near to them. These sessions are particularly focused which makes it more likely that the cues were used. During sessions in which mere is a stronger social emphasis, a lot of verbal cues were observed but this could perhaps have been at the expense of touch cues.

The variation in the number of times each object of reference was used reflects the activities that were taking place in classes. During discussions after the survey, staff raised the point that it may be more difficult to get into a routine of using objects of reference for activities that takes place only weekly. It seems that the more opportunity you have to use an object of reference the more likely you are to develop effective practice.

Staff had been aware that they had been much more conscious about using both touch cues and objects of reference during this self-review and felt they had probably used the cues more often than they would normally do. Although the observations of touch cues were made so that they had little impact on the class routines, the presence of the observer may well have affected staff by making them more aware of the use of cues. The self-recording carried out to evaluate the use of objects of reference may also have been affected by a heightened self-awareness and we needed to take these factors into account.

Our recommendations

We discussed our conclusions and made a number of recommendations to help us improve our practice:

- As part of their induction staff are introduced to the objects of reference and touch cues but we felt this training could be improved by including information about when and how often to use them. We also felt that we needed a leaflet of explanation that we could give to people in class who were waiting for their induction training or who were not part of the regular staff team.
- We decided that our regularly held team meetings were an ideal opportunity to remind staff about the importance of using touch cues and objects of reference.

We could also reinforce the use of low scoring touch cues by giving staff practical experience of what it is like to have something done to you without having a cue to prepare you.

- Copies of the touch cues are kept in the classroom but we felt that by displaying the pictures of certain cues in the relevant areas in the classrooms staff would be more likely to take notice of them and use them. A picture of the touch for 'drink', for example, should be in the class kitchen area.
- Staff felt that using the generic set of objects of reference did not reflect the diversity of the pupils' needs, so we needed to look into more pupils having their own set of objects of reference. We also felt our pupils would benefit if certain objects of reference were available in their relevant places, for example, a set of bells should be ready for use outside the multi-sensory room.

We were able to implement some of these recommendations straight away and others need time to be developed.

Overall, our staff thought this exercise had been very useful because it has raised our awareness of the importance of using objects of reference and touch cues to prepare our pupils for what is going to happen to them. Moreover, we felt it would be valuable to revisit this subject during a future self-review so that we continue to improve our practice by monitoring our progress and identifying how these changes have affected our practice and considering what further changes we need to make.

Chapter 20

Individual management plans in inclusive classrooms

Simon Knight

When considering how best to help children experiencing learning difficulties and showing inappropriate behaviour, a tension that has always been present is the extent to which the focus of thinking and support should be on requiring the child to make adjustments or whether it should be more on adjusting the context in which the child finds him/her self. This study by Simon Knight addresses the implementation of an individual management plan (IMP) in order to support the effective transition of a child, at risk of exclusion, from a mainstream school to a special school. It considers the existence of a tension between the ideals of an inclusive education system and the practicalities of working with children with learning difficulties within a mainstream context.

The purpose of this study is to consider the extent to which the curricular structures in place within mainstream establishments are themselves a barrier to learning and how they can be overcome.

The pupil with whom the project was conducted was a nine year old boy in an urban primary school who has an SEN statement. He was exhibiting a wide range of challenging behaviours. The aim of the intervention was to enable the pupil to remain in school and to help ensure that the transfer between schools was as positive an experience for the pupil as possible.

The main focus of the research is the impact of the pedagogical teaching and learning approach advocated by the implementation of curricular structures such as the National Literacy and National Numeracy Schemes. Wearmouth and Soler (2001) suggest these schemes are in direct conflict with the Government's Statement on Inclusion (DfEE, 1999) and its three key principles:

- setting suitable learning challenges
- responding to pupils' diverse learning needs
- overcoming potential barriers to learning and assessment for individuals and groups of pupils.

British Institute of Learning Disabilities for permission to reprint extracts from 'To what extent can an Individual Management Plan overcome barriers to learning in an inclusive classroom?', Simon Knight. Reproduced from *The SLD Experience*, Autumn 2008, Issue 52, 17–21, with permission of the British Institute of Learning Disabilities.

The aim was to identify and address some of the curricular and structural barriers to learning and implement a systematic and progressively developmental approach to managing the pupil's inappropriate behaviour.

The initial observation took place within the classroom during a morning literacy lesson that followed the recommended conventions: an introduction, a main activity and a plenary. This provided an opportunity to observe the pupil within a lesson that represented the typical challenges that both he and the staff faced in enabling him to engage with the learning process. The initial observation continued during a numeracy lesson within a class for pupils of a younger age than the pupil being observed. This was because the class teacher felt that the pupil would be more able to access the numeracy curriculum effectively if working on developmentally more appropriate tasks. This observation was completed in a context of a typical lesson.

Having observed the pupil, all the involved parties met to discuss the outcomes of the observation. It was felt that collaboration and ownership of the intervention was essential to ensure that the process would be valued. A frank discussion was held to identify which issues the staff felt needed the greatest attention in order to begin to reduce the significant barriers to learning.

The decision was made to implement an individual management plan (IMP). Its purpose was to resolve the issues of consistency and expectation from the point of view of the staff's approach and provide a clearly defined and accessible structure to support the pupil. The IMP consisted of a clearly written and highly focused explanation of how the behavioural issues should be approached to ensure that the pupil would be treated in exactly the same way by all staff. This was supplemented with a symbol-based communication strip detailing a reward for behaving appropriately and completing the work provided. The pupil would select the reward immediately before the work began and the communication strip would remain with him at all times. There were also identical versions for playing appropriately and for using the toilet sensibly.

The IMP was applied for two weeks. This is an extremely short period to effect change to learned behaviour and the nature and significance of the changes made were therefore expected to be minor.

After two weeks the pupil was again observed during an afternoon lesson on Design and Technology that was less structured than the previously observed lessons. The difference provided an opportunity to observe the pupil in a new learning environment in which the challenges and barriers he faced were contextually and pedagogically different. An informal discussion followed with the class teacher and two of the teaching assistants involved. It was agreed that the IMP was having an impact with some noticeable improvements and to adapt the implementation slightly, allowing the pupil to select his reward when half of his work was completed. The intention was to break up the time and reinforce the positive interactions with the opportunity to select and discuss the reward being worked towards. This amended plan was implemented for a further two-week period.

Outcomes

The findings of this research need to be considered from the point of view of their very specific context. It is important to acknowledge that ideologically trying to change the individual rather than adapting the artificial construct of the curriculum is questionable. In an inclusive classroom it is not just the placement that implies inclusivity but also the adaptation of curricula and teaching methodologies (Gibb *et al.*, 2007). In this case the child's short-term needs were perceived as being best met by moderating the socially challenging behaviours rather than adaptating the educational provision. This was a tacit acknowledgement that inclusion in this instance had at best been only partially successful. It would enable the child to remain in education for the duration of the transfer period, after which his educational needs could be met more effectively within a special school environment.

When the pupil was first observed it was noted that he was experiencing a level of passive academic exclusion. The nature of the curriculum enforces whole-class teaching and precludes the teachers' willingness and ability to differentiate (Wearmouth and Soler, 2001). The pupil was finding it difficult to remain on task when faced with challenging structures. A central reason for this was the expectation that his learning periods would conform to the conventions of the curricular structures. To sustain concentration for predefined periods of time combined to make the work prohibitively challenging to the child and in part led to outbursts of poor behaviour. The nature of the IMP and its application defined the expectations of time spent on task and the nature of a reward for doing so. While this did not address the wider structural barriers to effective learning, it considered the issue of arbitrary periods of time being spent on specific tasks.

With this is in place the staff commented that the pupil's behaviour began to change. The nature of a clearly communicated reward for completing more clearly defined periods of work, coupled with consistent expectations that inappropriate behaviour would be ignored and positive behaviour praised, meant that more time was being spent in the classroom. It was noted that this time was spent more productively.

There was also a concern that the pupil's behaviour, especially the incidents of more extreme antisocial behaviour, may have an impact on others within the classroom. This was addressed through the provision of a peaceful location that could be used should the pupil's behaviour become a danger to himself or those around him. The initial outcome of this intervention was that the pupil went from being withdrawn from the class approximately five times per day to once a day. The staff concluded that the time spent working within the lesson was more rewarding than the time spent out of the classroom. The consistent approach also meant that they felt more in control of managing the behaviour, and that this had led to more positive perceptions of the pupil. This meant that they viewed the situation more objectively and spent more time reflecting upon the pupil's learning needs as opposed to behavioural ones.

Another significant finding during the research was the marked difference between the nature of the behaviour when the pupil was working on broadly differentiated tasks alongside his chronological peers in Year Four and when he worked on identical tasks to his chronologically different but cognitively comparable peers in Year One. The curricular structures were similar in both classes, with each following the convention of an introduction, main activity and plenary. But when working on developmentally more appropriate tasks the number and nature of behavioural incidents were different. The pupil was on task for longer periods of time and when he did begin to behave in an unconventional manner, the behaviour was of a low level and quickly resolved with minor reference to the management system. The pupil seemed more socially and academically included and actively sought to be the focus of the learning. This contrasted with his partial socio-academic exclusion when working with his chronological peers.

It could be claimed that the pupil has had barriers to participation removed but the question is, has he had barriers to achievement removed?

Conclusions

The implications of this research are hard to state with confidence due to its limited timeframe. Within the context of behaviour management the positive impact of the management strategy may reflect the novelty of the approach rather than any deep-seated change to the negative behaviours witnessed. Had the research been continued, the behaviour may have regressed or escalated once the novelty factor dissipated.

One of the most significant changes effected by the intervention was the degree of confidence felt by the staff. Both the teacher and the teaching assistants stated that they once again felt in control of the situation with the security of a formalised framework. The structure enabled the staff to dissociate the behaviour from the child and in part led to the development of more positive relationships between staff and pupil. The increased ability to manage the behaviour enabled the possibility of long-term aims being pursued. This in turn reduced the staff's fear of failure of the approach and discussing the behaviour before the intervention enabled them to consider the long-term timescales of behaviour management. This led to a shift away from abandoning management plans if they did not resolve the issues in the short term. The awareness of a long-term view and the realistic timescales for change for other pupils presenting with challenging behaviour has led to increased skills of the staff.

From the pupil's point of view far more effective time is now spent in the classroom. However, the intervention has dealt with the symptoms of rather than the root cause. Having observed the pupil and discussed the pupil's ability to access the curriculum, it is clear that the model advocated by current mainstream pedagogies does not meet the pupil's specific needs. The outcome of this, as well as delayed development, has been disruptive behaviour and his needs have therefore been identified more easily due to the obvious symptoms. This raises the question of how many children with SEN are quietly being excluded by inappropriate curricular structures.

In many ways the intervention has been superficial, working towards resolving a problem in a reactive and short-term manner to keep the pupil from being excluded during the transition period. It seems, broadly, that the 'included' pupil is being made to fit the curriculum rather than, as stated by Porter and Lacey (1999), ensuring that the provision for children with behavioural or special educational needs is altered to meet their needs.

It may be time that for the 'included' pupil to be genuinely part of the mainstream educational structure we have to recognize that one curriculum cannot fit all.

References

DfEE (1999) *The National Curriculum – Key Stages 1 and 2* QCA: London.

Gibb, K., Tunbridge, D., Chau, A. and Frederikson, N. (2007) 'Pathways to inclusion: Moving from special school to mainstream'. *Educational Psychology in Practice* 23(2), 109–127.

Porter, J. and Lacey, P. (1999) 'What provision for pupils with challenging behaviour?' *British Journal of Special Education* 26(1), 23–28.

Wearmouth, J. and Soler, J. (2001) 'How inclusive is the Literacy Hour?' *British Journal of Special Education* 28(3), 113–119.

Part 4

Contexts for small-scale research

Children, adults and the primary curriculum

Chapter 21

Collaborative choreography

Sue Cottam

The belief that primary schools should focus very concertedly on 'the basics' in the form of maths and English has always had an impact on the time available for the arts. The prioritising of literacy and numeracy in recent years has, arguably, served to further marginalise the arts curriculum. 'Artsmark' is an award scheme which is managed by Arts Council England. The scheme encourages schools to increase the range, quantity and type of arts subjects that are provided to children. Successful schools are awarded formal recognition if they can show they are offering children enhanced opportunities in such areas as art, dance, drama and music. A strong element of Artsmark is artistic partnership and in this chapter by Sue Cottam, a freelance dance teacher, one such partnership is described. It involved collaboration between Sue, students from Royal Manor Arts College, Dorset, and teachers from Chickerell Primary School, Weymouth. The project aimed to stimulate the dance experiences of 110 Key Stage 2 children through their understanding of the behaviour of birds, especially their flight. Although not a research project *per se*, this initiative could be seen to have aspects of both developmental research and action research given that successive performances were documented and video-recorded in order to help gain insight and build upon and improve what had taken place.

Birds and Flight was part of the larger research project, Beyond Artsmark 2007, which aimed to encourage schools to apply for Artsmark. Dance was the focus in this project because many schools struggle to meet Artsmark criteria in this art form.

Project outline

Sue the dance teacher used the same stimuli for all participants, both adults and children: the observation of birds and excerpts from professional dance works on video. Led by her, the six groups then created their own performances using collaborative creative choreography.

Sue Cottam for permission to reprint extracts from 'Birds and flights; a research project', Sue Cottam, *Dance Matters*, Summer 2008, No. 52, 4–5.

The college students prepared the work they would do with the primary pupils. After performing their own choreography to each other, they worked in pairs with groups of primary pupils on the theme of birds and flight, enabling the primary pupils to create group work to add to the dance they had created.

The primary pupils loved working alongside the older students, gaining many new skills. The older students enjoyed leading activities and seeing how they could inspire younger pupils. The choreography was rehearsed and performance skills were improved before a final sharing.

The following lesson ideas are from the resource pack prepared for Key Stage 2 teachers. The same ideas were used with the older students with the addition of a variety of lifts and using long, flowing material.

1 **Preparation 'homework' for all participants**

- Look at the movement of a variety of birds in different situations: birds perched on wires or fences; birds flying together; birds flying alone; birds travelling on the ground; birds feeding.
- Look at the shape of birds in silhouette: from below, from above, when on the ground and when in flight.
- Look at the patterns and colours of birds' feathers.
- Listen to the sounds that birds make and try to copy them.

2 **Accompaniment ideas for dance work**

- Atmospheric instrumental music
- Recorded birdsong
- Live or recorded voices of birdsong created by pupils.

3 **Watch excerpts from**

- *Beach Birds* (1993) choreographed by Merce Cunningham
- *Swan Lake* (1995) choreographed by Matthew Bourne.

The discussion of different qualities and dynamics used by the dancers included: how dancers use their bodies to show the movement of wings; feelings of power, humour and emotions; floor patterns; relationships; the use of music, set and lighting.

Warming up

The first three sessions were preceded by a warm up inspired by bird movement: travelling steps – hopping, stepping, wading, swooping, hovering; the movement of contrasting birds – duck, hawk, swan, flamingo; head, arm and hand extensions; slow motion and acceleration to fast; balance; suspension; focus; specific bird behaviour – resting on wires, pecking, clawing.

Recording

Each session was videoed and also notated on paper with stick figures, words and floor patterns to aid recall. All work was videoed and edited to a final DVD.

Plan used for the project

Session One

1. The teacher selects exciting movements created by pupils during the warm up, building up a short Motif A, which the whole class learns and does together in unison. Share half class and half class.
2. Birds on a wire, Motif B: in small groups, pupils create their own short motifs using ideas from the warm up. Start and finish in freeze frame in a line as if on a wire. Give pupils a defined number of counts, e.g. 16, in which to move a short way from the wire, copying birdlike behaviour. Share half class and half class.
3. Discuss and experiment with ways of entering and exiting the performance space, inspired by birds in flight. In the same small groups, pupils create their own entrance and exit. Add this to Motif B. Practise: enter/Motif B/exit.
4. Link the above ideas together to form a choreographic structure, e.g. unison Motif A; groups gradually exit until the stage is empty; staggered entrances of groups to do Motif B followed by staggered exit; two groups left on stage start Motif A and others stagger their entry to create Motif A thus producing canon.

Homework: Each bird on a wire group chooses a bird for the next session and observes its characteristics and its shape when still and when moving.

Session Two

1. Practise work done in Session One.
2. Discuss how to form one large bird shape as a still image. Experiment with guidance from the teacher. Bring pupils out of the 'picture' to view. Discuss how to form the shape and dissolve the shape effectively – Motif C.
3. In their small groups, pupils form the shape of their chosen bird. Make a still image. How does it move on the spot? Practise and perfect. Share with the class – Motif D.
4. Join together Motifs A, B, C and D. This can be ordered in a variety of ways, for example:

   - Whole class start on stage as a still image bird – Motif C.
   - Swooping travel to unison work – Motif A – but pupils perform in their group spaces.
   - Some groups exit but leave two groups to peform Motif B followed by their own bird – Motif D.
   - Other groups gradually enter stage to do Motif B then Motif D.
   - Finish with unison Motif A but perfom solo so that the staggered start creates canon.

Session Three

1. Practise work done last week.
2. In twos, experiment with duo work on the spot which gives the idea of bird shape, bird wing movement, head isolations, claw movement, etc. Give each pair a spot

in the room to work in and 16 counts in which to improvise, select, practise and perfect – Motif E.

3 One duo performs to another duo. Encourage feedback.
4 Add this duo work to the choreography. The class can be asked to suggest where this would best fit. Practise.

Session Four

- Show pupils photographs of professionals dancing from dance programmes or posters, dance company websites, and books like *Airborne*: *The New Dance Photography* (1998) by Lois Greenfield.
- Encourage pupils to use descriptive words about the dancers and their bodies: strong, powerful, extended, tension, focus, relationships with others, facial expressions, shapes in space, balance, poise, alignment, posture, etc.
- Relate to the warm up below.

Warm-up for Session Four

Perfect freeze-frame dance shapes: class travel with bird movements of their choice. When the music stops they have four slow counts to make an amazing bird shape of their choice and four slow counts to hold it still before travelling on. (The teacher or a non-dancing pupil can take photographs here.) The teacher gives continual verbal feedback which encourages and teaches at the same time. Share good shapes as a class and encourage verbal descriptions.

1 Practise work done last week.
2 Solo work. Give pupils a solo spot. They create an entrance and exit to this spot using any bird travel they have enjoyed doing. They create a solo inspired by the photos and the warm up, in and immediately around their solo spot for 16 counts – Motif F.
3 Discuss where this section would best fit. Add this to the choreography.
4 Practise the whole dance, concentrating on performance skills.

Chapter 22

Singing together

Gitika Partington

Gitika Partington works as an organiser of music projects based at Camden School for Girls, London. This is a flexible advisory role which involves her in the musical curriculum of three primaries, a secondary and a special school, and also in the local community. In this chapter she focuses on school assemblies as a key time for including everyone in singing. The project illustrates, amongst other things, the way in which performance can be very motivating and the phrase 'I did not see a child or adult who was not engaged all day' is testimony to the potential inclusivity of singing. There are echoes here, of course, of the BBC television documentary series featuring the Gareth Malone who does much, wherever he goes, to break down the resistance of boys and men to participation in choirs. The Camden singing project is a further reminder that singing in a choir can be a very powerful personal and educational experience.

One of the plans for the first year of this music project was to serve and support singing – especially in the primary feeder schools. There was, of course singing happening already in all the schools, but to varying degrees, depending on the confidence and experience of the teachers and teaching assistants. The important issue was that there were not just small pockets of excellence happening but that all pupils and staff were having a positive singing experience.

We started to think about the idea of creating a repertoire of songs that the whole school community would know – by no means a new idea but one that we felt needed resurrecting. This could only happen if the school singing assembly became a place where all the school were singing – a difficult situation in many schools where the singing assembly is used as non-contact/planning time for most staff. Having run many singing assemblies I have noticed the positively marked effect whole school singing has on a school community, when pupils are singing with all the staff, not just the music specialist.

With Camden School's head of music, we decided to pilot Primary Singing Days in two primary schools. We planned to have one or two concerts (depending on

Peacock Press and Gitika Partington for kind permission to reprint 'Primary singing days', Gitika Partington, *Primary Music Today*, 2008, Issue 39.

form entry) so each class would perform a song for the rest of the school and then in the afternoon, students from the secondary school would come in and give a singing concert for the school.

The idea was to create a model that would not make too much extra work for any individual teacher but would give every member of staff the chance to be involved in singing with their class and be in charge of a class performance. The specialist music teacher and music coordinator from the two primary schools and I created a pack of about 12 songs for the teacher to choose a song for their class (they were of course free to make their own choice of song). I made recordings of the songs with and without vocals so the tracks could be used in the classroom, through the interactive systems. In both schools all the songs were put on the main computer system so were available in every classroom.

About a month after the songs had been given out and each class had decided on their song, I visited the schools for a day. Teachers were able to make appointments for me to watch them with their classes to see if there was help I could offer. In the first school, I parked myself in the staff room and thought I was in for a quiet day. But no! Almost all the teachers had signed up for me to visit for the half-hour slots.

My task was really just to give some feedback about what the class could do to move their song forward. All the children and staff had taken on their song with a real commitment to working towards a performance – classes were working on movement, gesture and even costumes. I did not see a child or adult who was not engaged all day. One of the Year 1 classes was so excited about singing for me, and did such an exhilarating performance of 'The Drunken Sailor' in two parts – with the boys as the sailors and the girls as the captains – that we had to have a class hug at the end of the session.

The other plan for the singing days was that the staff would also sing a song for the whole school. At each school I ran a singing workshop in a staff meeting and most of the teaching assistants were able to come too. When I came in to start the workshop the atmosphere was akin to a dentist's surgery. We started with a rhythmic warm up with lots of speaking, silly noises and chanting call and response. We sung 'My Bonnie Lies over the Ocean' in the style of the fruit and veg man, the Wicked Witch of the West, the small innocent child, the inconsolable (my pink puppy has just been flattened by an articulated lorry), and a wobbly diva. I also taught them an African song 'Mafuzulu' (collected by Colin Harrison in *Songs from South Africa*[1] in two parts) and 'Wade in the Water'/'I Wanna Die Easy'/'Sometimes I Feel like a Motherless Child'[2] by ear with only the aid of my trusty recorder and the words on an A1 sheet. Staff from both schools sung with real energy and passion and had fun. At both Singing Days the children gave the staff an enthusiastic ovation when they got up to sing. Both groups repeated their performance at their International Evening for all the parents.

One member of staff asked me what should be done as she felt she was singing on very few notes and that the signals I made with my hands to go up and down in pitch meant very little. Keep on singing was my reply. We had an interesting debate about the importance of the adult as a positive role model in the singing experience. It was agreed that it was important for children to see staff of all levels of singing experience joining in. We are still picking up the pieces from an era when teachers in the past often did not understand that only by singing regularly would a child develop pitch and rhythm, and that there is a natural singing development continuum which many of us get stuck on if we are not given the opportunity to sing regularly. So many of the adults I meet were divided into bluebirds or crows in childhood singing classes at school. Some, traumatically, were even made to sit in isolation on a mat and told not to sing at all. Staff who have experienced such negative experiences, or simply have never experienced good role models for themselves, are going to find it a real challenge to be a positive role model for the next generation of singers. At any time in a class you might have several children singing with real energy and passion something that not yet resembles the tune. Only by singing regularly in a group will the singer get more experienced.

Notes

1 Available from www.nickomoandrasullah.com
2 *Voiceworks*, Oxford: Oxford University Press.

Chapter 23

Mentor support for music and performance

Ruth Wright

As with Chapter 22, this chapter exemplifies the power of mentoring. Ruth Wright, from the University of Wales Institute, Cardiff, tells of a ten week music project in which primary children were supported by music college mentors. The project was based in Herbert Thompson Junior School which is located in an economically disadvantaged suburb to the west of Cardiff. With the personalised support of mentors, it enabled all children in one class to participate and also to establish a level of playing – with djembe hand drums, recorders, cellos, flutes and violins – that led to a performance at the Wales Millennium Centre.

In the summer term of 2007, the Music Development Team (MDT) for Cardiff County and the Vale of Glamorgan Music Service, led by Music Development Officer Emma Coulthard, began a 10-week project entitled Global Music Maker at Herbert Thompson Junior School in Cardiff. The project was designed to develop the musical skills of one Year Four class of pupils through whole class activities. The project was also intended to allow every child to develop their musicianship on an equal footing addressing issues of inclusion and equality of access to music in the school. The theme chosen for the project by the MDT was that of Native American music as this had been noted to be particularly appropriate for its use of circle activities and recurring patterns. Over a series of 10 one hour sessions of performing, composing and listening the pupils were invited to perform on the Tesco stage at the Wales Millennium Centre. The commitment of the school to the project was witnessed by the fact that a member of staff made costumes for all the pupils to wear for their performance. The performance was very well received by the audience and was judged to have been such a success by the school's headteacher Debbie Lewis, that she invited the MDT to return to the school at the beginning of the following academic year, this time to run a larger scale project with the original Year 4 class and their counterpart class, both now entering Year 5.

Peacock Press and Ruth Wright for kind permission to reprint 'Practice pals make perfect', Ruth Wright, *Primary Music Today*, 2008, Issue 41.

The intention this time was for the team to expand on the inclusive philosophy of the original project by allowing more children to have opportunities to play musical instruments. The team approached this through an initial 6 weekly sessions of musicianship development coupled with opportunities to hear and see a variety of different instruments including flute, recorder, violin, cello and African djembe drums. The thinking behind this was that it was important for pupils to have some background knowledge of a variety of instruments so that they could make an informed choice when the time came for them to select an instrument they would like to learn to play. After some negotiation, the final programme comprised two large group tuition ensembles on djembe drums and recorder, with groups of 4 cellists and 6 violinists.

Sessions took the form of an initial 15 minute group activity involving a warm up and learning a song, with simple instrumental accompaniment parts performed on the instruments. There then followed half hour group instrumental sessions and a final 15 minute plenary session where pupils and teachers shared progress and informed each other of their achievements during that session. Emma Coulthard emphasised the importance of sharing with pupils their progress at the end of each session as being vital to building pupils' confidence and self esteem about their playing. Due to the financial value of the instruments involved, all access to the musical instruments occurred only during school time under supervision. By Christmas time however many of the pupils involved in the project were very keen to be allowed to take the instruments home to practise. The school and the MDT could not easily allow this given the difficulty of replacing the instruments should they become lost or damaged. The issue was seen as presenting an unfortunate barrier to further development of pupils' technical and musical skill and, indeed, their motivation for the project.

Fortunately, two pupils received flutes as family presents for Christmas and one received a cello for her birthday. Whilst this was a wonderful indication of pupil enthusiasm and parental support for the project it raised the age old issue of lack of equal access to musical instrument learning for those pupils whose families were not able to afford to purchase instruments. Moreover the MDT had by this time been requested by the school to run a scheme for the whole of Year 6 based on rock band skills which was proving highly popular. The renown of the school for its musical prowess was also spreading, with increasing numbers of invitations to perform, including appearances at St David's Hall, to an audience of 2000 people and a tumultuous reception, and at the Senydd, home of the Welsh Assembly Government.

In an innovative move, Emma Coulthard the Music Development Officer approached the Royal Welsh College of Music and Drama (the conservatoire of Wales) and initiated a project entitled 'Practice Pals'. The Practice Pals scheme teams current students and recent graduates of the College with pupils from the school. College students then attend the school at lunchtime on one day a week to mentor junior pupils and supervise small group practice sessions involving 2 or 3 pupils at a time. It is hoped that this will allow pupils to access the skills of reading musical notation in addition to developing their technique on their instrument.

It appears essential that schemes such as this are initiated widely to address the issues of equality of access to musical learning. For schemes intended to result in progressive and sustained learning in the playing of musical instruments there are barriers to learning other than those raised by finance, important as this is. Closely related are the barriers raised to progress and enthusiasm by differential access to supervised practice. Pupils who do not benefit from practice supervised by someone with knowledge and understanding of music may not progress as do their peers. They are very likely therefore to lose motivation and even drop out of instrumental learning programmes.

Chapter 24

Analysing and presenting information

Min Wilkie

In a small-scale classroom enquiry you gather information (data), perhaps from several sources and in a variety of ways. In order to use this information constructively, you need to organise and present it so that you and others can interpret it. In this process you analyse your information, which means that you look for incidents, trends, patterns and themes. In this chapter, Min Wilkie describes four key activities which support this kind of analysis: *naming, grouping, finding relationships* and *displaying*. We have included this chapter because it provides practical examples of how to make an effective analysis of the kinds of information gathered 'in action' in classrooms, and because it uses research terminology (such as 'sample', 'validity', 'qualitative' and 'quantitative') in an accessible way. Min describes enquiries carried out by teaching assistants into children's learning in mathematics, literacy and ICT, and also into children's behaviour for learning. Her chapter encourages all those involved in small-scale enquiry to view their information from the perspective of others, and to communicate what is most important about findings.

Freeman (1998: 96) describes the process of action research as investigating what, as a researcher, you feel you know already, but in carrying out investigation, you push yourself 'to examine the sense of certainty, to expose, to scrutinise, to question, not because you are mistaken but to find out what is true and why'. To do this, he believes disassembling and reassembling data is a vital process that is both engaging and challenging. He identifies four activities that are necessary to analysis:

- naming
- grouping

- finding relationships
- displaying.

Very often, students gather interesting and vibrant data through observations or surveys, but then they seem at a loss to know how to handle the information and make it work, by applying it to their research aims. Early in her work for the Foundation degree in educational studies, Louise chose three children to observe (one each from the higher-, middle- and lower-ability numeracy groups from a Year 3 class of 27 mixed-ability pupils) in order to compare their strategies for addition and subtraction. She carefully recorded their responses and her initial interpretations, displaying them in a tabular format (Figure 24.1) that makes the information accessible, having introduced the task:

> I explained to the children that I was going to ask them some adding and taking away questions. We discussed the fact that there are different ways to do the same sum and I told them it did not matter how they did it, but that I would like them to either write down their workings out or describe to me how they had found the answer.

She then analysed her findings. Louise has perceptively assessed strategies in use, and told a 'story' that is useful in this small case study. In order to have done this, she was looking for incidences of strategies that she had 'named' as a result of learning about them. For instance:

- counting on
- using a derived fact
- partitioning and recombining.

Child A is in the highest ability group and showed a good range of strategies, although, perhaps, she did not always pick the most suitable. For example, when calculating 11+4, she used a strategy of approximating and adjusting, but it would have been easier to count on from the first number. Child A has taken on board strategies that are being taught in the class, and we can see that she is practising them and hopefully discovering for herself when best to use a range of different strategies.

Question	**Answer**	**Child's explanation**	**Comments**
11+4	15	11–1=10 10+4=14+1=15	Approximate and adjust
84+10	94	84–4=80+4=84 84+10=94	Got the correct answer but could not explain the beginning of the calculation. Said she had counted on in 10s in the second part
30+40	70	4+3=7 7+0=70	Using knowledge of place value
17+3	20	1+3=4 7+4=11	Her workings out are wrong but the answer is correct. I think she knew that 17 and 3 were a number bond making 20
48–45	3	40–40=0 8–5=3	Partition and recombine
60–30	30	'I just knew it'	Did this one mentally, using a known fact
15–5	10	10+5=15	Counting up – recognising that subtraction is the inverse of addition and using this fact to calculate the answer
50–25	25	50–20=30 30–5=25	Partitioning

Figure 24.1 Child A – higher ability

Child B has developed better strategies generally and seems to have a good understanding of mathematical concepts and strategies. He knows and uses his number bonds and recognises the link between addition and subtraction. He relied on counting on for most of the additions, but, perhaps, if the questions had involved larger numbers, he would have chosen and demonstrated different strategies.

Question	Answer	Child's explanation	Comments
11+4	15	'Put 11 in my head and counted on four'	Counting on from the first number in 1s
84+10	94	'Put 84 in my head and counted on 10'	Counting on from the first number in 1s
30+40	70	'Put 30 in my head and counted on in 10s	Counting on from the first number in 10s
17+3	20	'I just knew it'	Using a known fact – number bonds to 20
48–45	2	'I counted back'	He got this one wrong. First counting back in 10s and then in 1s. A better strategy here would have been counting up.
60–30	30	'I just knew it' cos if you add 30 and 30 that makes 60'	Using a derived fact (6–3) to work out a new one or use of doubles
15–5	10	'I just knew that one as well' cos 10–5 is 15'	Using a known fact, a very quick response to this question
50–25	35	'I counted on in 5s'	Counting up – recognising the link between addition and subtraction

Figure 24.2 Child B – middle ability

Child C, who is of lower ability, still tries to calculate by counting on, using her fingers. This worked quite successfully with the additions, but she did not appear to understand the subtractions, with the exception of 15–5, which she did by counting on the 100 number square that is displayed on the classroom wall.

Question	Answer	Child's explanation	Comments
11+4	15	11 in head, counted on 4	Counting on from the first number in 1s – using fingers
84+10	94	84 in head, counted on 10	Counting on from the first number in 1s – using fingers
30+40	70	3+4=7 and then put a 0 on the end	Using knowledge of place value, or this may just be use of a taught procedure
17+3	20	Counted on	Counting on from the first number in 1s – using fingers
48–45	6	No explanation	She guessed this one after telling me that she could not do it
60–30	4	Guessed	She had no strategy to work this one out
15–5	10	Counted on	Counted on using the 100 square displayed in the class
50–25	6	Counted on	Tried counting on with her fingers

Figure 24.3 Child C – lower ability

These *codes* (the comments row) can come from 'outside', as in this example where strategies are already identified, or they might be determined from the data itself.

Louise might have grouped together incidences from all three children, as in Figure 24.4, thereby enabling analysis of the most common strategies used by

Strategy	No. of incidences
Counting on/back	9
Using a known/derived fact	7
Partitioning and recombining	3
No strategy/guess	2

Figure 24.4 Codes for maths strategies

these children. In Year 3, where children are being taught to partition, only the most able child used this approach. Had Louise taken a greater *sample*, it would have been possible to see whether a relationship between the use of more sophisticated strategies and more able children was evident. This might have then affected the organisation of teaching.

Louise used her data in a *qualitative* way, but there was potential also to manipulate the data *quantitatively*. The *validity* of her small study rests on her interpretation of the children's actions and their explanations agreeing. Having a video of the action would have allowed for a third check on the *internal consistency*, which is often referred to as *triangulation*. The *reliability* of her study depends on the ability to replicate and generalise the work. The conditions of the activity were made clear, so replication would be possible, but one would need a far larger sample to be able to assume that similar findings could be generated in any such situation. Generalising findings to other situations is not usually expected in action research, where small-scale research is frequently reported in a case study format and often does not present numerical data. It is important, however, in any study, however small, to explain in enough detail for the work to be *replicated* if another researcher wished to do so.

Observation using codes

Chris carried out an observation in a Year 6 class. Numbers in parenthesis refer to suggested codes to be found at the end of the observation.

Throughout the observation, references will be made to children I shall refer to as C and D.

Introduction to lesson – seated in whole-class group on carpet.

C fidgeting/chatting/facing away from teacher. (1)

D staring at display. (2)

Discussion considered changes to Europe since the First World War.

C and D no involvement in group discussion, no interaction with teacher, as by eye contact/non-verbal gestures. (1)

As session progressed

D shows some signs of participation and puts hand up to answer question. (4)

C answers question – 'How did Hitler feel?' – inappropriate response. (4)

Teacher then explained what was required for the lesson – handing out two sheets, a map and an instruction sheet. Teacher asked children to listen carefully. The second sheet told the children exactly what they were going to do. Children asked to look at and read through the sheet.

C and D seem to be reading sheet. (4)

Group discussion took place on meaning of terms such as 'allies', 'neutral', etc.

C and D appear to be interested in map. (4)

Teacher explained instructions, i.e. in what order, how and in what colour.

C and D appear to be listening and attempting to read text. (4)
C and D chatting. (1)

Teacher then read the whole sheet to the whole class explaining what was required.

D not looking at map, instructions or the teacher. (1)
C able to contribute to discussion on reading key appropriately. (4)

The teacher explained that this was also a test of their ability to follow instructions appropriately. Children returned to their desks to start work on completing sheet. At this time, I checked child's understanding of task.

C shows good understanding of what was required. (4)
D appears to have understanding – however, (4)
also states that all cross-hatched should be red. (2)

Children commenced activity.

D sharpens pencil. (1)
C picks up a red crayon, starts looking around the classroom. (1)
C and D look around room – distracted. (1)
D initially colours Germany correctly, and (4)
then continues to colour all hatched areas red; (2)
hand up for help from teacher. (3)

C	does not complete in order – teacher had explained that this would help with recall.	(2)
D	needs reshowing what he should be copying.	(3)
C and D	teacher reiterates how instructions need to be followed in order so that they would understand how events had unfolded.	(3)
C and D	teacher moves away; both stop working and start a discussion.	(1)
C	tries to support D.	(4)
D	begins playing with pen.	(1)
D	playing with pen.	(1)
C and D	chatting.	(1)
C	starts to work independently when told to finish work before going out for break.	(4)
D	asks to leave room as has pen on face.	(1)
D	on return, teacher asks to finish instructions for colouring map; responds that he had done it, but in fact has coloured the whole of the map red.	(2)
D	when asked to do so, not able to find instructions that requested using blue/green.	(3)

At the end of the exercise, I asked each child what they had understood from the session.

C	able to explain why countries were coloured the way they were.	(4)
D	unable to explain why countries were coloured in a particular way.	(2)

Chris chose codes that arose from the observation itself, an example of identifying categories that is referred to as *grounded*, as they originate from the data, not from preconceived objectives. She has grouped responses, reassembling them where she has seen commonalities between them. The codes show that child D has almost twice as many instances where he displays non-engagement or lack of understanding. It is therefore not surprising that he cannot explain the lesson objectives at the close of the session.

Code	Includes	Child C	Child D
1. Off task	chatting/fidgeting/being distracted	7	10
2. Not participating	no interaction/inappropriate response	2	5
3. Not understanding	needing clarification/remodelling	1	4
	Total	10	19
4. Participating	engaged/interested listening/hand up	9	6

Figure 24.5 Codes for behaviour

Miles and Huberman (1994) suggest 13 ways to reduce data and begin to make meaning from analysis. These include:

- clustering information
- counting frequencies of occurrence
- seeing plausibility – using informed intuition to reach a conclusion.

As Patton (MacIntyre, 2000: 93) points out, analysis must enable the researcher to move beyond description. It is not enough to report. One should, even in small-scale research, be asking 'to what extent?', making comparisons and qualifying judgements. Obviously, in order to do this, you have to interpret the data, and even though you try to do this with consistency and integrity, no researcher is entirely free of bias. It is necessary therefore to retain an awareness of the effect of your choices may have, and explain why you make them.

Displaying data

There are many ways to display data purposefully to aid interpretation. Offering a visual depiction of findings enables the reader to form an impression with more impact than the reading of results. When deciding how to display results, it is a good idea to question your chosen method before determining to use it. Does it do what you want it to? Try getting someone else to 'read' your display and tell you what interpretations they can draw from it. Students may be impressed by the ease with which eye-catching charts and graphs can be compiled by a computer. They are sometimes tempted to include quantities of graphic material that do not enhance their work by aiding interpretation. Using block graphs to show the results of a questionnaire is a useful way (see Figure 24.6).

Presenting data in this way has allowed immediate understanding that many children consulted had real and valid concerns, particularly about the way they are cared for. Some of these might have been grouped together – for instance, sporting suggestions might have been entered next to each other. Discussion and comparison opportunities open up in this way.

In a study looking into the reading habits and preferences of a sample of Key Stage 2 children, Louise (not the same student as above) presented her data in both graphs and pie charts. In Figure 24.7 Louise can discuss the fact that the 'majority of pupils do, in fact, read a large number of books, outside school, for pleasure'.

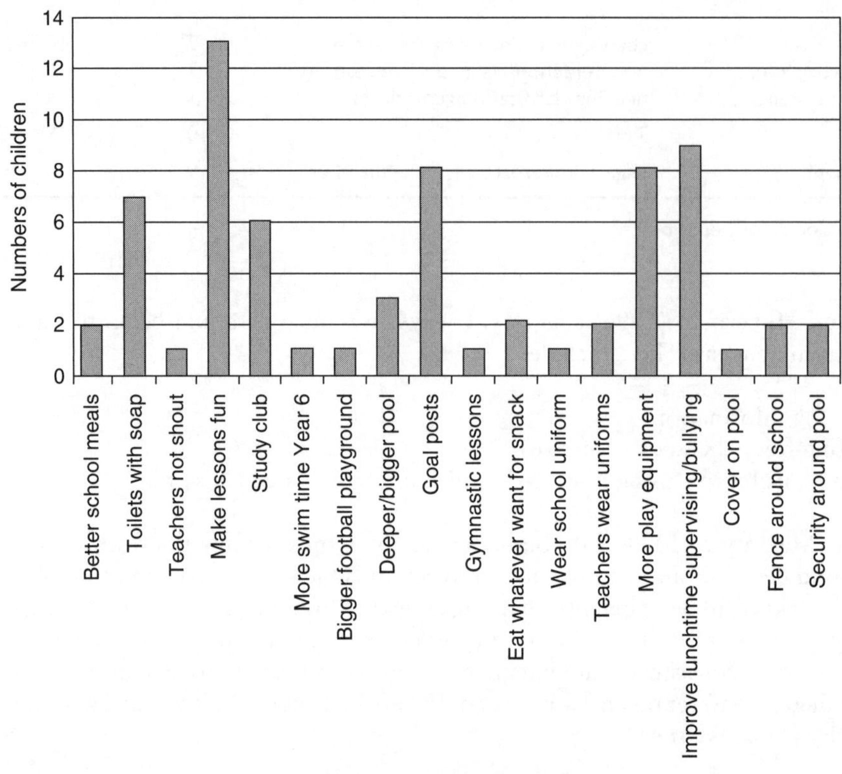

Figure 24.6 Questionnaire responses regarding issues that pupils feel require change

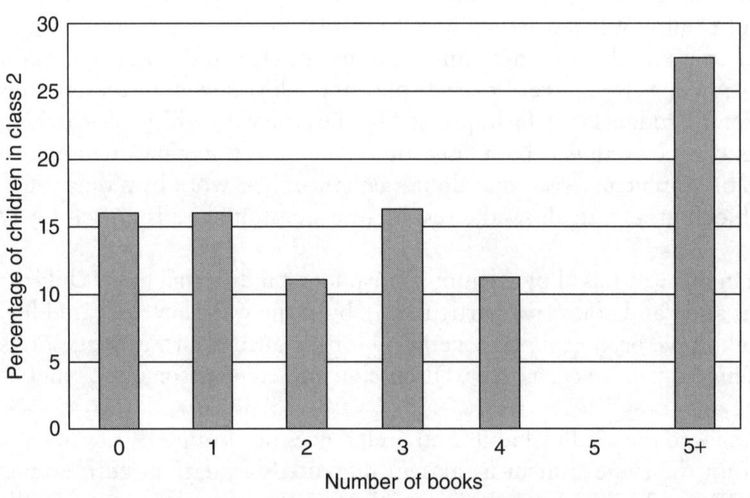

Figure 24.7 How many books do you read in a week?

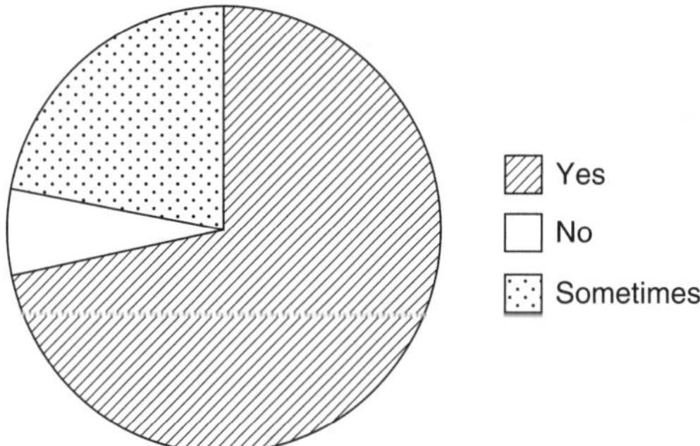

Figure 24.8 Do you enjoy reading?

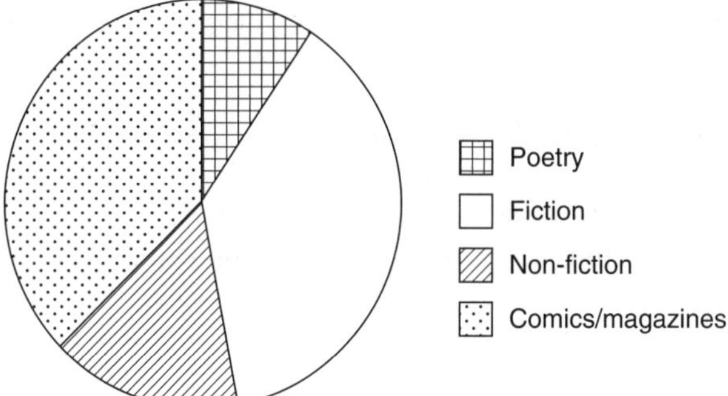

Figure 24.9 What do you like to read?

However, she realised that her graph also shows that almost half the class read two books or fewer per week, and in following this up with the children, she confirmed that the books were quite often their own school reading books. Hopefully, they did enjoy these, but she was looking for additional, self-motivated reading, which was not discernible from the display she produced. From Figure 24.8, it is easy to see that the majority of children asked do enjoy reading, and this impression may be enough. Even when it is known that 18 children responded, it is not easy to work out exactly how many answered 'yes', although it is possible to speculate that one child does not like reading at all.

Louise also showed in a similar way, that there is a spread in preferences for reading material (Figure 24.9).

But it is not possible from these pie charts to see whether those children who like reading are the ones who like fiction and poetry, for example. In order to do this, one must correlate results.

In small-scale studies, one has to temper inferences with caution, as the numbers involved are usually too small to be significant, or to be generalised. I agree with Drever (1995: 70) that, in general, it is better to use actual numbers than percentages, for this reason. Often a simple table is a most effective way of displaying results. But, inevitably, although gathering information together and collating it can help to

Name of computer game	**Number of times game requested during research period**	**Number of times voted favourite game in questionnaire**
Zoombinis games x3	12	11
Numbershark	6	2
Wordshark	1	3
Catch-up	1	2
Starspell	0	0
Task Master	0	0

Figure 24.10 The number of times each game was requested and the game the pupils voted their favourite in the questionnaire

make sense of data, there is also some 'degradation', some loss of quality. That is why balancing findings by reporting them using a variety of strategies will make the best of what you have. Jo, who works with dyslexic students in a centre apart from their school, examined the efficacy of various computer games in supporting learning (Figure 24.10).

Jo followed this examination with a discussion that began thus:

> We can see that the Zoombinis games were the most often requested and favoured. The pupils played on the Zoombinis games for an average of 15 minutes; the other games were played for an average of 10 minutes. It was noted in the observation sheets that the pupils remained more engaged with the Zoombinis games. They were often observed talking with a high degree of animation about the challenges and continued to play without pause until they were instructed to stop by the teacher.
>
> It was also noted that when one pupil was playing Zoombinis, other pupils were drawn from what they were doing to watch and comment. This game produced more collaboration, peer interaction and conversation than any other. This was particularly evident when new Zoombinis games were introduced. The most confident and skilled players led the games and remained in control of the mouse. Other pupils gave help and advice where they were able; little conflict or argument occurred. Some pupils simply observed and waited until they had an opportunity to play the game more privately. The pupils were happy to ask for help from those who had demonstrated expertise. However, little help was sought from the staff other than to read the initial instructions.

In this example Jo has given evidence numerically, by observation of their use, to justify that Zoombibis were the most requested games, as well as by asking the children directly about their preferences; this double approach strengthens the reliability of her evidence. She has further enhanced this by giving qualitative analysis from observations about the students' behaviour, which would have been lost if she had presented only tables, and which is vital to assess overall success. I believe Jo's study exemplifies the way data from a small-scale piece of research can be analysed by both qualitative and quantitative methods that complement each other.

Key points

Strauss and Corbin 1998 (Hopkins, 2002: 130) advise classroom researchers of four important steps.

- Obtain valid and reliable data.
- Recognise, and where possible, avoid bias in interpreting and presenting data. Explain why you take the steps you do.
- Critically analyse the data – and choose methods to communicate what you believe is most important.
- Try to view what you have from the perspectives of others. Then you can approach an evaluation of whether you have communicated the essential information.

References

Drever, E. (1995) *Using Semi-structured Interviews in Small Scale Research: A Teacher's Guide*. Edinburgh: SCRE.

Freeman, D. (1998) *Doing Teacher Research*. London: Heinle & Heinle.

Hopkins, D. (2002) *A Teacher's Guide to Classroom Research* (3rd edn). Maidenhead: Open University Press.

Macintyre, C. (2000) *The Art of Action Research in the Classroom*. London: Fulton.

Miles, M. and Huberman, M. (1994) *Qualitative Data Analysis*. London: Sage.

Chapter 25

Discussing friction

Anna Traianou

In this chapter, an extract from Anna Traianou's book *Understanding Teacher Expertise in Primary Science* arising from her doctoral thesis, Anna writes of an observation of a teacher, Coral, during a science lesson. The focus is on the way Coral discusses 'friction' with a class of 10 to 11 year olds, many of whom speak English as an additional language. Here, we present the initial part of the lesson which, in real time, lasted some 15 minutes. Although short in time, this part of Coral's lesson is not short on observational detail and exemplifies the important understandings that can arise from close observation of teaching and learning. We feel that the chapter provides insights into the nature of one teacher's teaching and the way she reaches out, often in exploratory ways, from her own understanding of friction to link with the children's thinking. We also note the way in which Coral encourages children to freely express their own thoughts which, of course, she cannot plan for or anticipate and which therefore requires that she too becomes a classroom learner.

As Coral indicated in her class diary, this early part of her lesson aims to generate children's interest in investigating friction. She achieves this by encouraging the children to offer their own explanations and ideas about friction in their responses to the following questions that were posed by her:

> What do you think has got lots of friction? What do you think has got less friction? What sort of things?

Some of the children's responses are offered as a tentative outcome of a practical test which was thought up and immediately carried out by the children. For example, one child (Paul), pushes his rubber across his table and reports his observation to Coral:

Paul When I push the rubber across the table it is difficult [Paul is actually pushing the rubber across this table].

Sense Publishers for permission to reprint an extract from *Understanding Teacher Expertise in Primary Science*, Anna Traianou, 2007.

Coral If you pick up a rubber [Coral picks up a rubber and she asks Paul if the particular rubber is okay for her to use. She then pushes it across the table surface which is at the front of the class]. It is very hard to push it across the table ... so you can say that there is a lot of friction there.

Paul does not seem to be certain whether what he has observed is an example of something that has got a lot of friction. He waits for Coral's response to his observation. At the same time, Coral does not appear to have a ready answer. Her answer develops as she increases her own understanding of what the child has observed. Thus, she repeats the practical test herself and she decides that pushing the rubber across the table can be an example of something that has got a lot of friction.

Although Coral has now given an answer to Paul's observation, this practical test generates a lot of discussion. Some of the children try to explain why there is a lot of friction between the rubber and the table. These explanations are not responses to a question asked by Coral. Rather, they are initiatives which aim to elaborate Coral's answer: 'there is a lot of friction because ...'. Children's explanations appear to be based on their everyday experiences of how specific objects and materials behave (for example rubber, plastic table, fabric):

Graham Miss... it's the same material ... it's like Paul says ... it's rubber and it's plastic on the table and plastic is like rubber and there is a lot of friction.
Coral So you think if two things are the same that will make a lot of friction. So what do you think will make less friction?
Graham Something like a fabric.
Coral Something like a fabric ... Sharleen.

Coral accepts Graham's explanation about the effect of having two similar materials upon the amount of friction between them, but she does not evaluate his idea. She seems to want to explore the pupil's idea further and for this reason she repeats the question 'What do you think will make less friction?' An interpretation of Coral's decision to find out more about Graham's thinking is that she is not entirely convinced that his idea is plausible.

During this time, some of the children in the classroom appear to repeat Paul's practical task (pushing their rubbers across the table) and one child in particular reports to Coral that her result is different from Paul's. This child (Sharleen) claims that it is easy to push the rubber across the table. Coral recognises a conflict between the children's observations and she decides to resolve it. She repeats the practical test and this time agrees with Sharleen's observation. At the same time another child (Kathleen) expresses the view that two objects that are made of similar materials do not have a lot of friction between them. Coral then turns to Graham and presents him with the evidence from Sharleen's observation, her own understanding, and Kathleen's idea about the effect of two similar materials upon the amount of friction. It is left to Graham (and to the rest of the children) to decide whether to accept the evidence provided or not. It is not clear why Coral decided to agree with Sharleen's observation. An interpretation of her response could be that Coral's ideas developed as the discussion about the effect of two similar materials upon the amount of friction developed or clarified.

The opening questions asked by Coral thus led to a discussion of a problem which was initiated by a child. The discussion, which involved many of the children in the classroom, led Coral to modify her initial response to Paul's problem. Both the teacher and the children seemed to 'co-construct' their understanding of the problem through their participation in the same activity. In turn, the problem shares some of the features of what is called within a sociocultural view of learning a 'dilemma', in that it is perceived by learners as a problem which has no unique solution. The children's willingness to extend the discussion suggests that the problem is personally meaningful to them because it is related to their experiences. Furthermore, the ways in which they participate in the discussion, by repeating the practical test and by offering their ideas and explanations, suggest that they are aware of how to make progress towards solving the problem. Coral's role is to accept and explore the different sorts of evidence and explanations offered until a tentative answer is found, even though it does not resolve all the conflicts (Graham, for example, is still left to sort out his views). Coral maintains her role as an authority in the classroom, in the sense that she is recognised by the children as the one who is expected to be the knowledgeable adult. Children respond to her and not to the particular children who ask the questions or offer explanations, and they expect Coral to give the final answer.

The outcome of the discussion concerns the effect of different materials on the amount of friction between surfaces. This emerged in relation to specific materials and in a specific context. During this time, only one child (Graham) seems to have been using the term 'friction'. The other children do not use the term in their explanations or observations, although Coral herself keeps using the term.

At this point, Coral asks again the initial question 'What things do you think have got less friction?' The question generates a number of responses which seem to represent children's everyday understanding:

Coral Now what things do you think have got less friction? Simon.
Simon Ice [other children say 'ice' at the same time].
Coral Right ice. Simon what do you think about ice then?
Simon Miss, it's easy to move.
Coral Right. Paul.
Paul You can't test it like card or other solids because when it slides along it gets water on it.
Coral However cold it is as soon as you have it out it starts melting. Well there is another reason you can't test ice today and that is we haven't got any.

As we can see, Coral accepts the children's responses about ice and she uses an additional question to explore their understanding, 'What do you think about ice then?' The first response seems to be a confirmation of the idea that ice has got very little friction. The second response is procedural, it says that it is difficult to compare ice with solid materials because ice melts. Both responses are accepted as valid by Coral. Following this, a hypothesis is offered by a child (Graham) based on a practical test which the child is carrying out in the classroom:

Graham If you push something really rough like my shoe it doesn't slide but on this floor it slides very easily.

Laura Miss, it's the floor, it's because it's a bit dirty that's why it's slippy [several children talk together].

Coral So if it's covered by little bits of dirt they act like ball bearings. Sharleen.

Graham notices that it is easy to slide his shoe across the classroom floor. However, he seems surprised by this because his understanding is that something 'rough' like his shoe should not slide easily. Before Coral replies to his idea another child (Laura) offers an explanation. Coral accepts and reformulates this explanation to make a scientific point. She uses a ball bearings analogy to explain how the use of particular materials helps to reduce the friction between different surfaces.

Next, Paul is pushing a piece a paper on his table and he observes that the paper slides along and then flips up:

Paul Miss when I push this paper on the table, the paper slides along and there isn't much friction.

Coral Come and do it on the floor. Paul is just going to push a piece of paper. He says that the paper slides very easily. It can't have enough friction. [Paul pushes the piece of paper, the paper slides along the floor and it flips up]

Coral What's happening there?

Rosie Is it gravity?

Coral So what's getting in the way of that paper?

Sam The air is getting in the way.

Coral Well I think that's what's happening to Paul. The air is getting in the way. So, if you've got air resistance it doesn't push up. It only pushes up when things are moving down. If you've got something moving that way the air resistance pushes it back that way [Coral shows the direction of the air resistance when things are moving horizontally]

In this extract, Paul is employing his developing understanding that friction is a force which opposes movement and that the less friction there is between two surfaces the easier it is for an object to slide, to explain his observation about the sliding of the paper on the table. This is the second time during the session that the term 'friction' is used by children in their explanations. Coral accepts Paul's observation but she decides to explore it further. She asks Paul to repeat the practical test in the front of the classroom. The paper slides along the floor and flips up. The 'flipping up' of the paper is the result of the force of air resistance, which depends on the surface area and the shape of the object. The concept of air resistance was discussed in detail in the first session on forces in the context of falling objects. Coral decides that Paul's observation is an opportunity to consolidate children's learning about air resistance. She then asks the children to explain what is happening.

It is clear from the transcript that Coral is searching for the 'right' answer here. One child says 'Is it gravity?' but her response is not validated. Coral gives another clue which aims to help the children recall the information she is looking for: 'What is getting in the way of that paper?' A child (Sam) offers the right answer. Coral then explains how the force of air resistance acts upon objects which move horizontally. Unlike the problem posed by the child earlier (pushing the rubber across the table), which generated a lot of discussion, this problem does not appear to initiate a large number of responses from the other children.

Furthermore, the kind of responses offered by the children in each case is different. During the discussion of the first problem children's responses seem to represent their everyday ideas and experience. During the discussion of the second problem, children appear to be trying to recall the correct scientific term (for example, 'Is it gravity?'). This is perhaps related to the way in which Coral deals with each problem. When Coral and the children were discussing the friction between the rubber and the table, Coral kept the discussion in the context of children's experience and her final response was the result of shared understanding between her and the children in the classroom. Indeed, in that situation, she did not appear to know the answer in terms of a straightforward application of a specific scientific concept. In the second case, the questions asked and the exchanges between the children and the teacher suggest that Coral knows the answer and this is provided by her, expressed in scientific language.

The discussion about air resistance could not have been planned beforehand. It emerged from a child's practical experience. Coral's understanding of the forces involved when objects move horizontally enables her to recognise an appropriate context to discuss this.

Coral's expertise is enacted in a different way during the following episode. Sue is asking a question about the friction between a ball and the ground. This question (or problem) is a response to Coral's question about 'What things have got less friction':

Sue Miss ... when you kick a ball there is friction there.
Coral Friction from what? on the ground you mean?
Sue Yes.
Coral Let's think about it. Let's think of a ball, just an ordinary ball, a tennis ball [several children say 'a tennis ball'].
You are talking about kicking a ball and it is going across the ground like that [Coral rolls a tennis ball across the table in the front of the class].
Paul Rolling miss.
Coral Friction is the force which stops things from moving. So the ball is moving and friction is stopping it.
Sue It's like a wheel.
Coral It is like a wheel. So what is the difference between a ball and a wheel and something that slides across?
Paul It rolls.
Coral So the difference is something to do with...
Adele Roundness.
Coral Yes, the fact that it has got all different bits on the ground all the time. Every little tiny bit it moves it's got a different bit of it on the ground [Coral rolls the ball across her arm] so it hasn't got force for a certain sort of time. So the rolling ball will never get off the friction I don't think.
Paul Miss can you put it on our table?
Coral Yes [Coral takes the tennis ball to Paul's table].

Sue asks a question about the friction between a ball and the ground. Coral's response, 'Let's think about it', invites the children to offer their explanations. At the same time her response is inventive and resourceful. She picks up a tennis ball and rolls it across the table at the front of the class. Some children begin to describe the situation ('It rolls', 'It's like a wheel'). Coral then uses her scientific understanding that friction is a force which opposes movement to explain a new situation, the rolling of the ball. She asks the children to think about the difference between rolling and sliding, and one child says 'roundness'. Coral accepts this answer and reformulates it to involve the concept of friction as a force which opposes movement. In this way, she relates children's everyday ideas to her own subject knowledge and produces a tentative answer. At the same time she seems to develop her own understanding at least to the extent that this is applied to the context created by Sue's question.

Coral's response to Sue's question differs from the way she responded earlier when she was encouraging children to offer their explanations. One interpretation of this is that it arises from Coral's personal interest in understanding the question. By making her thinking explicit to the children she offers the children a way to make connections between the scientific discourse and everyday situations. Paul's request to have the tennis ball on his table suggests that he wanted to repeat the experience for himself, which is an indication that the problem of the tennis ball is meaningful to him.

Discussion

In Coral's teaching, the elicitation of children's ideas, and the generation of their interest in investigating friction, took place during classroom discussion that focused on a range of practical activities or questions which were generated by the children, as a response to Coral's initial request to think about things that have less friction and things that have a lot of friction.

In this respect, Coral's expertise suggests a Piagetian view about the learner: in order to encourage children's learning, the problem that they are to investigate needs to be generated by the children, and not to be given to them by the teacher. It also seems to relate to the sociocultural idea that in order for learning to be effective, the children need to be engaged in activities that are personally meaningful to them. It is indicative of the learning environment that Coral has created in her classroom that soon after she asked the initial questions about friction, one child suggested and immediately carried out a practical investigation into the friction between a rubber and a table, which, in turn, initiated other children's interest in the problem, or generated other problems and questions.

Coral looked for opportunities in what the children said or did that could increase their interest in frictional phenomena and help them articulate their thinking about such phenomena. Her expertise enabled her to do this effectively. However, Coral enacted her expertise according to her judgment of learning opportunity. In the problem about the friction between the rubber and the table, she acted as a member of a classroom community of learners that were trying to solve a problem which did not have an immediately obvious solution. Thus, her role was to explore together with the children evidence and possible explanations, until a tentative answer to the problem was found which, nevertheless, did not resolve all the conflicts. Moreover, during this discussion, Coral made her own uncertainties explicit to the children, offering them in this way, opportunities to experience the uncertain nature of scientific inquiry. Later on during this phase, a child's question about the friction between the ground and the sand was interpreted by Coral as an opportunity to make a scientific point about friction. And, to achieve this, she used the ball bearing analogy to draw similarities between the ways in which the pieces of sand move against the ground.

One child asked Coral a question about the friction between a ball and the ground. Coral decided to respond to that child's question despite the fact that rolling friction was not part of her learning objectives or part of the primary Science National Curriculum. Her response was inventive and resourceful. She picked up a tennis ball, engaged children in discussion and used her own experiences about rolling friction, and children's experiences about wheels, to produce a tentative explanation. In doing this she appeared to develop to some extent her own understanding of rolling friction together with the children.

Chapter 26

Understanding evaporation and condensation

Georgina Harcourt-Brown

Primary school children learn about the water cycle through practical activities. In school they often learn about condensation and evaporation together as reversible changes, and of course many children also develop ideas about these scientific processes through their everyday experiences at home. In this chapter, Georgina Harcourt-Brown talks with children from Reception to Year 6 about their understanding of condensation and evaporation as they engage in four different hands-on experiments.

This enquiry explores age-related developments in children's scientific understandings, and in the experiments children's talk reveals a number of their misconceptions. We included this chapter because it gives examples of practical activities which adults can carry out with children in order to discover what they know, understand and what they may misunderstand. Based on her observations, the author makes recommendations for progression in teaching specific scientific concepts in order to better support children's learning in this important subject area.

Why did I investigate this?

Analysis of the progression of ideas has shown that children hold a variety of views about science concepts before formal teaching. Although children's ideas are personal, ideas often fall into groupable misconceptions (SPACE Reports, e.g. Russell and Watt 1990) suggesting that children have a common pattern of cognitive development. We need to be aware of what children's ideas and misconceptions are, as learning is affected by the pre-existing ideas that children bring to the classroom. Analysis of the progression of children's ideas can provide useful information about the ideas children are likely to hold at each age, which can then be used to plan effective lessons. Evaporation and condensation are key scientific concepts and their comprehension has wider implications for understanding many other processes. Complete comprehension requires knowledge of important concepts such as conservation of water and air, phase changes and the particulate nature of matter; therefore most pupils will not understand this

Primary Science Today for kind permission to reprint 'Progression in children's ideas about evaporation and condensation', Georgina Harcourt-Brown, 2004 in *Primary Science Today*, Issue 24.

process fully until the end of their secondary education. However, they are phenomena encountered in everyday life and are an integral part of the water cycle, so even the youngest children will be familiar with them. Therefore the progression of understanding of evaporation and condensation occurs over the whole period of pupils' formal education.

Evaporation and condensation are challenging phenomena to explain: because the child must understand the conservation of water, it can be counter intuitive that water can disappear or appear. This can only be understood if the child can conceive the presence of water in a state that cannot be seen or felt, which requires the ability to conceptualise events that are not perceptible. Therefore, the progression of understanding of evaporation and condensation is connected to the development of general cognitive abilities, so analysis of the progression of children's ideas about evaporation and condensation can provide insights to children's cognitive development and learning.

How did I find out?

The ideas of primary school pupils from Reception, Year 2, Year 4, and Year 6 were gathered. Four pupils from each year group were interviewed. As the youngest children in the study were only five, children's ideas were elicited using an individual open-ended oral interview. The interviews were recorded and later transcribed.

Each child was interviewed about their views on the four events below:

1. *Water evaporating from a glass at room temperature*
   A glass was filled with water to a marked level in the presence of the child. The glass was then left for one week in a visible place in the classroom.
2. *Drying a wet paper towel*
   The child made a wet hand print on a paper towel at the beginning of the interview. By the time the child was interviewed on this activity the towel had dried.
3. *Condensation forming on the outside of a glass of cold water*
   The child was shown a cold glass of water, and told it had been in the fridge. The outside of the glass was then wiped dry in the presence of the child. The child was then asked to observe what happened.
4. *Condensation formed as the result of breathing on a mirror and its subsequent evaporation*
   The child was given a mirror and asked to breathe on it and was then asked to see what had formed on the mirror and watch what then happened to it.

Each of these events lends itself to this research as they can be conducted in a short amount of time and can be demonstrated during the interview. This gives the child concrete evidence to comment upon, and does not require the child to remember events from the past.

The interview questions aimed to find out the following aspects of a child's views on evaporation and condensation: where they think the water has gone/come from, what they think made it go, whether the process can be made to happen faster or slower. The questions were open ended, and phrasing was given careful consideration to avoid providing any information or constraining the child's response. For example instead of asking 'Where did the water come from?' which tells the child the condensation is made of water, the question was phrased 'Where does it come from?' and instead of asking questions such as 'Where has the water gone?' which constrains the child's response to one that suggests a new location for the water, the child was asked 'What has happened to the water that was here before?' allowing the child to respond that the water no longer exists.

Children were asked to clarify what they meant if any of the following words were used: evaporation, condensation, disappeared, dissolved, dry/dried, shrunk as each of these words has a specific meaning to adults but may have a different meaning to the child. The words that a child used to describe condensation or water vapour were also clarified by asking children 'What is it made of?' These clarifications allow a clearer impression of what the child's ideas are to be gained than if the interviewer assumes the child has the same meanings of words as themself.

What did I find out?

Children's ideas about evaporation

1 *Evaporation from a glass of water at room temperature*

Children were asked what they thought had happened to the missing water. Their responses to this question fell into four categories:

A. Don't know.
B. It had moved to a downward location as water, e.g. the floor.
C. It had moved to an upward location *as water*, e.g. the sky, clouds.
D. It had 'evaporated', i.e. *changed to vapour* and gone into the air.

The number of children expressing each view was scaled against their age. Children in Reception and Year 2 could describe that the water level had gone down, but usually did not attempt to explain why. These children did not understand that water is conserved and so did not see any importance in accounting for the missing water and had no opinion about the new location of the water. The number of children that attempted to explain what had happened increased with age. If an explanation was given by the younger children it was that the water had moved to a downwards location. This idea shows understanding of the conservation of water, but does not involve a phase change, and so can be explained in simple terms.

For example: **Lewis, Reception:**

Interviewer: What has happened?
Lewis: The water came out.
Interviewer: What has happened to the water that's come out?
Lewis: It's gone on to the floor

This type of explanation is used by children in all year groups except Year 6. The next explanation to be given is the view that is closest to the scientifically correct explanation. Children only express this view in Year 4 and Year 6.

For example: **Thomas, Year 4:**

Interviewer: What has happened to the missing water?
Thomas: It's turned to steam.
Interviewer: Where is the steam now?
Thomas: Outside, disappeared.
Interviewer: When you say it's disappeared, does it still exist?
Thomas: Yes, but you can't see it anymore and you don't know where it is.

This view is more complex. It requires confident use of the conservation principle and the child must be capable of abstract thought. If can only be understood if mental concepts are developed about events that cannot be perceived.

2 *Drying of a wet paper towel*

Children in Reception generally made no attempt to explain how the paper towel dries, replicating the results of the evaporation of water from a glass. The response 'It dries' seemed a sufficient explanation to these children. Unlike the responses to the previous problem, all older children gave some explanation of what had happened and attempted to account for the location of the missing water. 75% of these children suggested that the water was inside the dry paper towel. When compared to the 0% of children who suggested the water had been absorbed in the previous experiment it can be seen that children's ideas about this event are context specific.

Of the children who thought the water was inside the paper towel, 75% used the term the water had 'soaked in' or been 'soaked up'. This is an example of a scientific misconception that has formed through of the use of everyday phrases. This conversation with **Ryan, Year 6,** shows how everyday language has led him to think that when a paper towel dries the water goes into the paper towel.

Interviewer: What has happened to the water?
Ryan: It is inside there (paper towel).
Interviewer: Why has that happened?
Ryan: Because paper towels are made to soak water up, it just soaks all the water inside of it.

This is an excellent example of how children's ideas can be a result of direct everyday experience and was shown by many of the children. Ryan's ideas also have another characteristic typical to children's ideas: he can explain the scientific phenomenon of evaporation correctly about water evaporating from a glass, but has not linked this knowledge to the drying process. Instead he added this to his conceptions alongside the idea of water being soaked up by the paper towel that works in everyday situations.

Children's responses in the interview about water drying from a paper towel were too context specific to determine the stages of progression in understanding evaporation. However, if the small number of children that did not express the idea that water is soaked up by the paper towel are considered, the results are similar to that of water evaporating from the glass.

A common misconception held by children is that heat is essential for evaporation. All Year 4 and Year 6 children mentioned heat as an important factor in evaporation, as did half of Year 2 and a quarter of Reception children.

For example **Kurt, Year 6:**

Interviewer: What does evaporation mean?
Kurt: If means the sun or heat's got to it and it's turned into water vapour and it's evaporated.

Out of these children only one child, a Year 6, thought that evaporation could occur in the absence of heat.

The view that heat is essential for drying the paper towel may be the result of direct everyday experience; children will have seen wet clothes being put in tumble dryers and on radiators, and things being put in a warm place to dry. This could result in children thinking it has to be warm for something to dry. The observation of boiling water may influence children's ideas about evaporation in some situations and this could be another reason children associate the process of evaporation with heat.

For example **Kurt, Year 6:**

Interviewer: What makes it [the water in the glass] evaporate?
Kurt: The sun and stuff.
Interviewer: How do they make it evaporate?
Kurt: They heat it up and like when you cook something it gets really hot and turns to steam, so it's got quite hot and turned to steam.

However, the view that heat is essential for evaporation prevails after children have been taught about evaporation. As '52% of teachers thought that evaporation from puddles is the same process as boiling' and '72% thought that puddles can only evaporate if they get energy from outside the puddle' (Pendlington *et al.*, 1993) this view could be a result of teacher's misconceptions being taught to pupils.

Children's ideas about evaporation progress as follows. First there is a shift from description to explanation. The youngest children make no attempt to describe what has happened to the missing water. As a child starts to understand that water cannot disappear it attempts to give a location for the missing water, this is when the child progresses to the explanation that the water has moved downwards. The next stage in the progression of ideas occurs when the child understands the transformation of water into vapour that goes into the air. This stage first occurs in Year 4. The final stage in the primary age range in the progression to being able to explain evaporation in specific circumstances, is being able to recognise it in various circumstances.

Children's ideas about condensation

3 *Condensation on the outside of a cold glass*

Most children could not correctly identify the condensation as water. The number of children who could identify the condensed water on a glass increased with age.

Other responses given were that the condensation on the outside of the glass was air, cold air, cold air mixed with warm air, ice and water, and coldness. Although a progression in ideas about where the water comes from cannot be identified, a progression in children's ideas about other aspects of condensation can be seen.

Three-quarters of children in Reception could not identify the condensation on the outside of a glass without guidance. This could be due to a lack of observational skills, but more likely it could be because the children do not recognise condensation on a glass as a phenomenon; it is just what happens, not something with a cause or explanation. They are therefore confused by being asked to look at it, as they don't understand what they are looking at.

For example **Natalie, Reception:**

Interviewer: Can you see anything on the outside of the glass?
Natalie: No.
Interviewer wipes the glass with a finger and discusses how it is being wiped away, but there is still some left in other places.
Interviewer: Can you see it now?
Natalie: Yes.
Interviewer: What is it?
Natalie: [No response]
Interviewer: What is it made of?
Natalie: Your fingers.

The response 'Your fingers' shows that Natalie still does not really understand the question she is being asked. She can see the lines being made on the glass by the interviewer's fingers, but does not realise these are the result of the condensation being wiped away. This conversation shows how Reception children were very confused when asked about condensation, suggesting that to them it is not a phenomenon and so they have no concepts about it. The children in Reception were therefore not even at an observational stage where they could describe what had happened.

By Year 2 the children recognised the condensation on the glass and understood the interview questions. Only one child identified the water but three children had ideas about the conditions that cause condensation. Three made reference to temperature being important for example that the condensation is made of 'cold air' or happens because the glass is cold. In Year 4, two children identified the condensation as water and all of them suggested that the coldness of the glass was important. By Year 6, some children had progressed to understanding that the condensation was a result of a temperature difference between the air and the glass, however still only three out of four could identify the condensation as water. Therefore progression in the level and accuracy of explanations about condensation is evident. However, even the children who identified that condensation as a result of a temperature difference between the air and the glass were often confused about what causes condensation. A child who had the best understanding knew that condensation was water vapour from the air and that it formed because the air was warmer than the glass. This was an unusually good understanding of the process, but even he gave some very confused responses to questions, such as 'the cold water (in the glass) is like frozen and the water vapour combines with that.' A more typical example of a response including both heat and cold is **Ryan, Year 6**. He understands that condensation is the result of warm meeting cold, but he expresses a variety of confused ideas and the meaning of the word condensation is not clear to him.

Interviewer: What do you notice?
Ryan: It's all smeared up, little bubbles.
Interviewer: What do you think it's made of?
Ryan: Air.
Interviewer: Why do you think there's air on the glass?
Ryan: Because it's cold air mixed with warm air making them little bubbles.
Interviewer: Where's the cold air come from?
Ryan: The fridge and the water, it's like condensation sort of thing. The cold air mixes with the warm air and makes the outside like water.
Interviewer: So the stuff on the outside, you said it was called condensation. What's condensation made out of?
Ryan: Cold air and warm air mixed together.
Interviewer: And the cold comes from the glass being cold?
Ryan: No, because the water's cold and the glass was warm before you put it in the fridge.

4 *Condensation of water vapour as a result of breathing on a mirror*

Only two children could identify the condensation as water in this event. A pattern of understanding was identified on the basis of children's reasons why evaporation was formed, as opposed to where the water came from. Children in Reception could identify the condensation, unlike condensation formed on the outside of a cold glass, but they lacked the vocabulary of the older children to describe it. The Reception children gave responses such as 'It does that' or 'I don't know what it's called'. The children in the older years all could find words to describe what had happened, often using the phrase 'steamed up'. This shows that the first progression is from being able to observe what has happened to being able to describe what has happened. This shift is facilitated by an increased vocabulary. The next progression is from describing the event to suggesting explanations for it. This occurs as children get older, and the number giving no explanation decreases with increasing age. Younger children give two explanations why the condensation can be seen on the mirror: because their breath is warm, or because the mirror is reflective or 'see through'. These explanations occur in equal numbers at Years 2 and 4.

When this information is triangulated with ideas expressed about the condensation of water on a cold glass, the conclusion is that it is probable that these explanations are a guess that seems plausible. This is still an important stage in the child's progression; it is a stage where they will attempt to explain events, even if they do not know the answer. The next view that children expressed was the one closest to the scientifically correct view, that condensation forms as the result of warm breath being blown onto a cold mirror. This was only expressed by two of the Year 6 children.

The progression of ideas about condensation that this research has identified is a very general progression with age. The child moves from having no ideas about the phenomenon at four to five years old, to then being able to describe it at six to seven years old. There is then an increase with age in the number of children who attempt to explain why condensation forms. The accuracy of this explanation increases with age. This progression is an example of how children move from description to explanation. It can also be seen that children develop their ideas from being specific to one situation to being linked to many situations. This progression was also seen for views about evaporation.

What are the implications of my findings?

This research has shown that children have ideas about scientific processes that are modified and progress with time. It has also shown what ideas children hold about evaporation and condensation at different ages throughout the primary school. Although it is important that teachers and support staff are confident in their understanding of evaporation and condensation so that they do not pass on misconceptions to pupils, children's ideas nave been shown to be the result of many experiences encountered. By being aware of these ideas teachers can provide new information and experiences at the appropriate level for their class. For example, children of about six years old are likely to think that evaporation occurs as a result of water moving downwards. Therefore, at this age range children could test this theory. However at this age teaching them that water can change from liquid to gas would be of little use as they would not associate it with the changing water level of a glass of water over time. Therefore the progression of children's ideas identified in this research could be used for planning what to teach children and when to teach it.

The progression in children's ideas about evaporation shows that young children think in a concrete manner, and that the ability to think in an abstract manner slowly develops over the primary school age range. This is confirmed by the order of development of the understanding of condensation, which appears to develop even more slowly than the understanding of evaporation. Within this shift from concrete to abstract thought there are progressions from descriptive to explanatory ideas. Children's descriptive ideas about condensation are often wrong, as they do not know the condensation is water. As this descriptive idea is wrong, it follows that when they progress to having ideas that explain the phenomenon these are also wrong. The formation of condensation cannot be understood without knowing that it is water that is condensing. Therefore it is important that we start children's education about condensation by ensuring that all children know that condensation is water.

Children's ideas start as ideas that are specific to certain contexts, They are then developed to link ideas to gain an overall understanding of how events and phenomenon are interrelated. Evaporation and condensation cannot be understood fully until certain pieces of information are understood and linked together. For example, to understand condensation it must be known that water vapour is permanently in the air. It must also be understood that water vapour can change state into water, and that this can occur as a result of cooling the water vapour. To understand the big picture about how all these link together the child must understand them individually. We therefore need to teach the components of the process before the whole process can be taught.

The results of this research suggest that evaporation should be taught before condensation, rather than concurrently as reversible changes. Evaporation is simpler to understand than condensation as it does not require knowledge of the permanent existence of water vapour in the air, and it does not require a temperature change. Children therefore should be taught about evaporation first. When they have a thorough understanding of this process, learning about condensation will be easier as they will only have to reverse a process that they are already familiar with. The only new pieces of information to be learnt are the conditions required, i.e. the existence of water vapour in the air, and cooling of the air.

Although this was a small study, it has produced reliable and valuable information about children's ideas about evaporation and condensation. The above suggestions for teaching could help to improve children's understanding of evaporation and condensation. This is important, as it is a fundamental aspect of science.

Bibliography

Driver, R., Guesne, E. and Tiberghien, A. (eds) (1985) *Children's Ideas in Science,* Open University Press.

Harlen, W. (2000) *Helping Development of Scientific Ideas.* Teaching of Science in Primary Schools David Fulton.

Johnson, P. and Gott, R. (1996) Constructivism and evidence from children's ideas. *Science Education* 80, 5, pp. 561–577.

Pendlington, S., Palacio, D. and Summers, M. (1993) *Understanding materials and why they change.* Primary School Teachers and Science Project, Oxford University Department of Educational Studies and Westminster College.

Russell, T. and Watt, D. (1990) *Primary SPACE Project Research Report, Evaporation and Condensation,* Liverpool University Press.

Tytler, R. (2000) A comparison of year 1 and year 6 students' conceptions of evaporation and condensation: dimensions of conceptual progression. *International Journal of Science Education* 22, 5, pp. 447–467.

Chapter 27

Knowing children's literature

Sue McGonigle and Olivia O'Sullivan

Do you read children's books? What do you know about children's authors? How does your knowledge of children's books help you to support children's reading development? These questions sparked the Power of Reading research project which began in 2005 at the Centre for Literacy in Primary Education. As of September 2009 the Power of Reading has involved more than 33,000 children, their teachers and teaching assistants, in more than 900 primary schools from Cumbria to Southampton and from Bristol to Hastings.

We have included a chapter on the key approaches and findings from the Power of Reading because it is a powerful combination of research and intervention, where primary school practitioners first audit their knowledge of children's literature, read for themselves a wider range of children's texts, and introduce to their classrooms new approaches and resources to promote children's reading development. Findings from the Power of Reading demonstrate that improvements in personal and professional knowledge of children's literature can have a significant positive effect on children's motivation and enthusiasm for books and reading, and on their literacy development in general. Key to these improvements is the enthusiasm that teachers, teaching assistants and other adults in school 'transmit' to children about books: when children are enthusiastic about reading, their rates of progress and achievement are higher. Moreover, as small-scale action research the Power of Reading promotes meaningful adult learning and professional development.

Reading, research and intervention

The Power of Reading developed in response to two observable trends: children's lack of engagement with reading and their decreasing attainment in reading, particularly for boys (Mullis *et al.*, 2003; Twist *et al.*, 2007). The apparent decline in children's motivation to read can be linked to a complex range of factors, including competing demands on children's time both at school and at home (Twist *et al.*, 2007) and changing patterns of literacy in families:

> Things have changed so much – when I was growing up there were only three channels on TV – we didn't have Play Stations and all of that. There's a lot of competition now for reading.
>
> (Teaching assistant, Southwark, 2007)

Another evident trend was that primary teachers seemed to lack knowledge about children's texts and as a consequence children's literature did not have priority in classrooms. In 2005 Power of Reading surveys, many teachers were unfamiliar with the wide range of children's poetry, picture books and award-winning novels such as *Skellig* by David Almond (Carnegie prize winner in 1999) and *The Other Side of Truth* by Beverley Naidoo (Carnegie prize winner in 2001). Teachers reported using a limited range of authors in the classroom, often ones that they remembered from their own childhood reading. For example 45% of 364 teachers surveyed in 2008 named Roald Dahl as their favourite author when they were children, and of these teachers 43% were currently or had recently read a Roald Dahl book to their classes. Only a minority of teachers had read new or current children's books themselves:

> If you don't have teachers who are readers then their impact on the children's reading is not as effective. Teachers have got to like reading themselves to be able to transfer the enthusiasm.
>
> (Literacy coordinator, Lewisham, 2006)

Teachers who participate in the Power of Reading begin by taking stock of their own knowledge about children's books, their experiences of reading and how they use children's literature in the classroom. You might like to do this yourself, and we have included the Power of Reading questionnaire at the end of this chapter (Figure 27.1). If you are not a teacher, you can reflect on the questionnaire in relation to your role in school and what you observe about the teaching of reading and book provision.

From this 'baseline', teachers extend their knowledge and experience of children's literature: they read books which challenge the adult reader such as *The Garbage King* by Elizabeth Laird, and they read a range of poetry, picture books and novels for use in the primary classroom. In 2008–09 only 16% of 210 teachers considered themselves knowledgeable or very knowledgeable about children's literature at the beginning of their involvement in the Power of Reading. By the end of the year this figure had increased to 95%:

> I feel I know a wider range of texts and I'm also using books I guess I wouldn't have used before. Even when I originally started reading *I Was a Rat* (Pullman, 2004) I thought it was possibly too complex for some of the children, and they've all got into it. They are really enjoying it.
>
> (Year 4 teacher, Hackney, 2006)

As they widen their knowledge of children's books, teachers are encouraged to carry out and sustain three interventions to support and promote children's reading:

1. create attractive book areas in their classrooms
2. read aloud to the class on a regular basis, within and outside literacy lessons
3. involve children in open-ended discussions about reading ('book talk').

As part of the research and intervention cycle, teachers measure the effect of these approaches on children's reading motivation and attainment by observing and keeping records on a small number of focus children as well as noting the impact on the whole class.

Whole texts not extracts

Prior to being involved in the Power of Reading many teachers had been using extracts of books to cover a range of literacy objectives. For example, in 2008–09 only 53% of a group of 40 teachers in Nottinghamshire reported using whole texts regularly; by the end of the year this figure had increased to 91%. Teachers report the value of being able to explore one carefully chosen book in depth over time, unfolding the book slowly so that children can 'step inside' the story, stopping to discuss particular aspects of language, characters and events:

> I haven't had so much fun for a long time ... from watching the children grow and books being a central part of their lives in school. They walk into class and they want to talk about books.
>
> (Year 2 teacher, Redbridge, 2008)

A book read aloud at the end of the day used to be taken for granted in primary classrooms but this practice declined in large part due to the overcrowded curriculum (Collins, 2005). Power of Reading teachers are encouraged to read aloud more often – both within literacy sessions and at other times during the school day. Teachers have reported that reading aloud has been especially significant in encouraging less experienced readers to engage with books, particularly boys. Children describe how hearing books read aloud helps their understanding:

> When you are reading yourself you focus on the words but listening to books being read means you can concentrate on the images that are being described.
>
> (Year 5 boy, Wandsworth, 2007)

Children particularly value the way that teachers 'perform' the book as they read aloud, bringing the page to life:

> She sort of does it in the character's voice and she makes noises of what's going on.
>
> (Year 5 boy, Lambeth, 2006)

Teachers and support staff may sometimes feel nervous about reading aloud but with practice become more confident, and this confidence and enjoyment is transmitted to the children. Teachers speak of reading aloud time as being 'special' and having an impact on relationships within the class:

> Children just love it when I read aloud, they absolutely adore it. The quality of silence and concentration is amazing as I've got more practiced. I start to engage them more with my eyes and I use gestures a lot. That's because I've been doing it so much, it's so much easier for me now.
>
> (Year 4 teacher, Southwark, 2007)

From children's responses it is clear that reading aloud helps them to engage with the book – to enter the story world. Because reading aloud involves children in books which they might not initially try or like, it can help children to develop personal tastes and preferences in reading. Reading aloud also deepens children's understanding, enabling them to imagine characters and settings by creating pictures in their minds. Reading aloud also exposes children to literary language which they might not be able to read and comprehend independently.

Book areas, book talk and longer teaching time

A book area with a wide range of texts displayed for children to read and browse is an important part of a primary classroom. It gives clear messages to children about how books and reading are valued. A key intervention in the Power of Reading is for teachers to review and develop their classroom reading environments and provision for reading, and to create exciting and well-organised reading corners. As a result, teachers have observed better use of book areas and increased motivation for reading:

> The reading corner in my classroom has become so popular that some children would rather stay and read in there than play football!
>
> (Year 5 teacher, Cumbria, 2008)

Support staff play a key role in developing and sustaining book corners; careful organization, labelling and displays of books help less experienced readers to find books they enjoy.

In busy classrooms it is easy to feel that time spent talking about books is a 'luxury' which cannot be afforded. Power of Reading teachers are introduced to methods of generating conversations about books, drawing in particular on the work of Aidan Chambers (1993). His work on 'book talk' starts from a simple sharing of responses: tell me what you like about this story, what you dislike, does anything puzzle you? Does this story remind you of any other story you know or anything that has happened to you? This approach demonstrates that the adult genuinely wants to know what the child thinks and encourages a sharing of responses which can develop into an interesting and open discussion. Teachers and teaching assistants have found this to be an effective way of generating talk which can be used in whole class discussions, when working with groups or with individual children.

Like adult reading groups, children's book groups provide informal opportunities for children to discuss books with teachers or teaching assistants. Children and adults alike enjoy the more informal atmosphere of the book group:

> At first, our discussions were quite stilted but after a few sessions the children became more confident and animated and many wanted to read aloud to the group. One boy, at the beginning of book club, was adamant that he didn't like reading, couldn't read, couldn't follow as we read aloud and did not want to read at home. A few weeks later, we saw him reading at breakfast club and he proudly volunteered, 'I'm on page 99, Miss!'
>
> (Two teachers from a Lambeth Primary School, 2008)

Using the three key interventions, teachers plan 2- to 6-week sequences of text-based literacy work which brings together reading, writing, speaking and listening, and active approaches to getting involved in a story or a poem such as drama, music, drawing, art work and dance. Working with extended teaching sequence based on books, teachers have noted both increased enthusiasm for writing and more developed use of the language of texts in children's writing:

> He is now a motivated reader and enjoys his reading. This has particularly become evident in his writing where he uses language and turns of phrase from his reading.
>
> (Year 6 teacher, Bexley, about a focus child, 2008)

Drama followed by writing in role (in the form of diaries, emails and letters) have been particularly significant ways of developing the skills of less experienced writers, particularly boys. Simple drama techniques such as hot seating, role play, conscience alley and thought tracking help children understand a character's feelings and motivation at key points in a narrative and can be an important preparation for writing, in particular writing in role as a character. Reading and performing poetry has also allowed children in their own texts to draw upon powerful images, settings and language, as this example written by two Year 5 children illustrates:

> *Fly Eagle Fly*
> Suddenly the world was ablaze with light
> Glittering gold
> Powerful sun in the sky
> Golden eagle stretching to the earth
> Magnificent claws
> Marvellous eagle stretching his wings
> Eagle clutching his claws on the rocks
> Great eagle on the high mountain
> Warmth giving life to the eagle
>
> (Year 5, Reinaldo and Ilayda, Hackney, based on *Fly Eagle Fly*, Gregorowski and Daly, 2008)

Drawing and art work have also played a central role in developing children's understanding of texts and teachers have noted the impact of drawing on children's writing:

> Drawing gets them inside the book in another way, deepens their responses, their understanding and their writing.
>
> (Teacher presentation, Lincolnshire, 2009)

> They couldn't have written the poems without the artwork.
>
> (Year 6 teacher, Lincolnshire, talking about his class's illustrations from *The Lady of Shalott*, Tennyson and Keeping, 1999)

As well as drawing in response to texts – recreating settings or events in the story – children can create annotated drawings of a character or maps of the story world; this is a form of drafting which many children find encouraging, enjoyable and useful.

Motivation and standards: books make a difference

Power of Reading teachers keep records of their classes and observe the progress of focus children. At the end of a year, a majority of teachers report on the transforming role of books, and creative teaching approaches in changing children's attitudes and achievement as readers and writers:

> September 2007: M is a reluctant, hesitant reader who considers himself to be bad at reading. He has a short attention span and groans at the prospect of writing . . . a nervous writer as well as a nervous reader.
>
> June 2008: We have been working with [the sophisticated picture book] *Varjak Paw* (Said, 2004) for 4 weeks now and he talks about the book a lot. It has really captured his imagination. He told me that when he hears cats fighting on his estate he imagines that it is Varjak and Ginger...
>
> (Teachers on a Year 4 focus child, Lambeth, at the beginning and end of the Power of Reading year 2007)

Over 5 years, data collected from classrooms show that children's reading motivation has changed in a number of ways in response to the key interventions: teacher knowledge about books, reading aloud, book talk, reading areas and extended teaching sequences. Common themes noted by teachers are that children:

- choose to read more often in school or at home
- talk about their reading to their teachers
- read at greater length or with greater focus
- are more confident to browse and choose books
- are more willing to seek out deeper meanings in texts
- show greater confidence in talking about books
- are more motivated to write.

Data from Power of Reading teachers for 2007–08 show that the percentage of focus children judged to be motivated 'can and do' readers increased from 50% to nearly 80% over a year, with the percentage increase for boys being over 7% greater than that for girls. Furthermore, data collected on children's National Curriculum attainment levels pre- and post-Power of Reading interventions show that whole classes made significant progress in reading. In 2008–09 in four Local Authorities:

- over 67% of children progressed by two or more National Curriculum sub levels in English
- over 33% progressed by three or more National Curriculum sub levels in English
- over 14% progressed by four or more National Curriculum sub levels in English.

The majority of these schools are in areas of high social need, have significant numbers of children eligible for free school meals and who use English as an additional language.

The Power of Reading draws upon a history of classroom-based research on the role of powerful texts in literacy learning, gender differences in literacy learning, and creative approaches to literacy pedagogy (Barrs and Cork, 2001; Safford *et al.*, 2004; Bunting *et al.*, 2005, 2006; Ellis and Safford, 2005; Safford and Barrs, 2005).

Its approaches to literacy teaching and learning reviewed here have involved whole schools, literacy coordinators, teachers, teaching assistants, pupils, and also parents who notice children's enthusiasm for reading. The pedagogic interventions – reading aloud, using whole texts, linked sequences of work, book areas and book talk – are practical and also, importantly for children and adults alike, they are pleasurable. The cycle of research and intervention demonstrates that improvements in personal and professional knowledge can result in positive changes to classroom practices and outcomes for children.

2009–10 The Power of Reading project Teacher Questionnaire Experience of Children's Literature	
Name	LA
School	Year Group
Number of years teaching	M/F
Role in school	
1. As a child Did you read children's books: Frequently ☐ Infrequently ☐ Not at all ☐ Name three of your favourite authors <u>as a child</u>: Name three of your favourite books <u>as a child</u>:	

Figure 27.1 Power of Reading Questionnaire

2. As a teacher

Do you keep up to date with children's literature by reading children's books:

Frequently ☐ Infrequently ☐ Not at all ☐

Name three of your favourite authors for children **now**:

Name three of your favourite books for children **now**:

3. How knowledgeable are you about children's literature?

Not very knowledgeable ☐

Fairly knowledgeable ☐

Knowledgeable ☐

Very knowledgeable ☐

4. Reading aloud

Do you read whole texts *(picture books, novels, short stories, poems)* **aloud to your class**

Daily ☐ Weekly ☐ Occasionally ☐ Not at all ☐

Figure 27.1 Continued

Name the book you are reading aloud now:

Name some of the books you read aloud last year:

How do you choose the books you read aloud to children?

5. Using children's literature within the literacy curriculum

In the last year have you used any **whole** texts (novels, poems, picture books) in your literacy planning?

If so name three of the texts you have used:

Do you base your literacy teaching on whole texts:

All the time	Mostly	Occasionally	Not at all
☐	☐	☐	☐

If you use a whole text – how long does the unit/sequence of work last?

Describe the main kinds of activities you have planned around them, e.g. drama

Figure 27.1 Continued

References

Barrs, M. and Cork, V. (2001). *The Reader and the Writer: The Links Between the Study of Literature and Writing Development at Key Stage 2*. London: Centre for Literacy in Primary Education.

Bunting, J., Nicholson, D. and Barrs, M. (2005). *BookPower Literacy through Literature, Year 5*. London: Centre for Literacy in Primary Education.

Bunting, J., Nicholson, D. and Barrs, M. (2006). *BookPower Literacy through Literature, Year 6*. London: Centre for Literacy in Primary Education.

Chambers, A. (1993). *Tell Me: Children Reading and Talk*. Thimble Press.

Collins, F. (2005). "She's sort of dragging me into the story!" Student teachers' experiences of reading aloud in Key Stage 2 classes. *Literacy*, April 2005, UKLA.

Ellis, S. and Safford, K. (eds) (2005). *Animating Literacy*. London: Centre for Literacy in Primary Education.

Graham, L. (1999). Changing Practice through Reflection: The KS2 Reading Project, *Croydon in Reading*. Vol. 33, no. 3, UKRA.

Mullis, I. V. S., Martin, M. O., Gonzalez, E. J. and Kennedy, A. M. (2003). *PIRLS 2001 International Report: IEA's Study of Reading Literacy Achievement in Primary School in 35 countries*. Boston, Mass: Boston College, International Study Center.

Safford, K., O'Sullivan, O. and Barrs, M. (2004). *Boys on the Margin*. London: CLPE.

Safford, K. and Barrs, M. (2005). *Many Routes to Meaning*. London: CLPE.

Twist, L., Schagen, I. and Hodgson, C. (2007). *Readers and Reading: The National Report for England* (2006) (PIRLS: Progress in International Reading Literacy Study) NFER/DCSF.

Children's books

Almond, D. (1998). *Skellig*. Hodder Children's Books

Gregorowski, C. and Daly, N. (2003). *Fly Eagle Fly*. Frances Lincoln.

Laird, E. (2003). *The Garbage King*. London: Macmillan.

Naidoo, B. (2000). *The Other Side of Truth*. London: Penguin.

Pullman, P. (2004). *I Was a Rat!: Or the Scarlet Slippers*. Corgi Yearling Books.

Sachar, L. (2004). *There's a Boy in the Girls' Bathroom*. Collins Educational.

Said, S. F. (2004). *Varjak Paw*. UK: Corgi Children's Books.

Woodson, J. (2004). *Locomotion*. Heinemann New Windmill.

Chapter 28

Children's online writing

Alison Kelly and Kimberly Safford

This chapter examines the nature of children's written contributions to a football weblog ('blog') during the 2006 World Cup. The information comes from a wider project which explored how a temporary, popular global sporting event could create opportunities for children's language development (Safford *et al.*, 2007[1]); it took place in two Year 6 classrooms and involved children, teachers, teaching assistants and university teacher-educators. We have included this chapter because the enquiry investigates how children can carry out 'real life' writing activities in the classroom.

The authors analyse children's online 'blogging' about football, in particular their ability to use complex sentence structures. Whilst children (and adults) use a range of grammatical forms routinely and unconsciously in speaking, being able to manipulate simple, compound and complex sentence structures on paper or screen is the mark of a skilled, confident writer. Concepts of audience and purpose – choosing words and sentences depending on who we write to and why we write – are central to literacy learning, and the authors use their data to discuss how blogging might refresh contexts for school writing and in particular the learning and teaching of grammar.

Kicking off...

> I think that if England are winning comfortably then I would put on Theo so he can get past the tired defenders. But if England were chasing the game, then I wouldn't put him on because it puts a lot of pressure on him and he'll get frustrated and lose the ball.

These are the words of eleven-year-old Alan, written during the World Cup, 2006. Alan is speculating as to whether the England captain, Sven Goran Eriksson, should try out the inexperienced young player, Theo Walcott. Alan was a reluctant writer, so our first response was one of delight at the enthusiasm and exuberance with which he articulated his opinion.

Literacy: A Journal of the United Kingdom Literacy Association for permission to reprint extracts from 'Does teaching complex sentences have to be complicated? Lessons from children's online writing', Alison Kelly and Kimberly Safford, *Literacy*, November 2009, 43, 3, 118–122. Reprinted by permission of the Journals of the United Kingdom Literacy Association.

A closer examination of Alan's writing reveals that this pupil, whose literacy folder in school was virtually empty, has expressed his ideas using multi-clause complex sentences which include adverbial clauses of condition, reason and result. What was making this difference to Alan's writing? He, and two Year 6 classes, were blogging; Alan was contributing to an online football web-log. Alan's contributions to the football blog prompted us to delve more deeply into the digital data from the World Cup project.

A byte about blogs

Blogging – online writing – is a world wide phenomenon: in 2006 *The Guardian* reported that one in four internet users make daily online blog entries. For many adults and teenagers blogging is a way of life and blogs flourish for all occasions and audiences: there are political blogs, events which trigger blogs, celebrity blogs ... the list is endless. However, despite this blogging fervour, little has been reported on the use of blogs in the primary school and the language of primary-aged bloggers. Huffaker (2005), working with pupils from primary through to secondary school identifies the communal characteristics of blogging where:

> ... 'comments' form a chain between the author and readers, and in essence, an online community. Communities are also built as bloggers link to each other, creating a group of storytellers that provide individualistic expressions, as well as interactions with each other.
>
> (Huffaker, 2005: 10)

The inclusion of a class blog in our World Cup enquiry reflected these ideas of social networking and an understanding of the open-endedness of blogging which Herring *et al.* (2004) say creates opportunities for a wide range of writing styles (genres) in accordance with the needs of writers and readers.

Levels of understanding children's online writing

The blog was set up and ran for the six weeks of the tournament. The two Year 6 classes had access to the blog at school (in the classroom and in the ICT suite) and for many, at home too. The blog was a secure, password protected site, and a teacher demonstrated how to post comments and explained that it would be monitored for unsuitable content. None of the children had blogged before but most had access to computers at home and were proficient users of ICT. Over the six weeks, members of the research team posted match reports and posed questions, most of which were ignored by the children who, once they began writing, were much more interested in presenting their own ideas and responding to each other's comments.

In our initial reading of the written data, we first recognised that children felt they were permitted to write in different 'voices' for a wide range of purposes. Some used the colloquialisms of a chat room:

> 'Hey Katie, did u watch da football on sat?' – 'Yes England vs Paraguay, England won 1-0. I knew they were going to win.' – 'but it was kinda borin on sat'.

There were calls of encouragement and exhortations to teams:

> England is the best team. I have faith in you'; 'Come on England do your best in the world cup you have to win the world cup again or another team like France will win the world cup.

Other children felt free to voice their dissent:

> watching TV is better than football I would watch tom and jerry. My best opinion on football is boring as snoring. If there were no rules I would watch it. I think football is a waste off time!!!!!!!!!!! What is the whole point of football?

Some children reflected speculatively:

> We are a little bit worried about England playing with Trinidad and Tobago because the way they played with Paraguay wasn't really a good performance. Even the goal wasn't their own goal, one of the players for Paraguay accidentally headed it in their own goal. We thought it was really embarrassing for their team.

and hypothesised:

> Wayne Rooney is a very talented young player. If I was as gifted as him I would consider myself lucky.

Herring's points about styles and genre hit home forcefully as we noted the immediacy and authenticity of the different language uses at work in this online community.

After this initial reading, we examined the vocabulary choices and phrases which the children used. We noticed numerous incidences of what we might describe as 'in-the-moment' language of football commentary such as *'the defence was sleeping'*, *'he skills up most of the team'* and *'bicycle kick'*. The blog was alive with the vivid phrases that belong to sport commentaries, both oral and written, in which the children were so immersed at the time. We noted the ebullience and enjoyment which characterised the children's contributions: a *'cracking goal'*, a *'classic match'* and *'great pace and first touch'*.

Finally, prompted by Alan's contributions, we analysed the sentence types used by the children across the blog. Remember that Alan was a disaffected writer: he was underachieving with a Level 3 in the Year 6 National Curriculum Assessments and there was no evidence of any writing of sophistication in his almost-empty literacy folder. And yet, as a blogger, he was making assured use of lengthy and complex sentences to articulate his speculative thinking.

In Alan's first sentence (at the beginning of this chapter), his main clause, 'I think', precedes an adverbial clause of condition – 'if England are winning comfortably'. The noun clause object – 'then I would put on Theo' is followed by another adverbial clause, this time of result – 'so he can get past the tired defenders'. The second sentence is also complex and includes adverbial clauses of condition and reason. This is clear evidence of written language supporting thinking: his use of the modals 'would / wouldn't' – reveal him considering the possibilities, projecting and thinking ahead. He is using the language of logic, cause and effect ('if ... then'). This is a powerful example of language driven by Alan's expertise and an informed desire to communicate accurately and forcefully.

Alan's contribution proved to be indicative of children's language use across the blog: out of 248 entries, there were 125 complex sentences (10% of which had more than one subordinate clause), 91 simple and 32 compound sentences. Further analysis of the clause types revealed a significant proportion (just over 18%) of adverbial clauses of reason, for instance:

- 'by keeping possession well and passing well and they were crossing well'
- 'because nothing much happened and the first goal was an own goal and in the second half we think the players were really hot and tired'
- 'as he was the only forward on the pitch'
- 'because he shot from far away from the goal and because they had better positions even though they missed'.

This confounded our original expectations that contributions to the blog would be elliptical and more akin to textese. Clearly this was language composed and constructed to fit its purposes – to explain, hypothesise and speculate. It seemed to be the dialogic nature of the blog that powered this language: perhaps it was the blog's communicative network that enabled the children to hypothesise and defend their reasoning and speculation using complex sentence structures.

The world in the classroom and the learning and teaching of grammar

Barrs and Cork (2001) identify the ability to use complex sentences as one of the 'countable' indicators of sophistication in children's writing, and within literacy learning objectives there is an understanding that the ability to manipulate sentence structures is the mark of a mature and thoughtful writer. For example, by the age of 8 or 9 children should be able to 'show relationships of time, reason and cause through subordination and connectives' (DfES, 2006: 29) and by the end of their primary education children should be able to 'express subtle distinctions of meaning, including hypothesis, speculation and supposition, by constructing sentences in varied ways' (DfES, 2006: 35). In writing assessment tasks, children can, for example (QCA, 2007: 32), gain higher marks for 'the controlled use of several subordinate clauses'. All of these elements were observed in the children's online World Cup writing.

Blogging offers a real-world digital medium for communication. It is multidimensional in that it does not just offer a 'container' for writing but has the possibility of multiple audiences and access points. From this small-scale enquiry we propose that the bringing together of the blog with a temporary, global event taking place in real time and with unpredictable outcomes, together with children's authority and passion about the subject matter, provided a moment of linguistic empowerment, fired particularly by the language and content of sports commentary.

Unlike much other school writing, there was nothing contrived about these audiences and purposes: the children were writing in the context of a real-life world event which their out-of-school communities were also watching and commenting upon. Children would blog from home as they watched matches, and friends and families were reading the blog's match reports and commentaries. Their enjoyment of the blog and the freedom it gave children to express their genuine thoughts and opinions was clear from the sheer energy of their writing and their reflective comments:

> I liked the web-log. You can write about how you felt about the game and how you think the match could have been better. I made a couple of comments. I said how England weren't playing as best they could but they still picked up a victory.
> (Kofi)

> The blog is the best part, because you can put your own opinions into it, you don't need your friends to do anything, you can just put your own opinions on.
> (Luk Ying)

But – and it is a big 'but' – this was a temporary moment. Blogs and sporting events are, by their nature, ephemeral, and digital data is elusive; all we have captured here is a linguistic moment in time, an example of what Elaine Millard (2006) has so usefully conceptualised as 'fusion literacy'.

Certainly the blog data goes some way towards challenging popular notions that technology is the cause of diminishing standards in children's literacy (e.g. Brown, 2007). As adults who support children's learning, what we also take from the World Cup project is that is it possible to offer children meaningful experiences and resources which create opportunities for them to demonstrate and develop their innate sentence-level knowledge. Just as Margaret Peters (1985) conceptualised spelling as both 'caught' and 'taught', our findings suggest similar possibilities for the teaching of sentence types. If children can so readily call upon these linguistic resources, we could then explicitly build on this spontaneous usage in the classroom by discussing and extending children's language choices and forms.

Furthermore, the data from this small project suggest that the confluence of a temporary, popular event and an online forum may offer something special: in this case, a context for communication where children articulated their ideas in a range of complicated linguistic modes. From observing children's use of complex sentence structures (as we have here), school staff could plan to build upon similar confluences of transience and interactivity with the explicit aim of promoting pupils' awareness, use and control of complex written language.

Note

1 *Exploring the Field* was a project which investigated the learning potential of a world sporting event. It took place in a multi-lingual, inner-city primary school with two Year 6 classes, each with an equal ratio of boys and girls. For the duration of the World Cup 2006, class teachers, teaching assistants and four teacher-educators from a nearby university developed a range of activities around football texts (stories, poetry, newspapers, role-play, writing journals). The aim of the project was to find out how a popular event might influence children's reading, writing and speaking and listening through engaging their 'funds of knowledge' (Moll, 1992; Marsh, 2005). For an overview of the project, see Safford *et al.*, 2007.

Bibliography

Barrs, M. and Cork, V. (2001) *The Reader in the Writer*. London: CLPE.

Brown, J. (2007) 'Computers Blamed as Reading Standards Slump' in *The Independent Education*, 29/11/07 http://www.independent.co.uk/news/education/education-news/computers-blamed-as-reading-standards-slump-760829.html (accessed 14/05/08)

DfES (2006) *Primary Framework for Literacy and Mathematics*. London: DfES.

The Guardian (2006) Editorial, 'I blog therefore I am' 20/07/06.

Herring, S., Scheidt, L., Bonus, S. and Wright, E. (2004) 'Bridging the Gap: A Genre Analysis of Weblogs', Internet WWW page at URL: http://www.ics.uci.edu/~jpd/classes/ics234cw04/herring.pdf (accessed 20/02/08).

Huffaker, D. (2005) 'Let them Blog: Using Weblogs to promote Literacy in K-12 Education' in L.T.W. Hin and R. Subramaniam (eds) *Handbook of Research on Literacy in Technology at the K-12 Level*. Hershey, PA: Idea Group.

Marsh, J. (2005) 'Introduction: Children of the Digital Age' in Marsh, J. (ed.) *Popular Culture, New Media and Digital Literacy in Early Childhood*. London: RoutledgeFalmer.

Millard, E. (2006) 'Transformative Pedagogy: Teachers Creating a Literacy of Fusion' in K. Pahl and J. Rowsell *Travel Notes from the New Literacy Studies: Instances of Practice*. Clevedon: Multilingual Matters.

Moll, L. *et al.* (1992) 'Funds of Knowledge for teaching: using a qualitative approach to connect homes and classrooms'. *Theory into Practice*, 3:2, pp. 133–141.

Peters, M. (1985) *Spelling, Caught or Taught*. London: Routledge.

QCA (2007) *English Tests, Mark Schemes, Reading, Writing and Spelling Tests, KS2*. London: QCA.

Safford, K., Collins, F., Kelly, A. and Montgomerie, D. (2007) 'Exploring the Field'. *Primary English Magazine*, 12.3, pp. 11–14.

Chapter 29 and Chapter 30

Creativity and language development

Ann Bailey and Brita Little

and

Who should ask the questions? Developing critical thinking

Adam Hickman

The final two chapters of this Reader come from a research project which took place in ten schools[1] where teachers from the Early Years Foundation Stage through Year 6 carried out small-scale enquiries into how children's work in the creative arts influences their language and literacy development. The schools were all developing 'creative partnerships' with a wide range of expert 'arts partners', providing children with frequent and sustained opportunities to work in dance, sculpture, textiles, music, animation, architecture, drama, painting, multimedia, storytelling and poetry. In this research, teachers identified themes and patterns in children's learning across such diverse projects.

We have included these two chapters because they highlight the benefits of a creative approach to the primary curriculum and they are first-hand accounts of practitioner-led enquiry. In Chapter 29, 'Creativity and verbal development', nursery teachers Ann Bailey and Brita Little discover how very young children extend their descriptive and imaginative vocabulary as they work in different media. In Chapter 30, 'Who should ask the questions?', Year 6 teacher Adam Hickman explores the ways in which collaboration with an opera company inspires children to become more thoughtful speakers and writers. In both enquiries, teachers use informal observation methods and look at samples of children's work (children's writing in Year 6, children's artwork in the nursery); they also refer to flexible assessment frameworks to help them evaluate and appreciate children's development.

Note

1 'Animating Literacy' was developed by the Centre for Literacy in Primary Education in collaboration with Arts Council England.

Chapter 29

Creativity and language development

Ann Bailey and Brita Little

The school

Triangle Nursery is a full-time nursery school run by the Lambeth Local Education Authority. There are 88 pupils on roll and the school offers 60 full-time places each session. We have 45% of children with English as an additional language and currently the school has 18 different languages.

The school is in an area of deprivation but attracts a mixed intake. The parents show a high level of involvement. The school has a flexible approach to literacy learning. We are responsive to the children's needs and interests and are open to new initiatives:

> We recognise that language is the activity through which children learn and express themselves and therefore we put great importance on giving children the skills to be able to do this.
>
> (Triangle Nursery Language and Literacy Policy)

We encourage our pupils to be creative and this is an underlying theme that runs through everything we provide for our pupils:

> Children who are encouraged to think creatively and independently become more interested in discovering things for themselves and are keen to work with others to explore ideas.
>
> (Triangle Nursery School Creativity Policy and Strategy)

The focus group

We worked with a core group of ten children. These children were both boys and girls from a variety of ethnic backgrounds. They had varying ability levels and differing interests in artistic activities. The only common factor for these children is that they were due to leave Triangle Nursery in September. From this group, we took a closer look at the development of two children, a boy and a girl.

Centre for Literacy in Primary Education for permission to reprint extracts from 'Creativity and verbal development in the early years', Ann Bailey and Brita Little, 2005 in *Animating Literacy: Inspiring Children's Learning through Teacher and Artist Partnerships*, Sue Ellis and Kimberly Safford (eds) London: CLPE.

Open expectations

We rented a space at Studio Voltaire, a short walk from the nursery. Our aims were for the children to own and run a space specifically for the arts.

We were unsure of what to expect at the beginning of the project. This was mainly due to the flexibility of the project and the temperaments of young children! To give us a baseline to work from we assessed the focus children using the Early Years Foundation Stage Learning Goals in Communication, Language and Literacy and Creative Development. We also involved parents and other Nursery staff and talked to the children about the project. Our certainty was that we would encourage the children to get involved as much as possible and we would be flexible in our methodology. Observations of children were mainly in the form of observational notes taken by adults during the activities; children were also occasionally filmed during the activities:

> The learning curve was quite steep. I was slightly apprehensive at the beginning of the project as art is not an area that I consider to be one of my strengths, but I have really noticed a difference in the children and my own enthusiasm for art has increased as well.
>
> (Brita Little, nursery teacher)

In the studio and in the nursery

The project began by children working in the studio, and around half way through we moved to work in the nursery.

We chose to begin by running initial drawing workshops where the children would experience different techniques and materials. This was also a good opportunity for the artists and children to get to know each other and build up their confidence in each other.

Ten children at a time were taken to the studio and the first two sessions were spent getting used to working there and using the space informally in the drawing workshops. These workshops included large scale collaborative work, using different drawing materials and worked up to using collage material alongside drawings.

The leading teacher (Ann) and the artists talked informally during the session. The sessions were held fortnightly due to the artists' time constraints. The sessions were very flexible, with artists responding to the children's interests and not necessarily what was originally planned.

We found that for a few children leaving the nursery to go to the studio – even though it was only a short distance away – was unsettling. Most of the children, however, understood and relished the purpose of the studio after only a few visits. One of the artists observed, "They used to come in and not know what to do – now, they come in and start drawing straight away, and for longer periods of time."

Children began by drawing around their hands onto fabric and then adding sewing onto the fabric. We used an overhead projector to look at their art work in a changeable, larger format. This led onto working with silk: drawing self-portraits onto the silk, adding a variety of collage materials and sewing onto the silk.

This part of the project took place in the nursery because the studio was booked for an exhibition. We chose to use a room in the nursery but the door was kept open and other children could come in and look at was happening and join in. The children were completely free to choose how they wanted to decorate their silk and worked on this project for two sessions.

It was observable that the children were very focussed and motivated during these sessions, and lots of children used this as "drop-in" time. The artists commented on how they liked the fact that the activity was open to all and not as exclusive as the studio sessions. They also liked that children (particularly the focus group) revisited up to three times during the session (for up to two hours). From these observations, we decided to continue the project in the heart of the nursery and develop the "drop-in" concept.

Working with the artists in the nursery had a great impact on the group dynamics. When the art activity became open to all the nursery pupils, children were free to drop in and out of the activity as they wished. Even though the core group members continued to participate and were encouraged to visit the art activity, they had the choice of whether or not they wanted to take part and how long they stayed. The benefits for all of the children were that they learnt to work together as a group, which included skills such as negotiation and accepting that your idea may not be the most suitable one. Other positive outcomes were a big increase in concentration and the children appearing to be more focussed.

A broad aim: for children to talk about and describe their art work

We wanted to develop the children's imaginative vocabulary and also encourage them to discuss what they were doing and the artistic techniques they used. This tied in with the Early Years Foundation Stage Learning Goals for Communication, Language and Literacy, i.e. "To use language to recreate experiences".

What we were interested in finding out was whether exposing children to different art forms would affect their drawing styles and themes and also their language to talk about these things. Through the art projects that were held at the studio and at the nursery, it became clear that exposure to a range of projects helped children express themselves creatively using a variety of media including drawing, sewing, clay, and drawing onto acetate. The children gained confidence in combining a variety of styles and media, working collaboratively and individually and using talk as means of explaining what they were doing.

Focus children

Catherine was chosen due to her great interest in art (particularly drawing). She is very confident in expressing herself creatively and verbally, and will often engage adults in talking about her art work. At the beginning of the project she mainly drew her family and past experiences in Australia. We chose her because we were interested to see whether taking part in this research would broaden her drawing themes and further develop her imaginative language.

What we realised from close observation was that even though she still has an extensive vocabulary which she uses in her everyday language, she only accesses this language when explaining themes that are familiar to her, e.g. Australia and family. She also has a fairy tale theme which is a combination of Australia, family and fairy icons (princesses and castles), as these two observations of separate drawing activities illustrate:

1 Catherine is drawing independently in the drawing area. An adult joins her and asks her about her drawing.
C: A palm tree, and octopus. It's got a squirrel inside.
Adult: Where are you?
C: It's just my dream in Australia. My daddy John's got loads of lines on his forehead. It's a nice beach. This is me. The sun looks like flowers but flowers have petals. They're too small. They're the rocks. That's the super bit coming out of the sun. That's me again. I stayed the night there but only in my dream, that would be nice wouldn't it.

2 *C:* It's my family and friends; they're all sitting down at the table. The Angel's serving the food. They're sitting down because they're staying the night at the angel's house.

In contrast when drawing purely imaginatively and not from own experience, her drawing is of a very high quality but her verbal descriptions are more limited:

> *C:* It's a monster and he's growling. A small person called Peter led Peter. The monster kicked Peter led Peter. Peter led Peter went away from the monster.

Our expected outcome was that Catherine's themes of drawing would become wider, and possibly her imaginative language would increase. Instead what happened was that Catherine showed an interest in learning new skills and persevering with techniques. This overlapped into her drawings, for example when she had worked with an adult at drawing a kangaroo, she was observed during the following week working independently redrawing a kangaroo to perfect the technique.

Matt was chosen as a focus child because he seemed to have difficulties expressing his needs verbally. He was very particular about who he worked with or approached at the nursery. When describing his art work he would take a long time, with adult prompting, to say what he had drawn and this description would normally be a one word answer. We were interested to see if this project would develop his inter-personal language and generate an interest in art.

This is an observation made at the start of the project (in October):

> Matt's Key Worker invited him to the drawing area and started drawing alongside Matt. This seemed to give Matt confidence to start drawing by himself. He made no attempt to explain what he was doing and when asked by the adult what he was drawing gave a one word answer, "Superman".

The second observation happened about a month later in the nursery:

> His Key Worker had noticed Matt drawing in the art area. When asked what he had done, he didn't respond. Ann asked him if she could guess what he had drawn, and he nodded.

Ann: Is it you?
Matt: No, I don't look like that.
Ann: Is it anyone in your family?
Matt shakes his head.
Ann: Is it an animal?
Matt: No.
Ann: Do you know what I think it looks like? A monster.
Matt: You're right.
Ann: What's his name?
Matt smiles and whispers: Mikee.

Matt had been working at the studio for two months on a large-scale art project that involved combining different media. This third observation happened in the nursery when Matt approached an adult:

Matt: Do you like this?
Adult: What have you made?
Matt: A boat, it's got 2 eyes here, actually that's the wheels.
Adult: Where is it going to?
Matt: Asia.

Matt continued to work on his picture, adding paint.

Adult: Why are you doing that?
Matt: Because that makes it beautiful.
Matt swaps the paintbrush for his finger.
Matt: If you dip your finger into blue, then this, then put it on there, it makes green. Let me mix it into this colour. I make it into black.

This fourth observation occurred in January, during a collaborative drawing project in the studio:

Adult: What are you drawing?
Matt: A thing that bites you, he's got a big head and a biiggg mouth and some big hair, its ear, its cheeks. I'm doing 4 cheeks and a big nose.
Adult: Everything in your picture is big!
Matt: Because that's what I normally do. A thing that's got 4 mouths and bites you hard. It's got 4 mouths and when the peoples touch it, it bites you hard.

From these examples of Matt's talk, we get a clear idea of the progression in his confidence levels. He is talking about his creative work, using a variety of media and accessing the creative areas in the nursery as well as in the studio. He also starts explaining his thinking behind the process and is beginning to plan his creative work. As Myra Barrs pointed out in "Maps of Play" (1988), Matt had *learnt that one could draw not only objects, but also action.*

Making art and emergent literacy

Due to the age of our children and the ethos of the nursery we felt that the most suitable way for us to evaluate the research project was to look at verbal communication, using the Early Years Foundation Stage Learning Goals as a point to work from.

Our ultimate goal was to provide the children with an opportunity to draw in a relaxed environment alongside adults and gain experience in expressing themselves creatively. We wanted the children to work without pressure and feel that they could set their own level of involvement. For example, during one of the sessions (silk collages) Matt's friend Jack watched the activity for 40 minutes (an adult repeatedly asked him if he wanted a go, but he shook his head). Eventually he approached an adult and asked for a piece of silk. He worked on this piece until the time was up and then returned the next week to continue working on it. He was so proud of his work that he had insisted that his mum come into nursery and look at it.

We wanted the children to have fun and to feel that their work was valued – we hoped that this would be a solid stepping stone for them to grow into confident artists.

Reflections and outcomes

Studies of play seem to indicate that boys' play is generally preoccupied with physical action, whereas girls' play tends to centre around relationships (Pidgeon, 1998). We have found this has been reflected in our focus children's drawings: Matt seemed to use his drawings as props for his narratives whereas Catherine appeared to use her drawings to tell stories and to make sense of her feelings and dreams. The work of such thinkers as Howard Gardner and Lev Vygotsky suggests that it would be valuable to adopt a broader perspective in relation to symbolic development, for instance in drawing. Both Catherine and Matt are definitely using drawing to develop their vocabulary, and symbols in their drawings often have deeper meanings in their narratives.

Both children have moved on in their spoken language and creative skills; we have monitored this through assessing them at the end of the project using the Early Years Foundation Stage Learning Goals. However, we are not able to determine whether they have progressed purely because of the art project or has this been a natural development? We would like to think that it is a combination of both, and that all the children involved in the project are confident artists who are aware that adults value their work and who will continue to develop their literacy and creative skills concurrently.

Professionally we have felt the benefits of being involved in the project; it has given Brita confidence in using the arts to support learning. It has also reinforced the belief for us both that children communicate in a variety of ways (including non-verbal) and that drawing is a great vehicle for expression. Ann noted an increase in confidence when the sessions were run in the nursery. She felt that because the children were free to access the activities and could stay for the period of time that suited the individual, it gave them confidence to join the project with no reservations. We felt that the children were aware that every contribution was valued and this in turn made them want to join in for longer periods and with more commitment.

We valued the fact that we were working with artists who had many new skills and ideas to teach us. The children appeared to benefit from these relationships and took on board a professional attitude that they were working with "real artists". Emma Derrick, one of the artists, commented that:

> The children's language has changed noticeably. They now use much longer sentences to describe their work or observations. They also seem less inhibited in expressing their imaginative interpretations of image or process.

In successful teaching for creativity, practitioners understand not just what it is they are promoting but also how to create opportunities for this to happen. Through our workshops with the artists we believe that our children have been given numerous opportunities to develop their creativity.

References

Barrs, M. (1988) "Maps of Play", Chapter 7 in *Language and Literacy in the Primary School*, (eds) Margaret Meek and Colin Mills; London: Falmer Press.

Gardner, H. (1980) *Artful Scribbles: The Significance of Children's Drawings*. New York: Basic Books.

Gardner, H. (1990) *Art Education and Human Development*. Los Angeles: The Getty Center for Education in the Arts.

Vygotsky, L. (1985) *Thought and Language*. Cambridge, Massachusetts: MIT Press.

Pidgeon, S. (1998) "Superhero or Prince", Chapter 6 in *Boys and Reading*, (eds) Myra Barrs and Sue Pidgeon; London: Centre for Literacy in Primary Education.

Chapter 30

Who should ask the questions?

Developing critical thinking

Adam Hickman

> In 54 lessons observed, where there were 1919 questions asked by teachers, only 20 questions were asked by children. Those questions that children did ask were mainly procedural, e.g. "Can I go to the toilet?" or "Shall I use a rubber?" When a child's question was related to their learning, the teacher often missed what the child was really asking and redirected the line of thought back to the teacher's agenda.
>
> (Debra Myhill and Frances Dunkin, 'What's A Good Question?' *Literacy Today*. No 33, December 2002)

School background and action research aims

Johanna Primary School is in central London directly behind Waterloo train station, located off a busy market street. We are a one form entry school and nursery with 180 children on roll.

Before becoming a teacher I trained and worked as an actor. The action research took place in my second year of teaching. I was eager to find creative ways of teaching literacy and opportunities to extend children's experiences in speaking, listening and drama.

Baseline data: attitudes, experiences and skills

After getting to know my new class and having some idea of their abilities I began to collect assessment data. I used a model devised by Gemma Moss of the Institute of Education (Table 30.1) which was an assessment of not only children's abilities but also their *attitudes* to reading and especially to writing. This framework helped me think about which children could progress from *Can read and write but don't* or *Can't read or write and don't* to *Can read and write and do* or *Can't read or write but try*.

Centre for Literacy in Primary Education for permission to reprint extracts from 'Who should ask the questions? How arts partnerships help develop children's critical thinking', Adam Hickman, 2005 in *Animating Literacy: Inspiring Children's Learning through Teacher and Artist Partnerships*, Sue Ellis and Kimberly Safford (eds) London: CLPE.

I took a writing sample from each child. I used these samples to assess the children according to both National Curriculum levels (Table 30.2) and on the *CLPE Writing Scale* (Table 30.3). Rather than purely a numerical score, the *CLPE Writing Scale* focuses on how children move from inexperience to experience as writers. It was this word *experience* which seemed so important and useful when trying to find ways of helping children to make progress. They need experiences, both inside and outside the classroom, to be inspired to write.

Who should ask the questions?

In January the children went to watch a production of *Skellig* at the Young Vic Theatre, based on a novel by David Almond. Afterwards they had the opportunity to ask the actors some questions. These questions were not planned beforehand as I wanted to assess their level of understanding of the performance. Here is a sample of their questions (b = boy, g = girl):

b – When you dropped, did it hurt?
b – When you were on the bus, were you really smoking?
g – What does it feel like being Mina's mum, and why?
g – Do you love birds in real life?
g – How does it feel being actors?
g – Do you feel nervous?
b – Is it ever boring?
g – What do you love most about your characters?
b – What's your next show?
b – What if you get a word wrong, what do you do?

The girls asked most of the questions, and these were mainly about how the actors felt. The few questions asked by the boys tended to be practical questions about the performance. I wanted the children to be able to ask questions that would further their understanding of the production and of the theatre.

I became interested in the nature of their questions. I realised that if I wanted them to become more analytical then I needed to help them learn about asking questions, to help them become more inquisitive. They needed to have a reason to ask questions, to want to find things out, but in order to know what questions to ask a level of understanding of a subject is needed beforehand. As the teacher I needed to provide experiences that would encourage the children to want to find out more.

I began to think about how children's questions – and not just their answers reflect their understanding. By helping them become better at asking questions, through modelling and explicit teaching, I hoped that they would become more independent learners. My intention was for them to ask questions about their experiences, their work and of themselves, and that this would enable them to take more control of their learning.

Working with the English National Opera

Before going to see and hear *Bake for One Hour* (a short opera about a chef, a maid, a hostess and a magical ring), children had an in-school workshop where they enacted the story of the opera as they learned about it. They became the characters and performed part of the story rather than sitting and listening to it. They began to feel that it was 'their' story. They were prompted throughout to be aware of the characters thoughts and feelings: "*What does your character think about ...? What do you feel when you see ...?*" They listened to an opera singer perform live and had a chance to try it for themselves. When they went to the performance it wasn't the first time they had heard these sounds which were quite strange to most of them.

The opera was specially written for children and was in English, but it was not only these aspects that helped to demystify it. The children were able to focus on the story and realise that opera is a different way of telling a story just as theatre is another way of telling a story. They were broadening their knowledge and experience not only of different art forms but the different forms of narrative.

The day of the journey to the London Coliseum to see the opera clashed with another date in the school diary, a football tournament where the Year 6 team were to defend a trophy they had recently won. I explained why I thought it would be beneficial for them to watch the opera and although they were extremely disappointed not to be playing many of the children were looking forward to the opera. The one boy later revealed:

> I really didn't want to go; I thought it would be rubbish, that I would probably be falling asleep.

The children had a tour of the auditorium and stage area before watching the opera. They were the only audience and were physically very close to the performers which made the whole experience more intimate and ultimately more personal. Later, the same boy told me that despite his initial reservations:

> I really enjoyed it. I understood what was going on and it was funny.

During the walk back to school from the Coliseum almost all the talk amongst the children was about the performance they had seen. The following day I facilitated a discussion about the opera in class but instead of asking the questions myself, *I* asked the children to think of questions they thought *I* might ask *them*. By asking them to come up with questions rather than answer mine, I had a clearer indication of their level of thinking and understanding of the opera:

- How do you think you could improve it?
- What did you like and dislike about it?
- What bit was funny?
- Was it the same as the story, you know, when the people came [for the school workshop?]
- How do you think the mirror was effective?
- Did you understand what the characters were saying?
- What costumes did they use?
- What did you think about the orchestra?
- What was the important thing in the play?
- What was your favourite part, and why?

During this session the nature of questions and the different types of questions that can be asked were made explicit; we can find out more information by adding *"and why?"* at the end of a question. It was from this point that the children became more aware of the quality of the questions that they were asking. I asked them "Why do you think I asked you to come up with the questions? The Big 'Why?'"

– Because we're gonna be writing about it.
– To help remember the story.
– Brainstorming, to remember the story.
– It would help you [Adam] and save time. Also on our SATs Test papers, they ask "why".
(Adam) But I could have asked you the questions; I could have made up all the questions.
– So we can think. So we can think MORE.
– It helps you think about what you might want to talk about and share with other people, so you can think about your opinion.

There was a mutual and infectious sense of enthusiasm and excitement in this question and answer session. I was beginning to make explicit that the children could ask questions not only of other people but of themselves as a way of helping them form their opinions and extend their learning. And we were facilitating this learning by making use of the opera experience.

I also used our focus on questions to share with the children some of the criteria for getting higher marks on their Key Stage tests. If they understood the type of question, they were more likely to understand the type of answer expected of them.

(Adam) There are two types of questions, listen for the difference:
1: Where did the chef hide the ring? and 2: How did you think the use of the mirror was effective? How are these questions different?
– The first one you can say: "the cake". The second one you give more information.
– The first one you need to find out, to remember and think back. The second one is about how YOU think.
(Adam) Which one could be right or wrong? Which one would be worth three marks on a SATs paper?
– To get three marks, you have to explain. For one mark, you just say yes or no.
(Adam) Which one makes you think more?
– The second one, because you have to think what YOU thought. You have to give your opinion.

A composer's visit

The following week we had a visit from the composer and conductor of the opera. The children decided on the questions that they wanted to ask him and the only support that I gave was in helping them to organise the questions into an order so that they did not ask the same question twice. Their increasing experience meant that they were now asking questions that would yield more information. The children again felt like experts with valuable opinions about the performance, and I observed that now they were asking open, not closed, questions:

> What's the hardest thing about being a composer?
> How did you feel when you got your job?
> Who was your favourite character and why?
> Why did you want it to look like the 1920s?
> Why did you choose to do *Bake for One Hour*?
> Have you ever had an opera disaster and if so what happened?
> What would you like to do in the future and why?

The role of the teacher

My classroom practice changed over the course of the year. I learned along with the children and developed as a teacher. I understood how important it was that before and after a cultural visit the children were given opportunities to talk and share their thoughts and opinions if these experiences were to be integral to their learning. As the teacher I had a strong role to play beyond organising visits and taking children on cultural trips. I had to facilitate their discussions and model the process of thinking and structuring thoughts, ideas and opinions. The teacher's role is crucial. It is how creative experiences are used for learning that makes the difference.

Assessment

I used the three frameworks at the end of the year to assess the children's progress at the end of the project (Tables 30.1, 30.2 and 30.3). Over 70% of the children moved on more than 2 or 3 National Curriculum Levels. Over 90% of the children now had a consistently positive attitude to writing and almost all children moved on at least one level on the CLPE Writing Scale (several children moved on more than one level). The children were more confident writers; they were asking questions about each other's work as well as giving their own opinions.

I began this action research project by asking whether working closely with arts organisations could help to improve children's critical thinking and literacy skills. Over the year I saw how the experiences children had, together with the teaching approaches that I developed, in fact influenced all areas of the curriculum. By coming to understand the importance of asking questions, and by having opportunities for self direction in their work, the children came to value and enjoy learning. My Year 6 class are now in secondary schools. I hope they will continue to enjoy learning and make the most of opportunities that come their way for the rest of their lives.

> Children need to go to the theatre as much as they need to run about in the fresh air. They need to hear real music played by real musicians on real instruments as much as they need food and drink. They need to listen to proper stories as much as they need to be loved and cared for…otherwise they perish on the inside. I'm not going to argue about this: I'm right.
>
> (Children's author Philip Pullman in *The Guardian* newspaper, March 2004)

Reference

Almond, David (1998) *Skellig*. London: Hodder Children's Books.

Data collected

Table 30.1 Assessment of children's attitudes to writing (with thanks to Gemma Moss, Institute of Education)

Children in October

Can and do	**Can but don't**
7 boys 8 girls	4 boys
Can't but try	**Can't and don't**
4 boys 5 girls	1 boy 1 girl

Children in June

Can and do	**Can but don't**
11 boys 11 girls	1 boy
Can't but try	**Can't and don't**
2 boys 2 girls	1 girl

(Two boys left the school over the course of Animating Literacy)

Table 30.2 National Curriculum Levels for writing

National Curriculum Levels			
Name	NC level for writing October	NC level for writing June	Progression of more than 2/3 level*
A	3b	4a	*
A	2c	3a	*
B	3a	4a	*
B	3b	3a	
C	3b	4a	*
C	3b	4a	*
D	3c	3a	
D	5	5	
E	3c	4a	*
G	3b	4c	
I	3a	4b	
J	3c	4c	*
J	1b	2a	*
K (focus child)	2c	4b	*
M	–	4c	*
M	1a	3b	*
M	2c	3b	*
N	3b	4a	*
N	3b	4a	*
N	4c	–	
N (focus child)	3b	4a	*
P	2a	3b	
R		3c	–
S	3b	4b	*
S	3b	4c	
S	3a	5	*
S	3b	5	*
S	2b	3a	*
T	1a	2a	*
T	3c	3c	

Table 30.3 CLPE Writing Scale (ages 8–12 years)

Level	Description	Children in October	Children in June
1 Inexperienced writer (NC Level 1-2c)	Experience as a writer may be limited: may be composing orally with confidence but be reluctant to write or avoid taking risks with transcription. Needing a great deal of help with developing own texts (which are often brief) and with the writing demands of the classroom. Relying mainly on phonetic spelling strategies and memorised words, with few self-help strategies. Seldom using punctuation to mark meaning.	Janice, Tanzir, Antonette, Michila, Paulina, Mohammed, Manuella	Janice
2 Less experienced writer (NC Level 2b-a)	Increasingly willing to take risks with both composition and transcription. Writing confidently in certain genres (eg simple narratives) and trying out different forms of writing, drawing on experience of the models available. May find it difficult to sustain initial efforts over longer pieces of writing. Mainly using language and sentence structures that are close to speech. Spellings of familiar words are generally correct and attempts at unfamiliar spellings reveal a widening range of strategies. Using sentence punctuation more consistently.	Danielle, Steven, Tiago, Conor, Nathan, Jake, Emmanuel, Kyron, Nourin, Chau-Long	Danielle, Steven, Tiago, Tanzir (+1) Pauline (+1) Antonette(+1) Michila (+1) Manuella (+1)
3 Moderately experienced writer (NC Level 3)	Shaping writing in familiar genres confidently, drawing on experience of reading. Widening range of writing and taking on different forms more succussfully. Aware of audience and beginning to consider appropriateness of language and style. Learning to revise own texts with support and to link and develop ideas coherently. Spellings of words with regular patterns are mainly correct and attempts at unfamiliar words show a growing knowledge of visual patterns and word structures.Using sentence punctuation appropriately.	Brandon, Glory, Shahina, Isley, Billy, Alejandro, Sorcha, Nara, Sharon, Samara, Isley	Brandon, Glory, Shahina, Isley, Connor (+1) Jake (+1) Kyron (+1) Mohammed (+2)
4 Experienced writer (NC Level 4)	A self-motivated writer who can write at length and is beginning to use writing to refine own ideas. Developing own style and range as a writer but needing support with the structuring of more complex narrative and non-narrtive forms. Likely to be reflecting on writing and revising texts for a reader, choosing language for effect or to clarify meanings. Using standard spelling more consistently and drawing on effective self help strategies. Increasingly able to use punctuation, including paragraphing, to organise texts.		Billy (+1) Alejandro (+1) Nara (+1) Samara (+1) Nathan (+2) Emmanuel (+2) Nourin (+2) Chau-Long (+2)
5 Exceptionally experienced writer (NC Level 5)	An enthusiastic writer who has a recognisable voice and uses writing as a tool for thinking. Making conscious decisions about appropriate forms and styles of writing, drawing on wide experience of reading. May show marked preferences for writing in particular genres. Able to craft texts with the reader in mind and reflect critically on own writing. Using mainly standard spelling. Managing extended texts using organisational structures such as paragraphing and headings.	Danny	Danny Sorcha (+2) Sharon (+2) © CLPE

Index